THE BRAINS . . .

Cary Cimino would supply the Wall Street experience; Jeffrey Pokross, the brilliant plan.

THE BRAWN . . .

Robert Lino would offer the aid of organized crime. The Mob would enforce.

THE BUSINESS . . .

The buyers on the stock market would never know what hit them.

Berkley Titles by Greg B. Smith

NOTHING BUT MONEY
MOB COPS
MADE MEN

NOTHING BUT
MONEY

How the Mob Infiltrated Wall Street

GREG B. SMITH

BERKLEY BOOKS, NEW YORK

THE BERKLEY PUBLISHING GROUP
Published by the Penguin Group
Penguin Group (USA) Inc.
375 Hudson Street, New York, New York 10014, USA
Penguin Group (Canada), 90 Eglinton Avenue East, Suite 700, Toronto, Ontario M4P 2Y3, Canada
(a division of Pearson Penguin Canada Inc.)
Penguin Books Ltd., 80 Strand, London WC2R 0RL, England
Penguin Group Ireland, 25 St. Stephen's Green, Dublin 2, Ireland (a division of Penguin Books Ltd.)
Penguin Group (Australia), 250 Camberwell Road, Camberwell, Victoria 3124, Australia
(a division of Pearson Australia Group Pty. Ltd.)
Penguin Books India Pvt. Ltd., 11 Community Centre, Panchsheel Park, New Delhi—110 017, India
Penguin Group (NZ), 67 Apollo Drive, Rosedale, North Shore 0632, New Zealand
(a division of Pearson New Zealand Ltd.)
Penguin Books (South Africa) (Pty.) Ltd., 24 Sturdee Avenue, Rosebank, Johannesburg 2196,
South Africa

Penguin Books Ltd., Registered Offices: 80 Strand, London WC2R 0RL, England

In an effort to safeguard the privacy of certain people, some individual and place names and identi-
fying characteristics have been changed. Events involving the characters and places happened as
described. The publisher does not have any control over and does not assume any responsibility for
author or third-party websites or their content.

NOTHING BUT MONEY

A Berkley Book / published by arrangement with the author

PRINTING HISTORY
Berkley mass-market edition / June 2009

Copyright © 2009 by Greg B. Smith.
Cover art by S. Miroque.
Cover design by Rita Frangie.
Insert photos by the *New York Daily News* copyright © New York Daily News, L.P. Used with
permission.
Interior text design by Kristin del Rosario.

ISBN: 978-0-425-22880-7

BERKLEY®
Berkley Books are published by The Berkley Publishing Group,
a division of Penguin Group (USA) Inc.,
375 Hudson Street, New York, New York 10014.
BERKLEY® is a registered trademark of The Berkley Publishing Group.
The "B" design is a trademark of The Berkley Publishing Group.

PRINTED IN THE UNITED STATES OF AMERICA

10   9   8   7   6   5   4   3   2

Most Berkley Books are available at special quantity discounts for bulk purchases for sales, promo-
tions, premiums, fund-raising, or educational use. Special books, or book excerpts, can also be created
to fit specific needs.

For details, write: Special Markets, The Berkley Publishing Group, 375 Hudson Street, New York,
New York 10014.

AUTHOR'S NOTE

Long before U.S. taxpayers began bailing out Wall Street with billions of their hard-earned dollars, there was the original Black Friday of 1869. It was spectacular and disastrous and caused millions in losses to investors from coast to coast, and it was mostly the work of one man—Jay Gould. When he died of tuberculosis at age fifty-six, one of his peers told reporters assembled on the doorstep of his Fifth Avenue mansion, "Wall Street has never seen his equal and never will."

In 1869 Gould was one of the richest men in America, a man who controlled one out of every ten miles of railroad in the nation. Although he was truly a very wealthy man, wealth has a way of making its owners believe there is always a little more just down the road. The source of just a little more, Gould decided, was gold.

His scheme was simple but inspired. He would run up the price of gold, which would, in turn, pump up the price of wheat. Western wheat farmers would then sell their wheat as fast as they could, which would require wheat to be transported East over Gould's railroads. He was counting on fear and greed to line his pockets. It was a clever idea, and therefore, it turned into one of the worst financial disasters in Wall Street history.

Gould and his co-conspirators began buying up gold, inspiring others who saw his investment choices as a bellwether to jump in, too. The price of gold began to rise at an alarming pace, awakening the administration of Ulysses S. Grant from its slumber. President Grant then tried to put the brakes on the runaway train, ordering a major sell-off of government gold.

The sell-off had a different effect. That morning gold had reached a peak of $162. The White House "sell" message reached Wall Street at five minutes past noon that Friday, September 24, 1869, and within 15 minutes the price of gold had dropped to $133. In the words of the Brooklyn Eagle, "Half of Wall Street was ruined."

In a system that relies on self-interest, these things are bound to happen. Gould had his reasons and explanations for his behavior, and he sought to make the case that he was just doing what capitalism demanded. Of course, this was not to be the final Black Friday or Unholy Thursday or Bloody Monday or whatever other modifier the press could dream up to illustrate the shock and horror of a sudden and allegedly unexpected crash. There would be many more, and although results of these market "corrections" were often different—sometimes the crash lasted awhile, sometimes there was a quick rebound—the underlying explanation often seemed quite similar. Everybody saw a run-up and wanted to get their's before the money stopped flowing. Sometimes that involved cutting corners here and there. Sometimes that involved breaking laws. But the logic of Wall Street was consistent—if everybody else is doing it, I'd be a fool not to.

Such was the case during the dot-com craze of the late 1990s, a time of irrational exuberance that, looking back, now seems merely irrational. This was a time when small "companies" with absolutely no assets went public and money fell from the sky. This was the dawn of "pump and dump," when the American Mafia decided it was time to take what they could out of Wall Street. It didn't last long. Just as Jay Gould's brilliant idea became Black Friday back in 1869, the party ended in a bad way. But if you were there when it all took off, for a while it seemed like there was nothing but money.

Greg B. Smith
March 9, 2009

CHAPTER ONE

December 17, 1987

Arthur Kill Road is the far end of nowhere in New York City. Running along the western edge of New York's smallest borough, Staten Island, it is not what you'd call a tourist destination. The camera-wielding busloads that flood Manhattan religiously check out the Statue of Liberty, the Empire State Building, the Brooklyn Bridge. These are icons meant for collecting. Tourists might even hop the ferry to Staten Island, but then—immediately—return to Manhattan. If any out-of-towner found himself on the winding curves of Arthur Kill Road heading into the heart of Staten Island, the borough of landfills and subdivisions, he would only be there because he got lost. Very extremely lost. There is really no reason to go there if you are a tourist, or even a regular person. There are no pleasant sights to see. There are no hip restaurants, no cutting-edge galleries, no timeless museums. This is the working edge of New York. This is where people dump things.

In the frigid darkness of almost midnight, there were no cars of any type—save one. A lone driver made his way down the road, his headlights knifing into the December darkness. He couldn't see it, but out there, just a few yards away, dividing New York from New Jersey, was the Arthur Kill, a fetid river that had been polluted by the captains of industry since the nineteenth century. The fish were dead; birds avoided the place. The water was the color of black coffee, and on this night, its petroleum content kept it from freezing. The driver passed refineries with peppery smells and midnight fires. He passed a ship graveyard where the sad skeletons of freighters and tugboats named after somebody's mother or girlfriend were left to rot. Nobody else was in sight. He was happy the road was so lonely. He could see if he was being followed. He passed an auto graveyard, capturing it in his headlights, and then, finally, a lone sign—"Island Wholesale Fence." The driver, Robert Lino, dutiful son of a hopelessly corrupt father, had arrived.

Robert Lino was twenty-two years old, and he had barely finished the sixth grade. His writing was like that of a fourth grader. He had spent his entire life in the middle of Brooklyn, where he learned what he learned and never thought that there might be another way to live. While other kids from Brooklyn thought about basketball scholarships or nailing their Regents exams in high school to go on to a decent college and all the rest, Robert Lino acquired different expectations. Robert Lino was going to be part of the American Mafia. This was an almost unstoppable destination. He had grown up surrounded by it. His father was in the Mafia, his father's brother, his father's cousin. All were made members of organized crime, the way that some fathers were vice presidents of international banks or partners in law firms or professors of French literature.

Robert assumed his father was already at the spot on Arthur Kill Road where Robert had been told to show up. His father was Robert Lino Sr.—Bobby Senior. He was a drug dealer. He dabbled in loan-sharking, collected protection payments, ran sports betting. He could also be called upon to shoot you in the head and roll you up in a rug. He had an official title in one of New York's five crime families, the Bonanno group. He was what they called a soldier, although the concept of rank and hierarchy was pretty flexible within the Bonanno group. Bobby Senior earned that title by being as devoted to a life of perfidy and deceit as a priest is to his order. Getting over was his religion. He loved the life, and he was hoping his son, Robert, would someday follow in his footsteps. That was why the father had phoned the son late on this December night and asked him to drive out to this desolate spot on the edge of the edge, on Arthur Kill Road in Staten Island.

It was heading toward midnight, and Robert Lino had to know what was about to occur. He was twenty-two years old now. No longer just a kid taking bets for his dad's sports-bookmaking operation. This was more than getting coffee for the guys at the social club. This ride in the middle of the night, this was the real deal. He knew his father well. He knew his father's friends and cousins. He knew that when they called him to come out here like this, he was now officially on his way to becoming just like them.

There was cousin Frankie Lino. Officially, he was another honored soldier in the legion of deceit named after Joseph "Joe Bananas" Bonanno. Frankie was a made guy ten years in now, one of the originals. He was famous among a certain set for a photograph in the newspaper from a long time ago. There he was being led by two detectives in that great New York tradition known as the perp walk, and Frankie was leering into the camera, his eyes black-and-blue, his cheek bruised, his hair wild. He was the very image of the stand-up guy. The New York City Police Department had dragged him to the precinct to ask him some questions about the shooting of a cop. This was 1962, and Frankie had said nothing, even when they enthusiastically applied cigarettes to his genitals. When Frankie limped out of court with his arm in a sling and his face all black-and-blue, Frankie's brother, Anthony, had hollered out for the benefit of the assembled press, "Lookit what they did!" Frank had dutifully scowled and muttered, "Shut up, you moron-ya!" and walked away. This experience with the cops and the cigarettes had a profound effect on Frankie. From that day, he would be unable to control nervous blinking, earning him a second nickname, "Blinky," among a small number of acquaintances from the neighborhood.

Then there was cousin Eddie Lino. Officially he was a proud member of the Gambino organized crime family, run by the world's most famous gangster, John Gotti. Eddie was considered a big deal within the Lino family. The FBI had told everyone that Gotti was Public Enemy Number One and that the Gambinos were the worst of the worst, more powerful than Bechtel or IBM. And Eddie was one of them. He told people John Gotti was one of his close personal friends. Plus Eddie was known to be crazy. He once decided to shoot a man in the head because the man said something nasty about the wife of one of cousin Eddie's friends. Actually Eddie shot the guy because he just didn't like him. In a few years Eddie would be found sitting in his Lincoln, shot in his own head, but for now he and Robert Lino's father and cousin Frankie were the best of friends. They broke all the laws they could find together—New York Penal Code, Federal Criminal Code, you name it.

Driving in Staten Island in the dark hours before dawn, Robert Lino knew what was coming. He pulled off Arthur Kill Road into the fence company parking lot he'd been instructed to find. His tires growled on the gravel, the spokes of his headlights swimming through a sea of blackness. The Island Wholesale Fence sign was the only object providing light, a ghostly presence in the claustrophobic blackness. There was nothing else out here but the lonely Outerbridge Crossing, the southernmost bridge in New York

City that took you out of Staten Island and into the wilds of New Jersey. In the headlight beams, Robert could make out a beat-up white trailer, probably the fence company's office, stacks of concrete barriers choked with weeds, rusting rows of abandoned vehicles with leering gap-toothed grills. And then he saw what he was looking for—a group of men standing around, rubbing their hands and stomping their feet against the cold. In the center of the group something lay on the ground, unmoving.

Robert Lino now knew precisely what he would be doing for the next hour. He got out of the car, and there was his father and cousin Frankie. There was also a guy everybody called Kojak because he'd shaved his head, along with a friend of Frankie's named Ronnie, and worst of all, a guy named Tommy "Karate" Pitera. Robert knew all of these guys, but sometimes wished he didn't know Tommy Karate. Tommy was the kind of guy who liked to kill people, really enjoyed it. Plus he liked what happened after, when he would personally cut up his victims into pieces convenient for disposal. He was known to have his own method. He'd shoot you in your house, drag you to your own bathtub, slit your throat to drain the blood, cut off your head and hands to eliminate identification issues, then go to work with a hacksaw to create four or five bagfuls of parts. On this night, however, Tommy Karate apparently did not have access to a bathtub because there, on the frozen ground, was Gabriel Infanti—dead, but in one piece.

This was the reason the father had summoned the son in the middle of the night. Not to take in a baseball game. Not to help paint the living room. Not to spend some quality time chatting about the best way to land a striper or who was the best athlete of all time, Babe Ruth or Muhammad Ali or Michael Jordan. This was an unusual father-son outing, one chosen by the father. And the son had done his part. He'd shown up. He had not questioned the father. Something needed to be done, and like any good son, Robert Lino did what he was told.

It was just a job. It was like everything else about this life. There was a problem; you fixed it. Take the guy on the ground, Gabriel Infanti. For years, Infanti was not a problem. He was a go-to guy within the family Bonanno, doing a piece of work when requested, kicking tribute up the ladder, the whole thing. He was one of the guys, a man of honor. Now he was just a problem. First he had failed what would appear to have been a fairly simple assignment. He'd been told to dispose of the body of yet another colleague. The colleague had been placed inside a metal drum and concrete poured in with him, and Infanti was supposed to make sure the drum and its contents disappeared. It didn't work out as planned, and the New Jersey State Police discovered this special little package inside a warehouse in New Jersey days after the homicide. Strike one against Infanti. Then, during another bad day at the office, Infanti—the only made guy on the scene—was supposed to be present when another victim was dispatched. If Infanti had been where he was supposed to be, he would have had the authority to call off the hit because the victim was waiting to meet another guy who wasn't supposed to be a victim. As it turned out, Infanti got nervous before the job and stepped out for coffee at Nathan's. As a result, the hit went forward, and now they had to kill two guys—the guy they were supposed to kill and the guy who showed up without making an appointment. All of this caused much anxiety for the leadership down at Bonanno corporate headquarters, plus it raised doubts about Infanti's commitment to the cause. If a person is a participant in a murder conspiracy, that person is as vulnerable as everyone else. He is a part of the team. If that person chooses to step out for coffee at Nathan's at just the right moment, questions are raised as to motive. The implications are that a person is attempting to extricate himself from criminal activity, something that implies the person may actually and truly be secretly cooperating with other organizations. Specifically, the FBI. The bosses of the Bonanno family decided Infanti was about to sign up as an informant and go on the government payroll, so it was decided that Infanti had to go.

Not surprisingly, Tommy Karate was the guy who did the deed. Everything was arranged. Infanti was supposed to meet a guy at an empty office space in Ridgewood, Queens, unaware that Tommy Karate was there already, waiting. So was Frankie Lino, who waited outside as lookout while Robert's father, Bobby Senior, waited inside in the dark. Cousins in crime. Frank saw Infanti driven up to the office in Queens by a Bonanno gangster named Louie, and he saw the two men walk into the building. Frank waited a minute or two, then followed them inside. There lay Gabriel Infanti on the floor of the empty office, blood pouring from a head wound. The guy Louie looked like he was going to wet himself. He'd been standing next to Infanti when he was shot. Tommy Karate was still holding the pistol with the silencer. They rolled Infanti up in a rug and carted him out to Arthur Kill Road.

And here Infanti was, stretched out on the ground, no longer a man of honor. And there was Robert Lino, ready to help out his dad.

It wasn't going to be easy. The problem was obvious. It was December, and the earth of Staten Island was harder than Arctic ice. Tommy Karate and Kojak were banging away with their shovels. Frankie Lino tried for a bit. So did Bobby Senior. Now Robert Lino stepped in and took the shovel in his hand. The only light came from the headlights of the assembled cars.

Robert Lino was a small guy—five feet two inches tall, squarish but not terribly bulked up. Little Robert, his uncles called him, mostly because of his father with the same name but also because of his size. He looked a lot like the other Linos—prominent nose, thick black eyebrows, hair black as a Lincoln. Here he stood, the youngest man in the group, ready to do his part. He swung the shovel and hit the ground and nothing came of it. Again and again. They all did. Tommy dug, Kojak dug, Frankie, Bobby Senior and Robert Lino—they all tried their best, chipping away at the hardened ground, all to no avail. It was like trying to clear a beach of sand with a tablespoon. You worked and worked and nothing seemed to change, and digging a hole the size of a man is a lot of work. Ideally you have to dig pretty deep so if the rain comes a hand or a leg or a head won't come popping out of the ground. In December, with the ground frozen, getting the job done right could take a long time.

And time was important on a job like this. For instance, it would not be a good idea to be standing out there with Gabriel Infanti lying on the permafrost when the sun came up and people started showing up to buy split rails or pickets or whatever they needed to fence in their little slice of Staten Island heaven. The men continued chipping away. In a few minutes, everybody was out of breath.

Tommy Karate and Kojak said they would handle the job themselves. Tommy was a very practical guy. He had brought along a bucket of lye. The lye would go on Gabriel Infanti, and in no time at all, Gabriel would be all gone. For Tommy Karate, Gabriel Infanti was just another job. Standing there in the headlights, he and the bald guy, Kojak, began to joke about how scared Louie looked the moment Tommy shot Infanti in the head. Kojak cracked up thinking about how he'd fished $2,500 cash out of Infanti's pants after Tommy had put a bullet in the guy's brain. All that was easy. This business of making Gabriel Infanti disappear, this was anything but. They'd thought they'd come out here and dig a hole and dump in Gabriel and the lye and then everybody goes home to their nice warm beds. Who would have thought they'd still be out here after two miserable, frigid hours, with nothing to show for it but Gabriel still lying there and the sun coming up at any time?

But they kept at it, and soon the hole was dug, the body dumped, the lye applied. The work was over. Robert Lino, the good son, said good night to his father, as if they had just watched a baseball game at Yankee Stadium and now it was time to go home. Bobby Senior and cousin Frankie drove off for a late dinner at one of their favorite restaurants, Villa Borghese in Brooklyn. They were hungry. That's what you did when you were hungry. Robert didn't quite have the appetite. He drove back to his home in Midwood, Brooklyn. The night's work was done.

It was different now for Robert. Now he was officially implicated. He was what the lawyers called an accessory after the fact, the fact being a homicide, the after being the digging part. And this was because of his own father. This was how the father wanted it for his son. In murder, if you're there when they bury the body and you don't run to the police, you're an official accomplice. A co-conspirator. That was Robert Lino's new relationship with his father; instead of "Hey Dad," or "Hey son," they could say, "Hey co-conspirator." Perhaps the father thought this would bring him closer to the son. Perhaps the father did not think at all.

In a few hours, the sun rose on Arthur Kill Road. Off the gravel road by the Island Wholesale Fence warehouse, a mound of freshly dug dirt could be seen—if you knew where to look. The crew had done a good job of making Infanti disappear. He was hidden by rotting wrecks and weeds and concrete barriers. Customers would show up and buy their wares, and business would be transacted as it had been yesterday and the day before. In a few days, Gabriel Infanti's wife in New Jersey would report Infanti as a missing person. She'd tell the police that he'd left the house with a big pile of cash. He was going to buy a car from a guy. That was all she knew. That was pretty much the extent of what she knew in general about her husband. He was always going off to see a guy about a thing. She was upset, but for the Bonanno crime family, it was as if nothing had happened at all. Christmas was coming, and Gabriel Infanti would be spoken of no more.

CHAPTER TWO

The young man of means awoke in his thirty-eighth-floor Manhattan aerie high above the East River. Below he watched the sun rise up over Queens and spread across the towers of the Upper East Side. He could see the millions just beginning to awaken. The lights on the 59th Street Bridge still twinkled in the gray dawn, and one by one, the good people of Manhattan were rising to face the day. Lights went on all around him. He was up at 5:30 a.m. every weekday, out the door by 6:30, at his desk by 7. He embraced his early morning enthusiasm. He couldn't wait to get to work. He was going to make money, lots of money, more money than a young man of twenty-seven deserved to make. This was it. He had arrived. He stepped into the shower and prepared to march forward.

He told people he lived on Sutton Place, an address synonymous with wealth and Upper East Side taste. He told people he lived down the street from the secretary general of the United Nations, who lived in a house built for the daughter of J. P. Morgan. Henry Kissinger was his neighbor.

Marilyn Monroe and Arthur Miller once lived within these city blocks of exclusivity. Sutton Place was a place unto itself, blocks from the subway but attractive to people who wouldn't think of riding the A train. Buildings designed by architects famous twenty years ago. A "TAXI" light from the 1940s on the corner of Sutton and 57th Street that hadn't stopped a cab in years. This was Sutton Place, a neighborhood that stubbornly clung to Old New York. An address steeped in old money. A place where guys who wanted everybody to know they'd made it might choose to live.

Of course, he really didn't live on Sutton Place.

Actually he lived a block away, on East 54th Street and First Avenue. But he still had the views, and for somebody who didn't know the difference, he could keep the line going. Sutton Place was where he lived, as far as he was concerned. And Sutton Place or not, he had come a long way.

When he started out, he had almost nothing. He had come to believe that, through sheer force of will and a good story line, he could do anything he wanted to do and be anyone he wished to be. Women inevitably loved him. Men wanted to be him. He was handsome in a predictable way. People often told him he looked like the actor Mickey Rourke, with square jaw and sly smile turned up at the corner. He was always tan—summer, winter, spring or fall. He knew how to turn on the boyish charm. He was a Wall Street buccaneer, the lone rider on the plains of Capitalism with no attachments, no real responsibilities other than to continue making money for people who already had plenty. He was up with every sunrise and ready to be at his desk at Oppenheimer by seven. That was the Wall Street way.

This was the 1980s. This was Reagan and supply-side and trickle-down. This was a market trading in the thousands after trading in the hundreds for decades. Money was the new frontier. Every day the heroes of Wall Street came up with new ways to make more and more money. And there was so much money floating around, you couldn't spend it all. There weren't enough hours in the day. Maybe the old guard still took the subway to work, but the new guard knew better. Why hide success? Screw the subway. Hire a limo. Order top-shelf, smoke Cubans, collect Italian suits. Spending theatrically sent a message, made a statement, proclaimed that you were a man of substance who spent only what he'd earned. Excess was acceptable, even expected. The young man's apartment may have been a block from Sutton Place, but the suits and the guy waiting to drive him down to Broad Street were real enough. They were what was required if you wanted to be somebody down on Wall Street.

Getting ready for the office, the young man was quite aware that he was the luckiest guy in the world. Ten years earlier a lot of guys his age would have been struggling to work their way up the ladder, nowhere near this wealthy this soon. His timing had been impeccable. He lived top-of-the-line, in a high-rise with a twenty-four-hour doorman in an old-money section of Midtown Manhattan perched over FDR Drive and inhabited by people whose money dated back to the robber barons of the last century. Some of these people had been born into it, but some had had to scrape their way up to be allowed to live on Sutton Place (or at least near it). Many of these people would have been shocked at all that the young man had assembled in such a short period of time.

There was the art collection. He knew almost nothing about art, but understood its ability to create credibility. He'd bought matching black Mercedes convertibles for himself and his sister. He owned a $500 Rolex. He visited a tanning salon once a week, no exceptions. The stove in his apartment was top-of-the-line, but he never turned it on. He ate out every night and placed himself in nightclubs and bars frequented by models. Models were part of the deal. You let models know you were a Wall Street guy and that got their attention. The sound of money always got attention. They may have had a hard time naming the president or filling out a customs form, but they well understood the ramifications of the Wall Street hurricane of the 1980s. In fact, all of America knew about the Wall Street buccaneers and the glamour and the glory. They worked hard, they played hard. They were doing lines of coke at midnight and were back at the office by seven, ready to reap the rewards they believed they so richly deserved.

On this day, the young man hoped for a little more reaping, although he was painfully aware that this Monday might be anything but a sure bet. The previous Friday had sort of been dubbed Black Friday. It was really kind of ridiculous, but it had spooked a lot of normally intelligent people. The Dow had gone and fallen more than one hundred points (108 points precisely), a feat it had never accomplished before in its history. The percentage drop, 11.7 percent, was not as bad as the 12.8 percent drop of the Crash of '29, and that disastrous moment in U.S. history had kept going for two days and then started a depression. This time the young man hoped it would be different. The Dow had been slowing since August, when it peaked at 2,700. It was down to 2,200 by the end on Friday, which meant a lot of the young man's colleagues had spent the entire weekend obsessing about what was going to happen come Monday morning. The young man tried to ignore it and go about his business.

Now here it was, Monday morning. He knew rewards required risk, and make no mistake, the rewards were endless. Just look at the numbers. He was making mad money. Crazy money. And there was no reason to believe he would not make more. Nobody had seen trading like this in the history of the New York Stock Exchange. No one had seen so many people getting rich so fast—even ordinary people investing their savings and pensions. Risk was good for the soul. Wall Street of the 1980s was spreading the wealth, and the young man was part of the mission. Here he was, a mere twenty-seven years old and already he had acquired and then walked away from a high-six-figure partnership at Bear Stearns—the biggest brokerage house on the Street. He would make a point of bringing this up and reciting the perks in detail as proof of worth.

"I came over to Bear Stearns as a vice president," he'd tell people. "It was right around my twenty-fifth birthday. I was given a private office. I was given a secretary. I was given a trading assistant. At one point in time, I had three trading assistants, and in the 1986 partnership announcements right before my twenty-sixth birthday, I was made partner at Bear Stearns."

He had a unique way of describing things. The language wasn't exactly Wharton School. He'd say he "purposely pushed the back of the envelope."

He wore his hair in a ponytail. He'd show up in the partners' dining room without socks. They called him "the kid" because he was the one who could spout financial judgments like he was at a spelling bee. They'd say, "Let's get the kid's opinion on where the market's going." At least, that was what he thought. It didn't last.

For some, leaving Bear Stearns would have been devastating. For the young man, it was just a means toward a more lucrative end. He knew things weren't working out as he'd planned at Bear Stearns. The lack of socks in the executive dining room, the ponytail—all of that was okay when he was making judgment calls that resulted in profit. But the calls weren't going his way of late, and "the kid" was now more of a nuisance than an asset. The partners were bored with the kid. He began to look around until he found a new spot—a tabula rasa opportunity at Oppenheimer.

Now on this unseasonably warm October Monday, he was headed into work at Oppenheimer, the black car picking him up outside his apartment for the slog from the Upper East Side through downtown traffic to Wall Street. It was good that Oppenheimer had made him a senior vice president, let him write daily financial futures reports and

given him a one-year payout that came to more than anything Bear Stearns had ever offered. It was a great job—
better than Bear Stearns. It was the kind of job he could
talk about to friends and family, let them see just how well
he was doing. He looked forward to going to work every
single day, even if it was the Monday after Black Friday.

The young man arrived at the office before his secretary and checked his messages. Usually he'd check prices
for commodities like wheat and soy and look at overseas
markets, where this stuff was sold, to see whether any new
wars or coups or assorted panics had screwed around with
price. Then he'd look at gold and silver and how the U.S.
dollar was holding up. Lately the dollar hadn't been doing
too well. There were a lot of people out there worried that
foreign investors were getting tired of its slow spin toward
the abyss and would start getting out of the American
stock market. This was something to think about in his latest line of work—derivatives.

At Oppenheimer, the young man was paid to foretell the
future, so he had to weigh all manner of factors. He was working as an analyst now, so he didn't have to deal with that in-
tense buy-sell nonsense of his early years, but he surely paid
attention to it. Dealing with derivatives was tougher. You
had to predict correctly all the time, and people tracked your
percentages. If your batting average hit a slump, you could
be out the door. If you were good at guessing, the client was
able to sell his futures contract when the per-pound or per-
ounce price was up, and everybody was happy and the Christmas bonus was in the bank. If anything unexpected or just
plain random happened, profit could go out the window and
then anything could happen.

In his office, the young man sat back, prepared. He
waited for the opening bell the way the bullfighter waits for
the bull.

One thing was clear: the young man certainly needed
Black Friday to turn into Sunshine Monday. He had much

to lose. He'd come so far and didn't want to go back. He hadn't grown up like the exclusive residents of Sutton Place. He hadn't been immersed in affluence, comforted by a sense of entitlement, possessing only an abstract notion of what it was like to have nothing. The young man had experienced living with no means of support before and was not interested in revisiting that period of his life. Anything good that had come his way, he had put there himself. And he knew one thing above all—everything you have acquired over years of hard work can go away in the time it takes for some fool out there to begin yelling "Sell!" at precisely the wrong moment.

His problem had always been timing. He was born into money that quickly disappeared. For his first eight years, he lived the upper-middle-class suburban life of bicycles and private school in Oyster Bay, Long Island. His mother had married a real estate developer who already had three children, so when the young man arrived, he became part of a family that wasn't really his. He had no idea his two older brothers and one older sister weren't blood relatives, because nobody told him. He learned about this the day his siblings' real mother showed up screaming and yelling about custody. A nasty battle ensued, and in the middle of it all, when he was a mere nine years old, his father collapsed on the kitchen floor of their comfortable home, victim of a fatal heart attack. When Dad died, so did the comfortable life.

Wall Street had been a pretty simple choice for a guy who'd suffered uncertainty for so long. It was not a question of what he *felt* like doing with his life, or whether he enjoyed one vocation or another. It was a matter of obtaining certainty. To do this you got and kept as much money as possible, as quickly as possible. He went to college, got a degree in biology, and naturally got a job with all the implications of Darwinism—a clerk at a commodity trading house. He took the Series 7 and became a registered broker, and in nine months he'd jumped to a new twenty-four-hour-a-day brokerage house with a higher salary. The money poured in, and as far as he was concerned, Wall Street was where he had always been meant to be.

"I would believe I had, I should say, I don't want to sound egotistical at all, there were points in time when I was the largest producer or second largest producer at Oppenheimer or at Bear Stearns and I believe during that time period I had only one [customer] complaint."

No way was somebody going to take it away. He had already come close to losing it all through no fault of his own. The way he saw it, you worked all the time and got only what you deserved—lots and lots of money. You benefited from rules that existed to ensure those with the most talent would receive the maximum profit, as long as they were ambitious enough to take it. But you could always lose it. His first job as a licensed broker was with a London-based firm, Johnson Mathie, one of four that fixed the price of gold and silver twice a day. It seemed like a sure bet, even if his abuse of the English language didn't exactly fit in at a London investment house.

"Everything was to be done correctly and articulately and properly. Clients' interests were at heart—to use a misnomenclature, the best way to describe it was, it was a class act. It was a nice place to work. Right down to the euphemism, they did have tea at twelve in the afternoon. It was a really nice place to work."

True he would always sound like a Yank, but he was making them money. That was a language anyone could understand. Then the biology major discovered a very biological fact about economics—one day you're here, the next day you're not. Mathie went bankrupt. He had to find a new job. It was his first time. On Wall Street, jumping around from employer to employer is not really that uncommon, but it's rarely pleasant. When Mathie shut down, he took what he could find and wound up at a smaller brokerage called Clayton.

This was difficult to explain on a résumé in a world where there was only one acceptable direction, but there was always a way to explain anything if you had the desire and imagination. He was particularly adept at explanation.

"I should say that Clayton was not an upward move. That was definitely a sideways or downward move. And I was with Clayton Brokerage for maybe nine months to a year and I became their biggest producer. But I want to define producer. Producer means commission dollars: how many commission dollars one is generating for the firm. I believe the last month—now this is 1985, the last month that I was at Clayton Brokerage, my commissions were approximately $150,000 to $160,000 a month, which my payout was 50 percent on. I had several months at Clayton Brokerage where I would earn that kind of money, right before my twenty-fifth birthday. I really didn't want to stay at Clayton Brokerage. It lacked a certain amount of sophistication."

Sophistication. Prestige. Sometimes it seemed these were more important than even the money. It was important to him that he be seen as sophisticated, a man of wit and worth. He never really spent much time acquiring the cultural education necessary to be truly sophisticated, because that would have taken away from the time he spent making money. And he had discovered that on Wall Street, you really didn't have to know a Mondrian from a Monet; you could pay someone to know the difference for you. What was important was the effect the Monet had on people who didn't know any better. It was Manhattan name-dropping. It was being part of something you could never really be a part of, simply by writing a check.

To be more precise, lots of checks. The need to improve the net was all-consuming. It was just as John D. Rockefeller had said when he was asked how much money is enough: "Just a little more." The hunting and gathering never ended. The young man was motivated by a desire to acquire, but once he'd begun acquiring, he learned a distressing fact: there was only one direction—up. You could never sell off property and you had to have more. Once you attained a certain lifestyle, you were obligated to maintain it and improve upon it as soon as possible.

"I was making very good money, and I was constantly broke. I never had a penny in the bank. I rented what I couldn't buy."

Whatever money he got, he spent. If he wanted more, he borrowed. He would never recommend a company that did business the way he lived. If he saw something he liked, he bought it. If he drank wine with his dinner, he'd never look at the price. That was something only ordinary people had to do. Cost was meaningless when you believed the supply of cash would never stop. And if he came up short, that was no problem. There was credit. American Express and MasterCard and Visa were delighted to help out, sending off friendly solicitations with zero-percent financing for the first six months. After that, you switch to another card. There was no reason to save. Saving was for fools. Sink some of your paycheck back into stock and get rid of the rest as fast as you can. The art hanging on his walls was worth a fraction of what he told people it was worth, but still he could use it as collateral to borrow more. Collection agencies hammered at the door, looking to seize first his Mercedes convertible and then his sister's. When he jumped over to Oppenheimer, most of the up-front payout went immediately to cover debts, some of which had been festering for quite a while. If Wall Street collapsed, that could be a problem. The revenue stream would have to be replaced immediately. Bankruptcy was not an option.

Which was why he was growing increasingly concerned as he watched the ticker on this Monday morning after Black Friday.

From the opening bell the Dow began to drop and didn't stop. It looked odd, the trading volume numbers he was seeing. He was used to seeing the same numbers every day.

A dip like this hadn't been seen since the worst day of all time, October 29, 1929. The idea that something like that could happen again was too much to think about. But here it was, and it wasn't slowing.

At 11 a.m., the Dow was down to 2,100.

The young man and all the other brokers and analysts and managers and clerks and receptionists at Oppenheimer sat transfixed, the numbers on their computer screens gliding by like tracer bullets.

For a while, there was hope. The drop stopped shortly after eleven and the Dow began to rise again, until noon, when it began to hold steady. Nobody went out on the street for lunch. The hot dog and knish guys on Broad Street outside the Exchange stood around scratching themselves, victims of slide. The shoeshine guys outside Trinity Church smoked cigarettes and talked Yankees and Mets. The usually bustling lunchtime crowd evaporated.

After lunch the drop started again. The execution of trades was beginning to get clogged in the machine. Trades were behind by two hours. Nobody knew what the hell was going on, so naturally everybody started to guess. Was it James Baker talking negative about the U.S. dollar? Was it the U.S. Navy choosing today of all days to blow up one of Iran's offshore oil platforms in the Persian Gulf? Was it millions of small-time investors spooked by Black Friday and fleeing the stock market altogether like lemmings into the abyss? Was it the dreaded program trading gone wild? Who knew? The Dow hit 2,000 at 2 p.m., then 1,900 by 3 p.m.

That was when the rumor started. The Securities and Exchange Commission was ordering the Exchange to halt trading. It could happen at any time. They had never done that before, and to do so now was surely a sign that the end of days was at hand for American capitalism. The fact that the rumor wasn't true didn't really matter. Rumor itself could easily have the same the effect as lightning hitting a pond. The panic began in earnest at 3 p.m. Investors began unloading as fast as they could. In one hour the Dow dropped from 1,900 to 1,800 and screeched toward 1,700.

At the closing bell of 4 p.m. the bloodletting stopped at 1738.74, and that was just an estimate because the trades were so far behind. They even shut down the Pacific Exchange a half hour before its usual 4:30 p.m. closing bell to stop further carnage.

It was over. There was nothing more to say. The Wall Street buccaneers sat back and looked at numbers.

This was history. This was big. They had witnessed the Dow skid like a kid on a sled headed for the interstate. You could almost hear the collective gasp. The money that everyone had made in the bullish eighties had swirled down the drain, all gone in six hours. Fortunes had evaporated between coffee break and lunch. The Dow had dropped 508 points—a 22.6 percent hit. That was well over the 12.6 percent of 1929, especially when you considered the scope of trading. In one day's activity, a stunning 604.3 million shares had been traded. That was nearly twice Black Friday's 338 million, which itself was a record. Who even remembered Black Friday? This was, by all accounts, a disaster. At close there were 52 stocks up, 1,973 down. The estimate was that the American stock market had just suffered a loss worth $500 billion in equity—more than the gross national product of India.

Nobody moved from his or her desk. Everyone knew what had happened, and no one could have done a damn thing to stop it—certainly not the young man who had much to lose, formerly "the kid," the guy who'd gotten quite used to making high six figures. The clients had panicked. Sell orders hit the desk like a tsunami. The buccaneers were overwhelmed. They watched the spectacle, absorbed the moment, put off all deep reflection. They sat in a catatonic trance. The market they all believed in, the good times that would never end, had collapsed right there in front of them in a handful of autumn hours. The weekend seemed far away. This was sea change. This was a turning point. This was the decline and fall, the end of the Temple of Boom. Clearly the young man had not seen it coming.

He was, allegedly, as prepared as anyone else making a fortune through his acquired knowledge of how money and people interact. He had taken macroeconomics, microeconomics, accounting, calculus. He knew about the Laffer curve, the multiplier effect, the nuances of supply and demand. He understood how it was supposed to work. He understood that at times it was difficult to anticipate arbitrary human emotion. He understood that voodoo superstition could sometimes play havoc with a system allegedly based on reason, but usually reason prevailed. Self-interest produced complex equations, but usually the answer was more or less equal to the sum of the parts. And it always worked out in the end. A bear was always followed by a bull. It had been that way since Alexander Hamilton established the first Federal Reserve. How had it come to this? Why hadn't he been on top of this?

For some of the young man's colleagues, the morning produced headaches, a deficit in the bank account, some heated arguments with demanding spouses or girlfriends or both. There might be some belt-tightening for a short bit, but they would weather the storm, wait until the seas had calmed, then wade back in and pull down the big bucks once again. Most had accumulated plenty of net and socked it away for events such as this. This would be a temporary setback, a speed bump. The money tree would sprout anew in no time at all.

For the young man, it was a different story. Surprise comes to those who seek the ends without heeding the ways and means. He knew where he stood.

If he thought about it, he knew it wasn't really his fault. It was the fault of unfortunate timing and, of course, his employer, Oppenheimer. In his opinion the firm had long been poorly managed and vulnerable to downturns like that day's implosion in ways it didn't need to be. If the company had not been so heavily leveraged, they would not now be facing the probability of severe cutbacks, which he knew were coming. He called it a "double whammy": making a "mistake" by leaving Bear Stearns (actually he would have been fired if he hadn't left) and then working for a company that was "grossly undercapitalized." Within days, he got the news.

It was just a job, of course, but work was his life. And when the market that would never end decided to self-immolate and bring half the economy down with it, "the kid" was quite aware that getting a new job as soon as possible was not just important—it was crucial. Oppenheimer had been comfortable, a serendipitous burst of good fortune. The Monday Massacre or whatever the *Wall Street Journal* was going to call it, meant good fortune was at an end.

His name was Cary Cimino. He was twenty-seven years old, and he knew it was time to start all over again.

CHAPTER THREE

Midwood, Brooklyn, in the late 1980s was Robert Lino's world. He grew up on East 13th Street near Avenue P, miles from Manhattan, south of the Hasidim of Borough Park, east of Italian Bensonhurst and north of Italian Gravesend. This was a neighborhood where strangers were immediately recognized and questioned. People shopped at stores owned by families. In the late 1980s, it was still almost entirely Italian, with a handful of Irish and Jews mixed in and almost no black or brown people. If they wandered in here, they'd be hounded out. The Hassidim were encroaching from nearby Borough Park, some Russians had moved in, but for the most part it was an Italian neighborhood.

Most of Midwood's residents had worked their way here from the tenements of Lower Manhattan and viewed this world as their own version of paradise. Robert's father, Bobby, was a gangster, but he also was partners in a popular neighborhood restaurant called Pizza Park that everybody in the neighborhood knew. In Midwood, if you were from the neighborhood and not from anywhere else, people knew all about you and who you were related to. They remembered whose brothers were star baseball players at Lafayette, who got drunk at his sister's confirmation party, and who was connected to organized criminals and who was not. This was a specific kind of America, where people from faraway places lived right next to each other and became not Italian or Russian or Chinese—they were just Brooklyn.

By the 1980s, the Brooklyn Robert Lino lived in was no *Tree Grows in Brooklyn* paradise of immigration and assimilation. Drugs were killing the tree at its roots. While crack cocaine was just beginning to chainsaw its way through black neighborhoods, the sons and daughters of Italy still preferred powder cocaine, quaaludes and heroin. There was plenty for all, and there was plenty in Robert Lino's family. Bobby Senior, after all, sold the stuff, although not formally, of course. The Bonanno crime group was very much opposed to selling drugs, if it was done officially. If it was done unofficially, the money to be made would have made Donald Trump blush. Of course, there was a downside to all of this. Robert Lino knew all about it.

For starters, his older brother, Vincent, had died at age twenty-three of a drug overdose. He took too much heroin and that was that. This was like a slap in the back of Robert's head. Vincent was a lot of things, but he would always be Robert's brother. Now the drugs were ripping apart the rest of the family. Robert's sister, Grace Ann, had addiction problems. Grace Ann was scoring from gangsters, informally. She would disappear for days at a time, sliding further and further away from the rest of the family. Only Robert had managed to stay away from it. It was a depressing time for him. He viewed the area and the era as dangerous to his family. He believed both drugs and the neighborhood itself had killed his brother Vincent. He was aware that his father would spend weeks at a time in Italy arranging drug deals. His father could only see all the money he was making and nothing else.

That was Midwood in the late 1980s. It was the Wild West. At one point there was a young couple from the neighborhood who'd come to the conclusion that robbing Mafia social clubs was a great idea. They would put on disguises and bust in waving revolvers and take as much cash as they could, then bolt out of there faster than red-blooded American shoppers the day after Thanksgiving. When word leaked out that this was going on, they became known in the press as Bonnie and Clyde of Brooklyn. This iconic tag was probably somewhat romantic, but the truth of such matters is messy and difficult to understand. To the reading public, the couple became a pair of antiheroes, criminals who robbed only criminals.

There was something appealing about this, but there was also a foreboding sense that Bonnie and Clyde—just like their namesakes—were headed for a nasty end. In Midwood, you certainly couldn't have found anybody who'd bet Bonnie and Clyde of Brooklyn were long for this world. People didn't really debate their motives. Who knew why they chose such a self-destructive career? It was clearly a deliberate act of suicide, and almost nobody thought the New York City Police Department should even bother with them. The criminals would catch the criminals, administer their own version of justice, and that would be that. The taxpayers shouldn't have to foot the cost of a trial.

The reaction to Bonnie and Clyde revealed a Midwood symptom: sometimes the mob becomes the criminal justice system it seeks to subvert. It is as much a part of the neighborhood as Nathan's Hot Dogs and Uncle Louie G's Italian ices. So when Bonnie and Clyde were shot in the head at a stoplight as they were driving home a station wagon filled with Christmas presents, there was no surprise and not a whole lot of effort to find out who did it. This was the correct ending to a peculiarly Brooklyn tale.

The way people from the neighborhood figured it, the crazy couple had ripped off the gangsters, so the gangsters were justified in killing the crazy couple. The gangsters had every right to, and in fact, under the rules of Midwood, they were obligated to do this. They had no choice. End of case. With certain residents of Midwood, the notion of what was criminal was relative. If you asked somebody if they thought it was a crime to murder your obnoxious upstairs neighbor, they'd say, "Of course." If you asked them if they thought it was a crime to murder a man and woman burglary team who had made a point of robbing Mafia social clubs, they'd respond, "What'd they expect?" There was common sense in it, and it was this Midwood logic—the "you get what you deserve" school—that Robert Lino carried around with him.

The Midwood logic shaped opportunities. In Robert Lino's world, where drugs killed your brother and were killing your sister, you had to get out or get with the program. You joined the army or got a job at the post office or ran a pizza parlor. Or you dealt drugs or became a gangster. With the last two choices, it was important to note the distinction. The drug dealer was a lowlife. The gangster was a man of honor. These options were clear in a neighborhood where you started off a few steps behind the starting line.

College was not an option. In school Robert sometimes had problems reading all the words. In class, he had a hard time sitting still. He wasn't the biggest kid, so football wasn't an option. He made it only as far as sixth grade. He never learned algebra or chemistry or the history of Western civilization. He dropped out of middle school when he was thirteen years old and nobody blinked. He wasn't expected to stick it out through high school. His father hadn't. His cousins Eddie and Frank hadn't. Few of the wiseguys he knew took school seriously at all. If anything, they derided it as a waste of time. What was the point? What did you learn there that you couldn't learn on the street? They knew where they were headed and school was not in the picture. The idea that you graduated high school, went off to college away from the neighborhood, got a big-money job and earned a real salary—it was all a big joke. Only losers and the kids whose fathers could afford to send them to military school or Poly Prep did that. For Robert Lino, stepping forward into late twentieth-century America with only a sixth-grade education was just something that was meant to be. There wasn't much you could expect to do about it except find another way.

So while other kids learned calculus, Robert Lino learned Mafia math—the best way to figure the line on college football; the quick way to calculate points of the vig when helping your cousins track the money they put out on the street. He was the kid who was always around, available to do the work nobody else was willing to do. He was the caddy, the ball boy, the sorcerer's apprentice. And these guys, these made men, they were his heroes. They were part of something special, something outside of the usual banal life of the dollars-per-hour working sad-sack drone. He believed that the myth of *The Godfather* was real. He believed that gangsters only hurt rats and deadbeats, only stole from people who could afford it, and did it all to feed their wives and children. He swore allegiance to the ritual of *omerta*, saw "the life" as a calling. Other teenagers memorized batting averages or spent all their unscheduled hours skateboarding. By the time Robert was a teenager, he knew the entire induction ceremony by heart—the business with the burning saint, the pin in the trigger finger, everything. "If you prick my finger, will I not bleed?"

From the first day his father had him collect bets from his lowlife bookmaking customers, Robert Lino knew where he was headed.

CHAPTER FOUR

June 1989

Post-crash, the Vertical Club on the Upper East Side remained popular among Wall Streeters. Those who paid the exorbitant monthly fees toned up abs and pecs and worked on keeping themselves fit and trim and in good enough shape to make more and more and more. They worked out whenever they could fit it in. The club was open from five in the morning until midnight, and there'd be people there when the doors opened and people there when they closed. It was a desirable place to be because more often than not there was the potential to make a connection that could lead to a deal or a commission or some transaction that ended with more money in your bank account. Between sets with the free weights and the four miles on the treadmill, if you weren't talking business, there was something wrong with you. After all, what else was there but getting and having? Or in the case of Cary Cimino, keeping.

In less than two years the market had recovered somewhat, leveling out and then beginning a crawl upward. The federal government had picked up some press indicting some of the innovators in the market like Michael Milken and Drexel Lambert, and a handful of brokers had been led off the floor in handcuffs, a true low point. Now everyone was cautious. Money was still there, only you weren't supposed to flaunt it. Investors had become conservative and regulators had become emboldened. Wall Street simply wasn't as glamorous and fun, but for most of those who worked in Lower Manhattan, it was no longer a scary experience going off to work in the morning. If you had work. At the moment, Cary technically had work. Technically.

It wasn't work that any government agency would know about, and it was extremely occasional. After the Crash of '87 he'd left Oppenheimer for what he thought was a better job with a six-figure sign-up bonus at Prudential Bache, but that lasted exactly nine months before the partners asked him to leave due to what they termed "lack of production." Then he got himself evicted from his apartment near Sutton Place for forgetting to pay the rent. Now he was constantly exhausted and depressed, running a fever, staying in bed all day because he didn't want to get up and face the world he'd created. And he'd become exhausted by the play-hard, work-hard life. He was popping every kind of antibiotic available, plus a myriad of antidepressants. His own good fortune was slowly killing him. "I was seeing a doctor twice a week," he said, proving that whatever ailed him was certainly physical and could never be a matter of personal choice.

No longer was he working hard. Playing hard was a different matter. Playing hard was mostly a way of not dealing with certain big issues such as career, a sense of purpose, growing up. The best way to avoid these things was to focus on little things, like a car.

"Summer was starting," he said. "I mean, I'm not going to have my convertible repossessed, God forbid."

Specifically, Cary was trying desperately to keep possession of his brand-new leased 1989 Mercedes 580SL convertible with the white leather seats and polished black exterior. Sometimes it was better to focus on the little things when the big things were getting you down. Maintaining possession of the 580SL convertible certainly qualified. If Cary concentrated on the car issue, he wouldn't have to look at the job issue. Or the housing issue. Or the girlfriend issue. The car issue was something he could get his brain around.

One morning when Cary was working out at the Vertical Club—Cary called it "a social club masquerading as a gym"—the solution to his car woes became apparent. A broker named Howie was there, who Cary didn't really know too well, although he'd done a couple of deals with him and made some money. Howie was telling him about this guy he knew, Jeffrey, who operated a car lease company with his father. Howie figured Jeffrey could help Cary work something out with the Mercedes. Howie made it clear that you didn't ask too many questions about Jeffrey, and you didn't need to know anyway. Jeffrey had a knack for getting things accomplished. In the locker room after their workout, Howie told Cary he'd get in touch with Jeffrey and get the two of them together.

At the time, Mercedes had demanded that Cary return the 580SL immediately. Again. The last time he'd managed to hold on to his vehicle by cobbling together enough cash to make a few back payments. But pretty soon the payments had stopped again, and now Mercedes was done with Cary Cimino and his many excuses. They wanted the car back. Although it was just a car, the idea that he might lose it was too much for Cary. It was the ultimate indignity.

Cary met Jeffrey for the first time in person at the offices of Three Star Leasing, the company Jeffrey was running with his father in New Jersey. The guy was maybe five foot six, a bit overweight and balding, with a nasty little mustache that looked like a leach lurking on his lip. He had tiny black eyes and it was hard to tell his age. He could have been thirty, but he looked forty. He cursed and talked a mile a minute, faster than Cary even. He threw around business words the way Cary dealt in the commodity of psychobabble. When he walked, the guy had a kind of side-to-side manner that he would call swagger and others would call waddle. He looked like a penguin with a criminal record.

"Jeffrey Pokross," he said, reaching out a hand.

Cary liked him immediately.

"Jeffrey had a rapier wit. Extremely quick. Extremely intelligent. He was one of the few individuals that I could banter with. He had a vast source of knowledge, a jack of all trades and master of none. I could see he had never done a legitimate day of work in his life."

Cary had a feeling that Jeffrey Pokross and his Three Star Leasing were not all they seemed. The place looked like a real business—there were secretaries and computer screens and telephones—but there was something odd about it all. When Jeffrey described what Three Star did, he was somewhat vague. He claimed the company arranged long-term leases of luxury cars for customers through banks. That was his story, anyway. The customer would lease the car through Three Star, which would obtain the lease from the car company and sell it to a bank. The bank would then assume responsibility for collecting the money and Three Star would get a fee. That was fine when the eighties were in full swing and people on the Street were a bit freer with their money. Now that was all over and Three Star was having a tougher time. Jeffrey still had his Wall Street customers, but far fewer, and now he was getting customers from different walks of life. Some didn't have the best credit ratings. At first, this meant Three Star had to say no to these people, but Three Star didn't say no anymore. They needed the business. They began offering a new service, which they never really put down on paper as a real service. It was referred to as "credit adjustment." This meant turning into a fiction writer when filling out lease applications. Cary could relate to that.

Three Star began to get even more creative. They came up with a new idea—one that Jeffrey did not mention to Cary. They were quietly selling cars they did not own to customers. The banks would raise a fuss and Jeffrey Pokross would funnel over a few payments from new customers to the bank to shut them up for a while before closing up shop and heading for another bank. It was a classic Ponzi scheme with Mercedes and Bentleys and Porsches as bait.

When they began talking about Cary's precarious Mercedes 580SL, Jeffrey assured him they could work something out. Cary was aware that Jeffrey Pokross and Three Star were not UNICEF, but he didn't much care. This was business, and he needed money. In business you sometimes cut corners to keep the operation running. You do it to help out the employees. They have babies to feed, car payments to make, mortgages to abide. Just because Jeffrey Pokross did some things that maybe weren't kosher every single minute, well, everybody's got something to hide, right?

Including, of course, Cary himself. He did not mention to Jeffrey certain aspects of his situation. Such as the fact that he was unemployed. Or that he was mooching free rent off his girlfriend. Instead, he told Jeffrey he was an independent financial adviser who'd quit Prudential because he'd felt cramped and unable to realize his full potential. He still had possession of his stockbroker's license, so he could wave that around, and he made mention that he had access to plenty of clients who'd invested millions of dollars with him over the years and trusted him like a priest. He dropped in his onetime employment as a Bear Stearns partner without mentioning how it all had ended up over there. Now he was claiming he'd gone to Stanford, without mentioning Boston University. BU had been replaced by the Ivy League and all its implications, without all the hassle of graduation. And, if it wasn't too much of a problem, could he borrow $3,000? He was having a little cash flow issue, temporary of course. No problem, said Jeffrey. And do you know about our "credit adjustment" feature we offer all our customers?

Whether Jeffrey Pokross believed anything Cary told him did not matter even a little, because he must have known that Cary was a guy just like him—a guy who looked at people to see what they had to offer. Cary was aware of this.

"I didn't come into that relationship with Jeffrey painting a true picture," Cary would admit. "I didn't tell Jeffrey, well, I'm totally broke and destitute. Jeffrey had an understanding that I was having financial problems, but Jeffrey is intelligent enough to know that I brought something to the table, which was—at that point in time—a legitimate résumé." Everybody involved knew it was a relationship based entirely on self-interest: "We both saw in the other individual an opportunity to make money together. I mean, to leverage off one another."

Jeffrey promised to take care of the Mercedes situation as soon as possible. In the meantime, he had a proposition.

There was this deal in the works that would make them all millionaires. Overnight. Guaran-fucking-teed. Cary would be getting $1,500 a week, a free office at Three Star and a free car thrown in. Jeffrey would just need to borrow Cary and his broker's license for a little bit. And if Cary had the temerity, he could make a lot of money in a short period of time. Cary said, "That's interesting."

Jeffrey went to work.

CHAPTER FIVE

Early 1989

Bobby Lino Sr. lay in a hospital bed in Brooklyn. Most of his life he weighed in around 180, 190 pounds. Now he was down to 90 pounds, with shoes. There were tubes and machines that beeped and nurses in and out scribbling on clipboards. An air of festivity was not present. At his bedside were his cousin Frank, and two old friends, Good Looking Sal and Big Louie. They had known each other for years, back from the old neighborhood in Gravesend, Brooklyn. They had lived the life of *la cosa nostra* every day, done pieces of work together, schemed their days away. Oh, the capers! They met all the big names—Tony Ducks, Rusty Rastelli, Big Paulie and even the guy on the cover of *Time* magazine, John Gotti. They strutted down Mulberry Street with a roll of bills and a smile and a slap on the arm for their fellow good fellows. But it wasn't the same now. It wasn't *The Godfather* anymore. It wasn't as much fun.

It all went bad with that business with Donnie Brasco, the FBI agent who'd conned them all. That was bad news for everybody. A lot of guys with families to feed had taken it in the neck on that one. Sure Bobby Senior had walked away from that mess. Donnie Brasco hadn't touched him. But look at him now. He was Bobby Senior, soldier in the Bonanno organized crime family of New York City, down to ninety pounds, the Big C hanging over his head. All the chemicals and tubes and machines weren't turning the tide. He was on his way. The current was pulling him downstream toward the big waterfall. True, he had done some very bad things in his life. Now it was time to set the record straight.

First off, Bobby Senior couldn't have helped any of it. He was born into the life. His mother and father and most of the Lino family had come from Sicily back in the 1920s when the Black Hand—a group of marginally organized criminals that would eventually become the particular version of organized crime called the American Mafia—did certain favors for people in the neighborhood, in exchange for which these people owed them for the rest of their natural born days. Way back in the 1930s it started with Bobby Senior's uncle, Frank Lino Sr. He'd done a big favor for a guy named Funzi. Funzi would someday become the boss of the Genovese crime family. At the time he was just a powerful man in the world of Brooklyn Sicilians, and if you asked him for help, he would help. In this case, a fellow Sicilian, Frank Ciccone, was facing the possibility of being deported back to the old country after being caught bootlegging. Ciccone needed to make sure his daughter, Louise, was taken care of here in Brooklyn if he needed to leave, so he went to the gangster boss. The gangster boss, being a practical man who knew a victim when he saw one, immediately embraced the Ciccone family as if they were his own. He immediately promised to arrange a nice marriage to a nice boy named Frank Lino. Frank's father was a friend of the boss, so there was no negotiation about whether Frank and Louise would begin this new life together. The blessed event, arranged by the boss Funzi, went forward, and thus forever linked the Lino family to *la cosa nostra.*

Years later there would be Bobby and Eddie and Frank Junior, all immersed in the life. All believed in the life, and in Brooklyn in the 1950s, 1960s and 1970s, it was something to aspire to. Bobby had enjoyed it, anyway. He would disappear for months at a time to Italy, arranging heroin purchases. He would sell marijuana, cocaine, whatever the demand required. He tried manufacturing quaaludes for a while but didn't make any money at it. And of course, he did a piece of work or two.

Lying in the hospital bed with the Big C looming over his head, it could happen that all of a sudden you saw all the people you'd clipped from a different point of view. Getting close to the end of the book had a way of doing that. Things you never spoke of had a way of coming back, even if you couldn't remember all the names.

One of the guys he remembered was Bobby C. He didn't really know the guy too well and somebody else did most of the work. It was explained that Bobby C owed everybody in Brooklyn money, and everybody in Brooklyn believed Bobby C was about to turn into a government rat. There were no documents or anything to prove this, just strong belief. Strong belief was usually good enough. When Bobby Senior was told to do it, he did it. Simple as that. He was also quite aware that if he didn't do as he was told, they would clip him and he would be the guy who winds up in Tommy Karate's bathtub. That's what happened with Bobby C, rest his soul. There was this two-family house on Bay 50th Street in Brooklyn; Bobby Senior couldn't ever remember the address. It was one of Tommy Karate's houses. Tommy had shot Bobby C while Bobby watched, and then they both dragged Bobby C's body to the bathtub, where Tommy went to work. In a way, it was pretty low-key. He didn't have to pull the trigger, and he didn't even have to do any of that business with the saws and knives in the bathtub. He just had to be around and lug first the guy and then the bags with the guy inside to a lonely spot in Staten Island, and then speak no more of Bobby C.

There was a reasonable explanation for what had to be done about Bobby C. This was also true about the other piece of work, the business with Sonny Black. Although in that case, it had almost been a disaster.

Sonny was a well-known man's man, a respected guy who many believed could one day wind up as boss. Everybody loved the guy, but everybody knew he had to go. Although it is true that in the civilized world, ignorance is not a sin, in Brooklyn, ignorance is a good way to get clipped. Ignorance was certainly the reason Sonny Black had to go. He had vouched for this knock-around guy named Donnie Brasco, even putting him on a list to get made. That would have been fine except for the fact that Donnie wasn't really Donnie. He was really Joe the FBI agent. And he'd been hanging around with Sonny Black and the rest of them for a very long time. Things were discussed. Conversations took place. Who knew that not every rat agent hired by the FBI looked like he came from Nebraska and hadn't laughed at a joke in years? This guy Donnie/Joe talked the talk, walked the walk, knew the game inside and out. Plus he was apparently very good at taking notes and sometimes even tape-recording. Sonny Black had been the one to embrace this guy, assuring everybody that Donnie was a stand-up guy who could be trusted. Sonny had confided in him, even asked him to do a piece of work. When Bobby Senior got the word that he'd be involved in clipping somebody and he realized Sonny Black might be the target, he understood why completely. You couldn't be a captain and open up the door to the federal government like that.

For Bobby Senior, the Sonny Black job was different. This time Bobby Senior had been forced to really pull his weight. Bobby had been around for a long time but never pulled the trigger. He would lure the guy to the meeting, or roll the guy in the rug, or dig the hole in the frozen ground of the fence company back lot. With Sonny Black, Bobby Senior had to do a little more.

The day of the job it was summer of 1981. It was not long after the FBI agents showed up at Sonny's bar and showed him a photo of this guy Donnie and asked, "Do you know this guy? He's an FBI agent. We just thought you'd like to know." There were a lot of meetings after that little interlude. Bobby's cousin Eddie approached Bobby and his other cousin Frank. The Lino family gathering got right down to business. Eddie inquired about finding a location for a murder. He didn't say who. Eddie said that Frank had been recommended for the job by a gangster in the Gambino family, which always had an interest in Bonanno family business. To Frank, this talk of setting up a meeting was probably bad news for Frank. Frank was always convinced that he was going to be the guy clipped. To Bobby, there was no back and forth. It was simple. They say do it, you do it. And there were certain pluses to these things. Being recommended for a murder could offer him some stability or even a promotion. Bobby and Frank said they'd find a convenient place right away.

A house in Staten Island was procured. It was like any other house, where people ate breakfast and watched TV sitcoms and fought and loved and lived. It was right next to another house and another house and was the kind of place you'd drive by and not think twice about. It was perfect for this kind of work. Twice the house was visited to make sure the layout was just right. There was a basement. This would be where the actual deed got done. Sonny would be lured to the house and walked downstairs, and would never again see the blue sky above, his final moments spent in a basement in Staten Island. The Lino cousins even acquired a body bag from the owner of a funeral home who didn't really want to know why they needed it. They set up tables and chairs in the basement to make it look like a meeting was going to take place. It was like choreographing a Broadway show, only with a different type of ending. Maybe more like Shakespeare. Everybody had a part to play, and if one guy screwed up, the reviews would be brutal. For Bobby Senior, who'd never actually pulled the trigger before, screwing up was a real possibility.

The day of the Sonny Black piece of work, Frank Lino got assigned the task of driving Sonny to the house in Staten Island. Sonny Black was a capable guy who knew he'd screwed up with the Donnie Brasco business, but they'd convinced him to attend this important meeting by assuring him that the mistake with Donnie Brasco was everyone's, not just his. To reassure him about attending the meeting, they had one of the top bosses of the Bonanno group, the consigliere of the family, a guy they called Stevie Beef, come along for the ride. If Sonny thought he was going to a high-level meeting, he would go. Everybody knew that bosses were never around when somebody got clipped. If a boss was there, Sonny Black was safe. Stevie Beef was the cover story. At least that was the thinking as Frank Lino showed up at a hotel in Brooklyn to pick up Sonny Black and Stevie Beef and drive them to the house with the tables and the chairs in the basement.

On that day Frank Lino drove a certain route to the house in Staten Island so he could pass by an intersection where a van was parked. Inside the van were Joseph Massino and another Bonanno gangster. Massino was the captain who had arranged the entire hit, and when Frank and Sonny and Stevie passed by, Massino saw that Sonny was on his way to another place. He followed in his van. This was gangster choreography.

At the house, Bobby Lino waited in the basement with gun in hand. He and another guy, Ronnie, were supposed to be the shooters. Standing in a basement waiting to use a gun on a guy you'd known for years was no easy task. They waited and waited, until finally they heard talking at the top of the stairs.

The door opened and Frank Lino emerged first, followed by Sonny Black and then the boss, Stevie Beef. As they began descending the staircase, somebody—Bobby Senior couldn't see who—pulled the boss back onto the landing and slammed the basement door shut.

Frank Lino grabbed Sonny Black by the shoulder and shoved him down the stairs. As he came rolling down, Bobby stepped up. This was his moment, the moment he'd been chosen for, a moment that would surely follow him around for the rest of his life. Bobby Senior aimed and fired. His first shot hit Sonny, but Sonny was still quite alive. Bobby fired again. This time, his gun jammed.

"Hit me again," Sonny said. "Make it good."

The other guy with a gun, Ronnie, stepped up and fired twice. Sonny Black lay still on the basement floor.

Frank Lino reached into the dead man's pants pocket to remove his car keys as proof. The keys were taken upstairs to show to Massino, while the rest of the crew went to work on Sonny Black. Bobby Lino had done his part, so this time he didn't have to stick around while they sawed off Sonny's hands so he couldn't be identified.

And that was the end of Sonny Black. Bobby Senior had, more or less, done what he was supposed to do, more or less. If the other guy hadn't been there, it might have been a different story. Bobby Senior had to know this. If Sonny had somehow escaped or some other horrific scenario had unfolded, Bobby Senior could have found himself in a different basement with tables and chairs. But it had all worked out. Months later Sonny Black would surface in a Staten Island swamp. The night of the murder there was supposed to be a hole already dug, waiting for Sonny Black, but the crew that showed up with Sonny Black couldn't find it in the dark. Instead, they dug a makeshift shallow grave, and all it took was one good rain for Sonny Black to resurface for all the world to see. There was a certain lack of dignity in all of this, but Sonny had chosen the life he'd led and died in a way he'd probably expected.

This would not be the way for Bobby Senior. He wouldn't be surfacing in any swamp in Staten Island without his hands. Instead he would die slowly from cancer. He was a physical wreck, trapped in a hospital bed, lingering. Natural causes were headed his way. There was little left for him. But as he lay there in a bed used by strangers, dying, his cousin Frank and pals Good Looking Sal and Big Louie at his bedside, he did have one last dying wish to impart.

"Frank," Bobby Senior said to his cousin. "Make sure Robert gets made."

Bobby Senior's heartfelt wish was that his youngest son, Robert, should carry on the traditions he had embraced his entire adult life. His eldest, Vincent, was gone, the victim of the drugs Bobby Senior himself sold in the neighborhood. Females weren't eligible. Robert was all that was left.

This was not a choice every father would make. Some of the old-timers felt that the whole point of *la cosa nostra* was that it was a springboard to legitimacy, a starting point to raise a little cash and then be able to participate with the Rockefellers and the Duponts on a level playing field. Look at Joe Kennedy. He started out as a bootlegger. Ideally you do what you have to do so that your children don't have to. Carlo Gambino never wanted his son, Tommy, in the life. Tommy was a bright businessman, on his way to being a multimillionaire in the garment trade. Why did he need the aggravation of kicking up to the boss, the sit-downs, the walk-talks? Vincent Gigante shook his head in disgust when John Gotti proudly boasted that his boy, John A. Gotti, had just got his button and was now a member of the Gambino family. Of course, Tommy Gambino ended up in the mob when his father died, and Chin Gigante's son Andrew would end up running a union in Miami and pleading guilty to extortion.

The allure was strong. In many ways, it made sense to have your own family next to you. A wiseguy needed somebody around he could trust, given that just about everybody else would cut your throat faster than you could say, "Leave the gun, take the cannolis." Who could Bobby Lino trust more than his own flesh and blood, his son Robert, a quiet, reliable kid?

Of course there was that part during the induction ceremony when you swore allegiance to your Mafia family above all else—even your blood family. That meant that if you were ordered to do so, you'd have to kill your own. And what if you were caught? Of course, you'd say nothing. Being a rat was worse than being dead. But maybe there would be reasons to be a rat and not be dead, and then you'd be facing a tough choice. The deal with the federal government was always the same: you tell all or you get nothing. So, for instance, if you called your son up in the middle of the night to come out and help dispose of a murder victim, you'd have to bring that up. You'd have to inform on your own son.

All of that was pretty abstract. Bobby Senior was asking his own blood relation, his cousin Frank, to do him this one last favor before he died. Frank was the perfect one to ask. He had a son, too, Joseph. Frank had taken him under his wing, put him in his own crew. So if anybody could understand, it was Frank.

"Sure, Bobby," Frank said. "I'll take care of it."

CHAPTER SIX

When he was out on the street, hounded by banks and credit card companies, facing repossession of his car, Cary Cimino had done what any grown man in his position would do. He found a rich girlfriend and moved right in. Her name was Jane, and—for a change—Cary's timing was perfect.

"Jane paid for everything for me to move my life forward and get myself back on my feet. I had had it. I had no interest in working hard anymore. I had an interest in getting healthy and playing hard."

It's difficult to judge couples. Cary and Jane seemed a mysterious combination indeed. She was a respected daughter of wealth, with a second home in Aspen and access to plenty of family money. He was a failed stock picker, bouncing from employer to employer, hustling to keep himself from Chapter 11 of the United States Bankruptcy Code. It was easy to see what Cary was getting out of the relationship: "She took care of me. Didn't judge me and probably was one of the few examples in my life of selfless unconditional love. I guess I didn't even know what that was. She supported me through thick and thin. Both emotionally, financially and intellectually. She was a marvelous and still is a marvelous person."

It was not so clear what Jane was getting out of the deal. It was probably very easy to see where it would all end up.

The first sign was the formation of NSPJ Financial Group. The acronym stood for Not So Plain Jane, Inc., something Cary had dreamed up himself, and it was to be founded by Cary but funded solely by Jane. She would appear on paper as the sole owner of Not So Plain Jane, Inc. Cary made it clear he needed to be in the background only. It was better for business that way. He still had his broker's license, but it had acquired a certain tarnish. The luster was diminished. His relationship with the prestigious world of finance had changed.

Working with Jeffrey Pokross had changed things for Cary. He was making money, but he was now burdened with a certain reputation that wasn't helping him get work at the big-name firms of Wall Street. If he was going to continue working in the securities world and scouring the earth for whatever goodwill he hadn't yet willed away, he'd have to do so behind the scenes. If there was anything he had learned in the eighties, it was that you could screw up and get caught and still make money on the Street. It wasn't easy, but it could be done. Not So Plain Jane, Inc., was to be Cary Camino's solution to this problem of reputation.

The idea was perfect: with Jane's family money, he would create from nothing a stockbrokerage company, and almost no one besides Cary would know what it was really all about. In corporate filings it was to be listed as the NSPJ Financial Group, which sounded as impressive as the rest of the scam brokerage houses that were again cropping up around Wall Street. It would seek out and reel in investors, promote hot stocks, make millions for everybody. Mostly it would make millions for Cary Cimino. Whenever Cary did any business, he would do it through Not So Plain Jane.

All the checks he would write or have written to him would come from or go through NSPJ. He would be called a consultant. His car was to be leased by NSPJ. His rent would come through there. His one gesture to Jane was to lease her a new red 1989 Jeep Laredo from Three Star, with her family's money, of course. NSPJ was the disguise that Cary the biology major would use to make his way in the world without the hassle of being seen. The Securities and Exchange Commission wouldn't see him. The United States Internal Revenue Service wouldn't see him. The banks and the credit card companies wouldn't see him. They wouldn't see him, but he would be there.

"Jane paid for everything. I used NSPJ Financial Group as a means to conduct business. Checks were written to NSPJ for consulting work when I worked with Jeffrey. I started expanding my consulting business and started taking checks in as I started to raise money for other start-up deals."

In truth, Jeffrey Pokross was the real genius behind Not So Plain Jane. Partnered with Cary, Jeffrey had now branched out into the stock promotion business, specializing in start-ups, companies that were just about to go public. Jeffrey knew all about the stock promotion business. The way Jeffrey planned it, Cary, with his broker's license, would look for people to make insider commitments on these companies, including his girlfriend's rich family. Cary had no problem getting them to invest in Jeffrey Pokross's once-in-a-lifetime deal, without having to explain details or let them know that Jeffrey hadn't made money legally since he quit his paper route at age ten.

The deal had started at the Vertical Club when Jeffrey and Cary ran into a broker named John who was a senior partner in something called Lowenthal Financial Services. Cary would say he and John formed what he termed "a tacit partnership, and what I mean by tacit, we never had anything formally in writing. It was a handshake partnership." Translation: his girlfriend's family also bought Lowenthal Financial Group. His girlfriend's family took the risk—not Cary. Thus did Cary's girlfriend and her family become central to a little performance choreographed by Jeffrey Pokross. What is clear is that the purpose of Lowenthal from the day it was purchased was to act as a fig leaf to cover up something Cary and Jeffrey didn't want everyone to see. It was covering up a reverse merger.

"I had no idea in 1989 what a reverse merger was," Cary said. "I was trying to get myself up on the yield curve, so to speak. On different methodologies available to me to raise money."

The reverse merger was Jeffrey Pokross's idea. The first time he pitched it, Cary had to ask him to slow down. When Jeffrey was pitching he often dropped into business jargon and cranked up the speed. He'd start jabbering like a chipmunk, presenting ideas as sure bets, big wins, profits guaranteed. This particular sure thing started with a reverse merger and relied heavily on Chinese action films.

Here the pitch could make your head swim. The company was to be called MPSC for Motion Picture Service Company. It would offer one-stop-shopping for making movies. You want to make a movie? You come to MPSC and they hand you a producer, a director, a film editor, a casting agent and everybody but the actors. Jeffrey claimed he was putting together heavyweight investors. MPSC would make a quick killing and he and Cary would walk away like lottery winners. There was nothing to it. They had two guys involved in producing and directing a TV crime show signed up. They even had a guy who'd directed some of the old *Lost in Space* TV episodes with the robot and "Danger Will Robinson!" and all that. They just needed a few more big-money types willing to commit some money up front so they could all be rich by Wednesday. Something like that.

But to reel in the big checkbooks, they needed Jeffrey Pokross to remain out of sight. They couldn't offer even a hint of Jeffrey Pokross. That was where Cary came in. He could still claim to be a high-powered broker with a real broker's license. He could still claim to be a former partner at Bear Stearns, a graduate of Stanford University. When you met him, you might think he was a paragon of legitimacy. Here was a guy, you might think, who knew what he was doing. Here was a guy who could bring in the serious investors who have the good sense to jump on an opportunity when it presents itself. Three million dollars would be great, $3.5 million would be better.

The fact that MPSC had absolutely no assets to speak of was not a problem. Jeffrey Pokross proposed a classic bit of "lead into gold" legerdemain—the reverse merger. Cary—the guy with the broker's license—was learning from the guy who'd taken a few graduate business courses at Monmouth College, home of the Fighting Scots. He listened and learned.

Jeffrey's plan went like this: They started with a publicly traded company called Unicom Distributors that owned 250 Chinese martial arts movies and sold its stock in the loosely regulated, highly speculative over-the-counter market. Unicom had a key piece of paper necessary when creating the aura of legitimacy—an audit signed off on by Arthur Andersen, claiming the Chinese action flicks were worth $38 million. Step one complete.

Step two: Unicom "bought" MPSC, a company that existed only in the minds of Jeffrey Pokross and Cary Cimino and possibly the guy who directed the robot who says "Danger Will Robinson!" Now MPSC was a wholly owned subsidiary of the heretofore nonexistent company that was really just Unicom. Now MPSC could claim Unicom's $38 million in assets as its own and MPSC could borrow against that to build up the company's appearance before taking the company public and then selling MPSC as a separate entity. Unicom—the money behind the façade—told investors it was going to make a killing in the emerging video market by putting its entire kung fu collection on video.

Step three was where Cary's girlfriend and her rich parents came in. The family's purchase of Lowenthal was specifically intended to generate more fees for Cary and Jeffrey and all the others involved in the deal. Lowenthal was to be the financial underwriter that would handle the reverse merger of Unicom and MPSC.

There was only one problem: in 1990, the market for Chinese action movie videos was going nowhere. The only "assets" behind the whole Potemkin Village were useless, worthless. The company behind the company was losing money and credibility. MPSC went bust about seven months after it was born.

"Well you had delusions of grandeur back then," Cary recalled. "Of course Jeffrey and I were deluding ourselves that eventually we were going to spin off MPSC into its own and we were going to make millions of dollars. Unicom acquired MPSC and the deal died on the vine. The Chinese films weren't selling. MPSC backed out. Then Lowenthal also went out of business—a loss for Jane and her family."

Under most circumstances, such a drubbing might undermine the relationship between a future son-in-law and his future family. Jane's parents, for one, would certainly have had good reason to encourage their daughter to dump the loser and find herself an orthodontist or bankruptcy attorney right away. They had, after all, lost thousands of dollars on a deal presented to them by their trusting future son-in-law as easy money. When the Chinese kung fu movies took a dive, so, too, did the future son-in-law's credibility.

When it comes to Cary Cimino, some women just don't know where to look. Jane stood by her man. Somehow Cary convinced her father that he had other sure deals. There were medical companies that weren't anything like the movie business. For sure, medical investments were just starting to look hot on Wall Street. Not-so-plain Jane's family didn't kick Cary out into the street.

If only Jane had checked the ownership of her brand-new red 1989 Jeep Laredo, a present from her one and only, sort of. He'd found it and set it up so her father could buy it, but it was an amazing deal. After MPSC and the kung fu movies went away, Cary and Jane took a little well-deserved ski vacation to Aspen, paid for by Jane. While they were there, she learned that the Laredo she was driving was in fact a stolen vehicle. The bank owned it, not Cary's good friend Jeffrey Pokross.

She was furious. Her father agreed to buy the Jeep for her from the bank, but it was incredibly embarrassing. Cary suddenly remembered he had a business meeting he had to attend. He flew back to New York, leaving Jane in Aspen.

While Jane was still in Aspen, Cary quickly moved all his belongings out of her apartment and into his own. He was making enough money from his many stock promotion deals. He obviously felt he didn't need Not So Plain Jane anymore. He moved out without telling her he was going to do it. When she returned from Aspen, he was gone.

"I destroyed her emotionally, being careless with my relationship with her. By leaving her," he said. "This was my methodology of repaying a woman back who was nothing but kind and considerate to me."

Not long after he ditched Jane and left her family absorbing the trail of debt he'd created while passing through, Cary walked out to the private garage where he kept his prize 1989 Mercedes 580SL. The space was empty.

The repo man had cometh.

CHAPTER SEVEN

June 7, 1989

Bobby Lino Senior was dead. The wake took place at Cusomano and Russo's in Brooklyn. Because Bobby Senior was a made man, the scene attracted a parade of wiseguys from most of the families. There were guys from the Genovese family and guys from the Lucchese family. John Gotti showed up with a crew. At the time, he was still the Dapper Don, the Teflon Don, the boss of the most powerful mob family in America, the Gambinos. He became boss by arranging to kill his boss and had beaten prosecutions again and again. He was riding high, talking to his underlings about how his "public" needed him and wallowing in his brief status as a national celebrity. It was all very strange, considering that the American Mafia was supposed to be a secret society that existed below the radar screen of law enforcement. This guy was running around with a target on his back, shouting, "I'm a gangster! Come and get me!" And here he was, strutting around Bobby Lino's funeral like a rock star, all the sycophants lined up to kiss his ring.

Outside, across from the parking lot, the FBI had brought along plenty of film.

The family of Bobby Senior—what was left of it—was assembled in grief. His wife was gone, and so was his eldest son, Vincent. All that was left was Grace Ann and Robert—a drug addict and a wannabe gangster. There were many ways to view this. Some might say Bobby Senior was a lousy father, maybe even the worst ever. He was a drug dealer whose eldest son died of a drug overdose and whose daughter was now deeply involved in destroying herself with the substance he'd sold to make money. He had shot Sonny Black and helped bury Bobby C and Gabriel Infanti. He had cheated and lied and made these choices while raising a family. But sometimes, when you thought about him, it was tough to suppress a smile.

Robert Lino believed his father had tried—in his own way—to be a father. Sitting here at Cusomano's Funeral Home, with the organ music and the flowers and the silk-suit parade passing by, it was easy to look back and smile at just how crazy his father could be. It was way back in 1979, Robert remembered, that the incident with his sister and the guy everybody knew as Mikey Bear occurred.

Back then heroin was king in certain neighborhoods of Brooklyn, thanks in part to Bobby Lino. Some of that heroin wound up with a guy associated with the Colombo family everybody called Mikey Bear. Mikey had been selling drugs all over Brooklyn, and one of his customers wound up being Grace Ann, Bobby Senior's little girl. Sometimes they would use drugs together. It was an ugly time, and the two would spend days inside Mikey's run-down apartment near Avenue C off Ocean Parkway in Flatbush. They'd cook it up and shoot it up and go off into that *Alice in Wonderland* world, unaware of anything or anyone around them. Bobby Senior got wind of Mikey Bear and didn't see the connection between the fact that he personally smuggled kilos of this stuff into his own neighborhood and the fact that his daughter had wound up hooked on it, spiraling into a self-destructive, claustrophobic state of permanent pain. The issue wasn't heroin. The issue was Mikey Bear. As Bobby Senior saw it, if Mikey were removed from the equation, there wouldn't be a problem anymore. The solution was that simple.

One of Bobby Lino's partners in Pizza Park was a guy named Nicky Black. Nicky was a Colombo soldier and professed to disapprove of drugs, although he was in favor of extortion, loan-sharking and, on occasion, murder. Bobby told Nicky all about Mikey Bear and his daughter and the drugs, and Nicky, too, agreed that the solution was simple. From that moment, Mikey Bear was no longer an associate of the Colombo organized crime family of Brooklyn. Bobby and Frank Lino had permission and so they set to work.

The lesson of Mikey Bear was this: clipping someone you don't really know is much more difficult than clipping someone you do know. The Lino cousins had to figure out Mikey Bear's schedule, which often consisted of scoring drugs and then spending weeks at a time holed up in his rancid apartment. They watched him to learn his patterns and discovered he had none. The only way to get him was to lure him outside. Two of Mikey's friends, the guy Kojak with the bald head and another guy named Vito, made some calls and a meeting was arranged. Mikey would emerge from his hellish little hole and hook up with Kojak and Vito on the corner of Avenue C and Ocean Parkway. It would be safe because it was a well-trafficked area with working people coming and going.

The day of the job there were three cars filled with guys and guns cruising along Ocean Parkway. Bobby Senior was in the crash car, the car that pulls in front of the cops if they show up. Cousin Frank was a backup shooter in the car a few parking spots away from the sidewalk meeting locale. The third car contained the two shooters, the Ronnie who shot Sonny Black, and Tommy Karate, at the time both wannabe gangsters who were itching to become made men. Kojak and Vito stood on the corner of Avenue C and Ocean Parkway, waiting for Mikey Bear.

Soon Mikey emerged from his apartment and could be seen shuffling up Ocean Parkway. This was a major street in Brooklyn, with lots of cars and numerous bus routes and shops and people all over. Lots of people. Here comes Mikey Bear toward Kojak and Vito and here comes Ronnie and Tommy Karate with guns drawn and they pull up next to him and shout out, "Hey Mikey!" He looks over and it's too late. Tommy shoots at the Bear's massive body, but his gun jams. Ronnie pumps several bullets into Mikey. He slumps to the pavement. An older couple, a man and woman who just happened to be walking by, observe the entire proceeding from about ten feet away. The shooters screech away. Mikey Bear lies on a crowded sidewalk in Brooklyn.

Mike Bear is alive.

For days the Lino cousins and all the rest of the hit team are unhappy fellows. Mikey Bear is lying in his hospital bed, still breathing, and Bobby Senior wants to get somebody in there to finish up what was started on Ocean Parkway. He had done this for his daughter, and he had to make sure his daughter never again saw this Mikey Bear. One day passed and then a second, and Mikey Bear still lived. Word was out that one of the cars had been identified and confiscated by the police. Perhaps all of this helping your own wasn't really worth the trouble. Then Mikey Bear decided to die, and everything was all right again. The job was done. The problem was solved. Bobby Senior had accomplished what any loving father would seek to accomplish— coming to the rescue of the beautiful daughter he'd raised from a baby.

Of course, Robert Lino knew better. His sister, sitting next to him now in the funeral parlor, still had problems with drugs, long after Mikey Bear had gone to that great rehab clinic down below. Grace Ann just seemed to deteriorate more and more. A few months before, Robert, the dutiful son, had signed a form that gave him power of attorney over Grace Ann's affairs. She was a grown woman who could no longer take care of herself. Robert was now, in effect, her father.

Bobby Senior was dead. Robert now officially took up the role as head of the family. He would turn twenty-four in two months. It's hard to say how many choices he had about the journey he was about to embark upon. His bearings were determined by locale. His context was organized criminals. He'd done poorly in school; he could barely read. He had not graduated high school, never mind college. He was not really Robert Lino, anyway. He was Robert from Avenue U. His cousin Eddie was a gangster. His cousin Frank was a gangster. His father died a gangster and told anybody who'd listen that his dying wish was for Robert to embrace the life he'd led. Robert was like a boat on a strong current, headed for the cataract. Most who knew him felt he was basically a decent guy. He had his own set of rules within the rules. He was quite aware that plenty of gangsters, including his late father, rest his soul, were involved in selling drugs, but he would have nothing to do with that. He saw shylocking as a necessary evil. People needed money and somebody had to provide it. It was just capitalism at work. He could see nothing wrong with gambling. Taking sports bets was a way of life where he grew up, like getting married or hating the Red Sox. And when a piece of work had to get done, it was always for a reason. Usually it was a rat, an informant, some guy who was betraying his friends and denying his colleagues the ability to provide for their wives and children. That, anyway, was the thinking.

His father's wake came to an end. John Gotti and his entourage were long gone, even the FBI agents had packed it in. Robert Lino and his sister stepped out onto West 6th Street deep in the heart of Brooklyn. He wore an uncomfortable suit in the summer swelter. It was June. The summer of 1989 lay ahead like the bejeweled blue Atlantic twinkling off of Coney Island. It was the end of the eighties. The stock market boom had crashed. The country was heading for a recession and was being led by a country club Republican who talked about "a thousand points of light" and then raised your taxes. America was marching toward the millennium, and the Brooklyn that Robert Lino had grown up in was changing dramatically. Indians and the Chinese were beginning to move into Italian Bensonhurst. Who knew where it was all headed? Robert Lino had a lifetime ahead of him and no father to lead the way. Now it was just Robert Lino against the rest of the world.

CHAPTER EIGHT

The Nineties

Cary Cimino was back. The eighties were so over, the ski slopes of Aspen beckoned. He was now driving a Ferrari, flying first class, spending as fast as he earned. He was enjoying yet another long weekend on the slopes, playing hard and ordering only the best of everything. Everything he bought he laid off on his clients anyway, so what the hell? His partner, Jeffrey, did the same thing. And jetting away from New York for a weekend in the winter was always a good idea. Especially this year. This had not been the best of years for Wall Street or for the city itself.

The 1990s already looked like the kind of decade in New York that would never be regarded in the sentimental glow of nostalgia. The forties had the abstract expressionists, the fifties had the Dodgers, the sixties had the World's Fair. The nineties were beginning to look like the seventies, with "Ford to New York: Drop Dead," Son of Sam and the garbage piling up in the streets. Just like those sordid days, the 1990s were all about chaos and anarchy in the streets. Murders were way up, surpassing two thousand in one year for the first time since the New York City Police Department bothered counting. Crack cocaine was killing certain poverty-wracked neighborhoods, turning ordinary people into raging sociopaths. The more out of control the city appeared, the more out of control it became. A tourist from Utah was stabbed in Midtown on the way to a tennis tournament in Queens. A new street name had sprung up for the innocent people shot while walking down the street: "mushrooms." The squeegee man reigned, shaking down motorists at stoplights all over. Hundreds of homeless people took over Penn Station every night. Activists were distributing free sanitized needles to drug addicts to halt the spread of AIDS. *Time* magazine ran a front page proclaiming New York City the "Rotten Apple."

The glory days of New York seemed distant and remote, like a great baseball pennant race that would never happen again.

Down on Wall Street, the 1980s were definitely over, but a new economy was emerging. Perhaps it was the general atmosphere of criminality pervading the city or a creeping belief that New York was no longer governable, but as the Dow recovered and the pace of trading again began to increase, a new white collar underworld began to emerge. As the Dow began to rise again, people like Jeffrey Pokross abandoned their car lease scams and check kiting operations and Ponzi schemes and set up shop on Wall Street. If money was to be made, they were going to be part of the party.

For Cary Cimino, the return of the Dow meant a second chance. This time, however, he was going to do things differently.

Considering the circumstances, Cary was doing pretty well. The end of the eighties had turned into a head-on collision for his career. He'd exhausted any currency he'd accumulated in the industry, jumping from firm to firm, swallowing up-front bonus after up-front bonus, failing to produce while amassing mountains of debt. Job offers had stopped coming in. Headhunters no longer called. A legitimate firm was simply no longer an option for Cary Cimino. He had gone from being a partner at one of the most prestigious brokerage houses in America to an unemployed stockbroker nobody wanted to touch.

No problem.

It was time to adjust the methodology. After he was fired from Prudential Bache for lack of production, Cary decided to remake himself entirely. His days as a partner or even as senior vice president were over, and that was just fine. He told himself the opportunities for brokers working for big or even little firms were too restricted. You always had to kick up a percentage to the boss, and he had come to believe that was not his style. He decided the only way to go was to be independent. He decided to transform himself overnight into a stock promoter.

In the 1980s, stock promoters were considered a kind of second-tier player on Wall Street. They were kind of public relations pimps who plugged small companies headed for public offerings in the over-the-counter market. Now in the 1990s, Cary decided stock promotion was the only way to go. Only suckers stayed with the big brokerage houses. Stock promoters were basically guys without broker's licenses who would promote the stock of a specific company. They essentially hyped specific stocks, for a fee. This was different than the supposedly objective world of the stockbroker, who wasn't supposed to have an allegiance to one particular company or another. Always a master of jargon to make something sound greater than the sum of its parts, Cary put it this way: "I would do financial PR. I would try to get retail buying or establish retail interest in their company."

Cary was well aware that his newfound vocation had the potential to drift from the purely legal into the clearly questionable, but he was willing to take his chances. He had come to believe that truly successful people did not get where they were by following every little rule and regulation. Sometimes you had to push the envelope, take risks. There were too many rules, anyway. Nobody followed every one. Just watch people driving. People ease through stop signs without coming to a complete stop every day, and rarely does that cause problems. People switch lanes without using their blinkers every minute of every day. Probably once in a while that causes an accident, but the numbers aren't overwhelming. You're already signing up for risk when you get behind the wheel of a car. The same holds true for Wall Street.

The biggest problem was all those disclosure requirements.

Stock promoters were really children of the night. Rarely did they stand in the sunlight of full disclosure and tell the trusting investor that they were being paid a fee by a particular company to promote that company's stock. Brokers were never supposed to be wedded to a company financially, and if they had any such ties they were obligated—required—to make that known to their clients. Stock promoters had no such requirement because they were never supposed to be in direct contact with the clients. They worked behind the scenes, and were useful in facilitating any number of transactions. Mostly they were about making a company appear to be the next McDonald's. They were capitalist weathermen, using charts and graphs and most importantly numbers to prove their case. They implied exclusivity. They made the investor feel like he was getting something the other poor loser was not. They made the investor feel the superiority of the insider, the guy who gets past the velvet rope. They used the euphemisms of business to reassure nervous investors that they, and only they, held the key to massive and easy affluence.

And 1991 was a good time for stock promoters. Hardly

anyone in the world of government regulation paid much attention to them at all. As far as Cary was concerned, that was okay. And he'd convinced himself that promotion was a legitimate way to make lots of money. He would tell friends the big firms like Bear Stearns did almost the same thing when they bought blocks of stock in a specific company they had an investment banking relationship with. The firms would designate the client's stock as the stock its brokers would now push as "stock of the week." In return, the brokers pocketed commissions. Sometimes the clients were aware of the fiduciary relationship between the brokerage house and the company. Sometimes they weren't.

"The stock would then be in my partnership account and that stock would then become the stock of the week. Then our four hundred and sixty retail brokers would get on the phone and use any other words you want, pump the stock, hype the stock, and we had, at one point in time, we had five hundred brokers. When I say 'we,' I speak of the partnership at Bear Stearns. We had five hundred retail brokers, which were the highest producing brokers on the Street. And this wonderful retail sales force would go out, all right, and recommend the stock that we had in our account. And there would be whatever sales credit, there would be whatever extra commission the firm would give."

He described the "stock of the week" companies feting brokers at the Four Seasons, pumping them up about selling the stock that the brokers owned themselves. It was called a "dog and pony show," and, Cary was quick to add, it was all legal financial PR.

That was the way Cary saw being a stock promoter. He was still working with Lowenthal Financial Group, but it didn't really matter who he was working for. If there were any problems, he was a stock promoter. Lowenthal, for instance, had been caught by the NASD "forgetting" to make payments in arbitrated disputes. They'd been fined and reprimanded, but Cary's fingerprints were nowhere in sight. He was under the radar; he was living on the edge.

Cary had reason to believe the edge would soon be mainstream. In the middle of 1991, with the city spinning out of control and the mayor of New York insisting that his city was not Dodge City, there were whispers of a Wall Street revolution in the wings. The word was the financial markets would never be the same because of a little known entity that was growing year by year. It was called the Internet, and Cary believed it was going to be huge.

In 1991, the Internet was still used mostly by university professors and scientists and Department of Defense employees, but it was growing every day. The first microprocessor had been around for twenty years. Apple Computer had been around for thirteen years. IBM had produced its first PC a decade earlier, and Microsoft was now its operating system of choice. By now, Microsoft had split twice and was trading just under $5, up from the pennies it started with. The web had been in existence for two years, and already people were talking about using it to let investors know about investments. The over-the-counter market, which had been powerful during the 1980s, would soon be the over-the-web market and the opportunities would be endless.

Or so Cary hoped. Anyway, he couldn't complain. In his new role as stock promoter, he was making a killing, which was why he could afford to be spending a long weekend in Aspen. His new gig also allowed for more flexibility. He wasn't working for a brokerage house anymore, so he was his own boss. If he wanted to spend a four-day weekend in Aspen, he could just buy the first-class tickets and disappear for a bit. His clients could leave messages with his phone service, and he'd get back to them quickly. They usually didn't need him on an emergency basis anyway, so when the phone rang at the hotel where he was spending his well-deserved cash, he figured it was not about work.

His sister Andrea was on the line. She kept it simple.

"Mom is dead."

CHAPTER NINE

July 1, 1997

The fourteenth-floor apartment on Central Park South was the kind of art deco address Rodgers and Hart dreamed about. Right at the southern edge of the park, between Seventh and Eighth Avenues in the heart of the island of Manhattan, it faced Frederick Law Olmsted's masterpiece in all its splendor. In the daylight the park presented an ever-changing seasonal panorama: a forest of pale green in the spring; a glorious wonderland in winter; a carnival of maroon, yellow and orange come fall. In the summer it was an emerald carpet, the castles of Manhattan peeking out at the edges. And at nightfall, the view from the fourteenth floor really came into its own. The park became a great black sea ringed by the jewelry boxes of Central Park West, a twinkling armada headed uptown to the northern tip of Manhattan. This was the view Francis Warrington Gillet III had purchased for himself and his new family. An address to envy. A castle in the sky. Far below, yellow taxis competed for tourists, their horns and screeching brakes a distant symphony. Up here on the fourteenth floor, Francis Warrington Gillet III lived above it all.

As he stood in the dark alone at midnight, gazing down upon the park, *his* park, Warrington remembered his birthday. It was something he usually tried to forget. In October he would turn thirty-nine. In some ways, thirty-nine seemed worse than forty. Any year with a nine in it meant you were looking back and trying not to look ahead. Thirty-nine meant this was the last year he could say he was in his thirties. After that he'd be middle-aged. You might even say halfway done. Halfway done meant you had to take stock of what you had accomplished. You had to make comparisons, reflect on certain choices. You had to add things up and see whether you were greater or lesser than the sum of your parts. In the summer of 1997, Francis Warrington Gillet III believed he was destined to beat that equation. He had found his calling, and it was money.

The great-stepgrandson of the cereal heiress Marjorie Merriweather Post and the scion of the Gillet family, a family of United States senators and old horse country money, had arrived at his destiny. He was a stockbroker. A maker of big money. He was clearing $300,000 net, and he'd set his sights on much more. Looking over at the lights of Central Park West, he could remember what it was like when he first arrived in May of 1996, still a bachelor stockbroker living large in the all-night party that was Manhattan. At the time, he was swimming in opportunity. A chart of the Dow from the Crash of '29 to 1996 looked something like a ski slope that no towrope could climb. Starting in about 1995, the trading volume had begun to rocket skyward, and the increase was reflected in Warrington's rising commissions. The Dow, which had traded under 5,000 for sixty-five years since the crash, was headed for 10,000 and nobody was going to stop it. The fabulous flop of the 1980s now seemed like a speed bump. There was no way to go but up, and Warrington had managed to wangle himself a front-row ticket to ride.

Life was good. He'd worked his way up from a rookie at Smith Barney in 1989, when the market was in the toilet. He bounced to a small shop called Global American, which went out of business. He suffered fits of unemployment, but that was the way it was on Wall Street. He jumped to Ladenburg Thalmann & Co., then Grunthal & Co., then Baird Patrick & Co. in 1995, just as the market began to take off. Most of his clients were wealthy overseas customers he found through his connections from private school and steeplechase and growing up around extremely wealthy Maryland horse country people. He bought and sold stocks for large institutional investors like the Bank of Monaco. He earned a mention in a *New York Times* gossip column as a "prince of the moment," right alongside John F. Kennedy Jr. and David Lauren.

And 1996 was looking even better. He'd hooked up with a small-sized outfit called Monitor Investment and was practically the top producer at the place in no time. His contacts were golden. He bought a Lamborghini. He hung out at Harry Cipriani's on Forty-second Street. He was on top of the world. That very night he'd gone out drinking with friends and it reminded him of those days when he was still single. The giddiness you got hanging around models, the freedom you acquired with your corporate expense account, the belief that you were invulnerable. Then he remembered—1996 also included the arrival of Warry the Fourth.

Warry the Fourth had shown up in May and changed everything. For his entire adult life, Warrington III had done pretty much what he wanted when he wanted. His childhood was kind of a dream. He'd grown up around money in a house with its own name—Tally Ho Farms. His kingdom consisted of rolling green hills, miles of clean white fence, Thoroughbreds prancing in the morning sunlight. He never had to think about attending public school. His sports were steeplechase and polo. He knew people who wore cravats without irony. There were yachts and servants and winters in Monaco. It was a perfect little world, far removed from mundane middle-class existence or the scary world of the poor. It was the world of the Gillets of Worthington County.

Staring out at the darkened park in the heart of the big city, Worthington County seemed pretty far away. It surely had been one surreal trip. He'd bummed around Europe endlessly until he was bored out of his mind. He'd tried competing professionally at steeplechase until he failed but told himself he was bored out of his mind. He'd immersed himself in acting school and, for the first time, was not bored out of his mind. He truly loved it. He had a vague sense that if he put his mind to it, he would succeed. It would just happen because it always did. People in his world were simply bound to succeed. They were blessed with so many advantages; the idea of failure was not to be considered. At least, that's what he'd been told.

It wasn't that simple, of course. He'd only made it through two years at Villanova, bored by his chosen subject, economics, so he was wandering through the world without a college degree. And when he went to acting school, it was his father who paid his rent on Sutton Place. And he wasn't a very good actor. He wound up doing mostly TV commercials. His best role was a nonspeaking part as Jason in one of the *Friday the 13th* horror series. He got the part because he didn't make the cut for a speaking role.

And now he was a father and husband.

He had met Martina at the Coffee Shop in Union Square. At the time, back in 1995, this was a happening place. It was one of those spots that become hot for a year and then are as empty as the Canadian wilderness when someone—no one knows precisely who—declares the place dead. The Coffee Shop was, in 1995, the kind of place Warrington could relate to. Young people—mostly younger than Warrington—trying to talk on cell phones over the cheerful din. Everyone always on their way to something else. And lots of models. In 1995, Warrington spent lots of quality time in places like that. In 1995, if you were an up-and-coming Wall Street guy trolling for rich clients and aggressively pursuing a certain image, you were expected to be out pretty much every night of the week talking to beautiful women.

Martina was a Swedish model. She was gorgeous in a way that made people—both men and women—stop and stare when she strolled into a room. They were a beautiful couple. He was a handsome fellow, a good-natured guy who liked to have a good time and could charm people simply with the warmth of his ebullient self-confidence. When Martina got pregnant, Warrington hesitated. He wasn't sure if he had what it took to be a father. Look at his experience with fathers. His real father was a guy who sometimes confused philanthropy with philandering, and his stepfather wouldn't know if he was jailed, bailed or dead unless it was printed on the front page of the *Racing Form*. Nevertheless, Warrington proposed; he and Martina were married in a matter of months. By May, little Warry the Fourth had joined the entourage, and Francis Warrington Gillet III became a new man.

Of course there was still time for discovering which bar made the best martinis on Thursday nights. On this night, Martina was on vacation in Europe with Warry the Fourth. His progeny and namesake was now about fourteen months in this world, and although Warrington loved him to the core of his soul, little Warry the Fourth could wear you down with his caterwauling all around the apartment. And the apartment didn't help. No, not at all.

Truth be told, Apartment 14N with the drop-dead views of Central Park was, in fact, tiny. Sure, when you mentioned the address—240 Central Park South—people stopped yammering on about themselves and actually listened. Central Park South was a big deal. Not just anybody could land there. Of course, rarely did he invite people up. In fact, never did he invite people up. And he certainly never told any of his good buddies down on Wall Street that he lived with wife and child in a studio apartment. Not two bedrooms, or one bedroom and a half, where the sophisticated Manhattanite pretends a closet is a bedroom. No, this was *no* bedrooms. One room. A kitchen, living room, dining room, den, master bedroom, child's bedroom—all in one room. Only the bathroom had a separate space with a real door and everything. His castle was a studio. It was a cold, hard fact.

Even though he was making a million dollars investing other people's fortunes, Warrington was quite aware that you never know what can happen. It was always a question of maintaining the net. Warrington had rented a studio because he was never sure if fortune would take her smile away from him. Sure he was making good money, but in a year, he could be on the street. He'd been unemployed twice in the last three years. He'd handled a couple of major deals, but that was it. Although the market was trending in the right direction, it all could change. You had to be a fool to think otherwise. That was why he got the studio.

And he wasn't going to be like his father. He was going to provide. He was going to succeed on his own terms. He hadn't married rich; he'd decided he would be the source of his own success. He figured with the market headed in the direction it was heading, he'd soon be clearing upper six figures and be able to buy a bigger place on Fifth Avenue or down in Soho. In fact, he expected this. He believed in this. He planned to send Warry off to prep school, just as he had been, and then on to the college of his choice. He would probably buy a second home in the Hamptons. Or maybe at Telluride. Who was to say where the horizon ended? That was the only way to look at things. You had to make yourself see unlimited opportunity.

As he stepped away from his glorious view of the wondrous toy and dumped himself into bed, Francis Warrington Gillet III knew in his heart that he would make it after all.

He couldn't remember his dream when he awoke suddenly to the sound of pounding at his front door. He looked at his watch—7 a.m. Who the hell would bang on your door at this hour? He stumbled out of bed and toward the door, blinking and trying to understand what some guy was hollering out in the hall.

"FBI! Open the door! Now!"

Warrington hastily ran to the front door, all the while pleading, "I'm here! I'm coming!" He had seen so many TV shows he was sure they were about to bust down the door and charge into his tiny studio, guns drawn and breathing hard with adrenaline. He slid back the door and stood facing a man he recognized immediately.

The guy he was looking at was Nick Vito. He was a stockbroker working out of a small office in the World Trade Center with whom Warrington had tried to do a deal. They'd discussed ways to wire money into a Bahamas account so that both could reap the benefits of the 1996 bull market. Warrington still had his business card: Nick Vito, Thorcon Capital. It looked like a real business card presented by a real stockbroker who worked in a real office. Only none of it was real. Reality struck Warrington hard: Nick Vito was actually the FBI, standing in Warrington's doorway at an ungodly hour holding up a different kind of business card— a gold badge that said "Special Agent D. True Brown." Nick Vito/True Brown was reciting TV banter about how Warrington had the right to remain silent and all that, but Warrington was mostly trying to remember as much as he could about Nick Vito and what he might have said that would give True Brown reason to put him in handcuffs.

It was tough to remember. Most of it seemed so innocuous. Warrington had been introduced to Nick by a colleague. The colleague said he knew of an aggressive young broker with plenty of big-money clients looking to take new companies public. He just needed a little encouragement, usually in cash. The guy's outfit, Thorcon, was small, but he would be happy to chat with Warrington. It all sounded like a win-win proposition, so Warrington had done what any hungry stockbroker would have done and tracked down Nick Vito to see if they could work something out.

First they talked by phone. Then they met face-to-face at Nick's office in the World Trade Center. Nick seemed like a decent guy, maybe a little stiff. He was certainly knowledgeable about the market, and they soon were able to work out the details. There would be discounted stock handed over to Nick as commission. There would be money wired to an account in the Bahamas. The arrangement was essentially a bribe, but Warrington felt it was, at that time, an extremely common practice among small brokerage houses that dealt with over-the-counter stock. You could even argue it was leaning toward legal, or at least hidden behind a façade clever enough to fool the average drone at the NASD.

But perhaps not the FBI. Here Warrington stood in his underwear in his fabulous studio apartment, unable to remember precisely what he'd said to Nick Vito or Special Agent D. True Brown or whoever was standing right there in front of him. It had been nearly a year since Warrington had last seen the guy, so remembering what he'd said wasn't so easy. In fact, the more he thought about it, the more confused he became.

Warrington alternated between anger at himself and a growing sense of dread. The anger came from the fact that the deal he'd discussed ad infinitum with Nick Vito, with the Bahamas bank accounts and free restricted shares, hadn't even gone through. Discovery Studios was a big bust. But it was difficult to escape the fact that the conversations about said deal had, in fact, taken place. And when Nick Vito, now Special Agent D. True Brown, began reading off a description of the charge filed against Warrington, the sense of dread began to overwhelm Francis Warrington Gillet III. The anger morphed into raw fear.

"Francis Warrington Gillet III did conspire, confederate and agree together with others to commit offenses against the United States," Special Agent True Brown intoned. "To wit, to commit wire fraud in violation of Sections 1343 and 1346 of Title 18 of the United States Code . . ."

And so on and so on.

The phrases floated by. "Commercial bribery." "Part and object of the conspiracy." "Unlawfully, willfully and knowingly." Each was like a shovelful of dirt on a coffin. Here he stood in his own apartment, a privileged son of affluence and influence now facing up to five years in prison for committing a crime. Several crimes. And the documents Agent Brown was reading even made a point of alleging that his actions were "against the United States."

As far as he could tell, Francis Warrington Gillet III was still standing in his own apartment in his own country. He had always believed in the system of checks and balances. He'd always embraced the idea of a criminal justice system that protected those who worked hard and paid their taxes from the seething, blood-seeking criminal hordes. Until this very moment, the police, the judges, the prosecutors—they were all on his side. They were all his friends. Now here he stood, on the other side. He could think many things. Whose fault was it? What if he'd done things differently? Suppose he'd never met Cary or Jeffrey or James "Jimmy" Labate or Sal Piazza or any of the rest of them? He thought of these things but he kept coming back to another, darker, more impenetrable question that buzzed and whined inside his skull like a gnat. And that question was this: What would his family think when they learned the truth about Francis Warrington Gillet III?

CHAPTER TEN

May 1976

Warrington awoke in a stranger's house, as he did every school day morning. It was not his house, and it was not his choice. Warrington was seventeen, in his junior year at the Gilman School, an exclusive all-boy prep school located on sixty-eight acres in an affluent corner of the city of Baltimore. It used to be called the Gilman Country School for Boys, but the trustees—in an effort to make the school seem a bit less pretentious—dropped the "Country." It was one of those schools that made a point of wearing its history on its sleeve, rhapsodizing about its founders and insisting that it catered to students "from all backgrounds and segments" when it really served only the sons of the affluent and influential. They were Warrington's classmates, and—truth be told—he fit right in.

He and his peers were being prepared "for college and a life of honor and service." This was not a matter of choice. They were to become "men of character," although the type of character was never specified. They would learn to go out and conquer the world, or at least acquire as much of it as possible. Some of Warrington's peers had started Gilman in kindergarten and were planning on making it all the way through to the bitter end, spending twelve of their most formative years lugging satchels of books across the rolling green lawns that took them from grade to grade. Warrington was one of the Gilman lifers.

He and his 971 classmates all wore identical navy blue suit coats, white shirts and school ties, usually accompanied by khakis and Top-Siders without socks. Some—like Warrington—had their initials monogrammed in shirt cuffs. They were the sons of senators, CEOs, tycoons, moguls, big-time lawyers, big-money doctors. There was lots of old money and even a little new. He fit right in. He was just like nearly all his classmates—white, wealthy and without restrictions to opportunity. Nearly every one of them saw the world as his for the taking.

Like everybody else at Gilman, Warrington read the entire *Lord of the Rings* cycle, smoked massive quantities of dope and listened to Neil Young records day and night.

But Warrington also knew he was unlike his classmates. Almost every student came and went to school every day, being that it was a day school. Only two students actually lived on the Gilman grounds, in a little apartment that was part of the headmaster's home. One of those two was Francis Warrington Gillet III. Warrington was aware that the other kids got to go home and see their moms and dads and siblings and dogs every night. All the other kids were well aware that Francis and his roommate, the son of a United States congressman, did not.

The symbolism of his involuntary living arrangements sometimes gnawed at Warrington's very soul. Mostly he tried not to think about it, especially on these days in the middle of the 1970s when he was late once again for the morning chore known as algebra II.

Every junior had to take it. Warrington hated it. It did not highlight his strengths. It was unpleasant. He was pretty lousy at it. The combination of waking up alone in the headmaster's house and the prospect of wrestling around with algorithms was enough to make him want to hide back under the covers and stay there for the day. But he could not. He was, after all, a Gillet.

Being a Gillet could be something of a chore. It seemed, on its face, quite impressive. Often people assumed he was the heir to the guy who invented the razor blade, or something like that. He was not. He was, instead, the great-stepgrandson of the cereal heiress Marjorie Merriweather Post. On his mother's side were two United States senators, Millard Tydings and Joseph Tydings. His father's father was a big war hero in World War I. His stepfather, John Schapiro, owned racetracks and lived with his mother and siblings on an enormous horse-farm estate. Warrington's home was not just a home; it was Tally Ho Farms in Worthington Hills, four hundred acres of stark white fences and green, with the Schapiro/Gillet family horses cantering in the misty dawn. It was a lot, this image of impregnability. And what was worse? It was just that—an image.

There was a part of Warrington that was happy that he lived at the headmaster's little apartment. He was aware that if he were, in fact, living at home like all the other kids, he'd never see his mother and stepfather anyway.

They were always away at events—fox hunting, charity parties, that sort of thing. His stepfather preferred to spend his time at his racetracks rather than at Tally Ho. Whenever Warrington ate dinner at home, he'd sit down at the table with his real sister and stepbrother and the food would be prepared and presented by servants. Mom and Dad simply weren't part of that scene. Even calling them Mom and Dad seemed wrong. Thus Warrington had convinced himself that staying at the Gilman School was not such a bad thing. At least you didn't have to confront the empty chairs every night at the dinner table. At least you could pretend that you didn't really care.

"Those values did not get instilled," Warrington said. "Everybody's busy on a highfalutin lifestyle. They're too busy. The kids of these types of families get lost in the shuffle. The parents are too busy to sit down for three hours to do math homework . . . Rich people do not have time to run around with children, to run around to Little League and soccer and football. On the weekend, you'd go fox hunting. You were misled into thinking that you were just like everybody else."

Of course, not caring wasn't so easy on this particular morning. The schism between the Gillet family image and the Gillet family reality had hit home hard the previous weekend. At the age of seventeen, Warrington III had met Warrington Junior for the first time in his life.

His real father had just shown up, out of the blue. He might as well have been the last emperor of China. Here he was presenting himself to his son, who was by now a junior in high school and who had not seen his father during his entire conscious existence. Kindergarten, elementary school, junior high school, almost all of high school—no father. Now here he was, this stranger with the same name, blown up on the doorstep like a guy with a subpoena. Of course when Warrington saw his father for the first time in seventeen years, he knew immediately who he was. This stemmed in part from the fact that Warry Junior looked exactly like Warry III.

He was a handsome guy, this stranger, with a Kirk Douglas chin and all his hair at age forty-five. The man had perfect posture for a tall guy, and even more perfect teeth. He wore a very nice suit jacket but no tie and appeared self-confident and yet informal at once. He was charm personified. He was the prodigal dad.

Warrington couldn't really call him Dad. He knew the man solely through washed out photographs and bitter stories told by his mother. When he was a toddler, probably two years old, his mother had discovered that Big Warry was screwing around as much as possible with as many women as he could track down. Warrington's mother, herself the daughter of money and privilege, wasn't going for that. Out the door went Big Warry, and off to Palm Beach he slithered, living la dolce vita without so much as a postcard home to his namesake or anybody else at the Tally Ho Farms that Warrington called a home.

Seeing his father out of the blue was like a shot to the chin.

Here was a guy his mother referred to as "the bon vivant playboy-about-town who never worked a legitimate day in his life." The closest his father came to actual work was at one point becoming president of the Game Conservancy USA, a nonprofit effort to support wildlife conservation and raise money for anti-poaching efforts in Tanzania. Otherwise he spent his days hanging around other people's houses and trolling for a wealthy woman who might want to marry him. It was difficult to explain why Warrington would even give the man a second thought, but he did. His explanation would have been that he'd always wanted a father, even one who forgot about him for nearly his entire childhood.

His stepfather, John Schapiro, didn't really count. Granted the man wasn't abusive. In the two years after he moved into Tally Ho, he hadn't beaten Warrington or sent him to bed without supper even. He just wasn't what Warrington imagined a father was supposed to be. He owned racetracks and spent nearly all his time there. When he was home, he could speak passionately about only one subject—information contained in the *Racing Form*. He got Warrington—who'd begun riding at an early age—reading it by the sixth grade. There was some connection. They could talk horses, which to Warrington were about sport and to Schapiro were about money. Sometimes his stepfather would pick him up at Gilman and take him to the Pimlico Racetrack for the day. He'd let him use his allowance to place bets. He put Warrington in touch with one of his bookies to bet on the football spread. Twice he flew Warrington and his siblings out to Las Vegas and let Warry roll the dice at the craps table. Warry, his stepfather explained, was lucky.

"The last thing a real father would do—the last thing I would do with my child—is let him call a bookie on the telephone. But if I was married to some babe with renegade kids, you wouldn't care about them. They're not your kids."

For Warry, the equestrian kinship with his stepfather ended there. In all the years from middle school into high school that Warrington competed in steeplechase, he could not remember his stepfather (or his mother for that matter) showing up to cheer him on. They were elsewhere, along with his real father and any sense that he would be allowed to have a family life that involved actual family.

Yet when his real father showed up, Warrington could not simply turn away. He wanted to. It would have been justified. He could not. On this morning, he should have tried to forget the entire weekend. He was late for algebra II. Thinking about algebra II was somehow more inviting than thinking about his father's visit. He knew he had to focus and couldn't be distracted by familial sideshows. Every year about 10 percent of the class would not make it to the next year, and each year Warrington wondered if he would make the cut. He'd gotten almost all the way through junior year, and figured he could stick it out to the end. But as he dressed himself for class, he couldn't help remembering one particularly strange moment during Dad's sudden weekend visit to Tally Ho.

The two were alone, and Warrington suddenly realized that this guy in front of him was trying to give him advice. That was strange, given that the guy had forgotten he had a son through three presidential administrations and Watergate. But there it was, his father—his real father—giving

Warrington advice. Was it about how to become a man of character? Did it involve a "life of honor and service"? Not quite.

"Son," he said, "never marry for beauty. Always marry for money. With money, you can always get beauty on the side."

May 20, 1978

Preakness Day at Pimlico, the biggest race in Maryland. This wasn't your average day at the track. This wasn't just a back alley crap game. This wasn't three-card monte. This was Pimlico, where the United States House of Representatives once adjourned for the only time in its history to attend a horse race. Nobody remembered the horses—Parole, Ten Broeck and Tom Ochiltree—but everybody called that day the Great Race. And the Preakness was the Great Race on an annual basis. It was the high church of high stakes. It reeked of history, from its place as the second jewel in the Triple Crown to the tradition of painting the wrought iron horse-and-rider weather vane atop the Old Clubhouse cupola the colors of the victorious horse's silks as soon as the race was run. On this day odds were the painter was going to be dipping into his cans of pink and black—the colors of Affirmed, a three-year-old Thoroughbred out of Harbor View farms who was favored to win.

Tradition was not on the mind of the nineteen-year-old Villanova freshman named Francis Warrington Gillet III who stood at the cashier's window, trying to convince the guy behind the iron bars that placing a bet with a $5,000 personal check from a teenager was a perfectly normal occurrence. The guy wasn't buying his pitch.

The clock was ticking and Warrington knew he had to do something drastic. He wanted Affirmed to win and Alydar to place, and the guy behind the window was practically laughing in his face. The guy had his suspicions. Five thousand dollars was a lot of money for a kid Warrington's age, regardless of the last name involved. Warrington was dropping every name he could think of to sway the guy, but it wasn't working. Then he got an idea: why not take the check directly to a trustee of Pimlico his stepfather knew?

Warrington knew that being the stepson of John Schapiro might make the difference. John Schapiro was a devoted gambler. It made him feel alive. He spent most of his waking hours thinking about the next horse race, the next poker game, the next interlocution with his bookie. He knew everybody at the tracks, from the stable boys to the trustees of Pimlico.

There was only one problem with the whole scenario: Warrington knew very well that there wasn't a thin dime in his checking account. He was betting it all on the idea that the stars in the heavens would fall into alignment just for him. He craved quick cash (who didn't?), but he also sought that feeling of euphoria that comes when you take a chance and you're right. He knew he wasn't taking the biggest chance of all time. Affirmed had already won the Kentucky Derby with Alydar placing, and he was favored to do the same today. But you never knew what was going to happen when you plunked your money down at the cashier's window. Alydar, after all, was the only horse to have actually beaten Affirmed. You were always taking a chance. And Warrington liked taking chances. Of course, it helped if you actually had some money to bet. With only a few hours to post time, he did not.

He did, however, have his stepfather's name to drop. He went to Plan B. He managed to talk his way into the trustee's office less than an hour before post time, and dropped Schapiro's name as many times as he waved the check in his hand for the important man to see.

"Now, son," said the Pimlico trustee, "are you sure you have enough money to cover this?"

"No problem," said Warrington, and the deed was done.

Warrington knew that was a lie. He knew he'd crossed a line, but he was testing the difference between recklessness and confidence. He was nineteen years old. That's what you did.

He made sure to return to the same cashier, just to see the guy's face when he noticed the trustee's signature on it. The guy said, "Are you sure you want Affirmed to win?" Warrington nodded, and walked away with his tickets, filled with both excitement and fear. He got as close to trackside as possible to watch his life either soar into the heavens or crash into the mud. It was now out of his hands as the horses assembled in the paddock and the race time buzz began to grow.

The way nineteen-year-old Warrington saw it, pretty much everything was out of his hands. He'd gone to Gilman as his mother had instructed and somehow managed to graduate. No high honors, but a diploma nonetheless. He'd been accepted at Villanova and was planning on declaring a major in economics. All of this made his mother quite happy. Outside his mother's view, he lived a different life. A second life. He lived his stepfather, John Schapiro's, life.

He read the *Racing Form* daily and bet on horses with his stepfather whenever he could. He would regularly visit his real father in Palm Beach, where he learned what it's like to live well, but he had come to terms with his stepfather. He was learning some interesting things. The man introduced him to the adrenaline of high risk, and it was as addictive as any narcotic. He had come to love taking chances, and the bigger the better. He really had no expectations of failure. He was absolutely positive he would do well, be rich, meet lots of beautiful women. He was nineteen. He had all the time in the world.

The gates crashed open and the Preakness was off. Believe It—who'd finished third behind Affirmed and Alydar at

Kentucky—took the lead along the rail. Affirmed remained along the outside, running head-to-head with Believe It by the first turn. Warrington appreciated that moment. He knew Affirmed had been trained by veteran Luz Barrera and Believe It had been trained by Barrera's son, Albert. At that moment, it was father against son.

An also-ran, Track Reward, pulled ahead in the first quarter mile, but then Affirmed took his place out front by the first half mile. Alydar was still well back. By 1:11, Affirmed led Noon Time Spender by a length, followed by Believe It and then, close behind, Alydar. And then Alydar began to move.

At the five-sixteenth pole, Alydar pulled into second place.

Warrington's stomach began to roil and quail. Five thousand dollars he did not have. What would he do? What would happen when the check bounced and his stepfather got a call from the president of Pimlico? Would he be banned from the track? Would his stepfather? Would the police be summoned? What would they call the crime? Fraud? Deceit? A stupid teenager trick? Would he be kicked out of Tally Ho for good? Would Schapiro sit down that afternoon and rewrite his will?

Affirmed and Alydar were now neck and neck. Heading into the final stretch, Affirmed was in front in the middle with Believe It coming on strong at the rail, and Alydar pulling up fast on the outside. The jockey riding Alydar began hitting his horse with the whip in is left hand, then switched to his right to slap furiously away. In the upper stretch, from where Warrington was sitting, it was tough to see which horse was out front.

Then it was over, and Warrington was leaping into the air, howling like a dog, ecstatic. Affirmed by a neck. A neck! Alydar placed. Just as Warrington had hoped and prayed.

"The race was unbelievable. The turns are going up and

down, up and down. If Alydar had won, I'm out. I collected $15,000. I took $5,000 of the winnings, went over to the window and got my check back and ripped it up."

He stepped back outside and looked up at the cupola to see the painter going to work, coloring pink and black on the weather vane that glinted in the sun. Pink and black were now Warrington's favorite colors. He looked at the $10,000 in his nineteen-year-old hands. He couldn't wait to tell his stepfather what he'd done. He would appreciate the temerity, the fearlessness of such a crazy stunt. Turning $5,000 he did not have into $10,000—now *that* was the difference between recklessness and confidence.

CHAPTER ELEVEN

Now that she was dead, Cary suddenly realized he'd spent a lot of years talking to psychiatrists about his mother.

He'd seen one when he was just eleven, on orders from his mother, and then after he got out of college he'd begun formal analysis. He spent hours with the guy, trying to figure out why his childhood seemed more complicated than everyone else's. His running theme was that he was basically a good guy who was constantly foiled by external forces. He learned all the phrases. Choices weren't choices. There was no right and wrong. There were the "methodologies." The "methodologies" involving his mother had taken up quite a bit of time.

Of course they had. Was there anything more complicated than the relationship between a mother and son when there was no father in the picture? His stepfather the doctor didn't count. The real force in his life, the real mystery, was clearly his mother. At one time she was a model, but when a real estate developer came along with the promise of material comfort and security, she got married instead. That's where it got complicated.

When Cary was nine years old, a woman he'd never met before showed up at the Cimino family's comfortable little home in suburban Oyster Bay, Long Island. She claimed to be the former wife of his father. This was news to Cary. It was also news that his brother and sister weren't really his brother and sister. They were stepsiblings. His only sibling by blood was his sister Andrea. The woman wanted custody of *her* children. Cary's father said no, and an ugly dispute migrated to the courts. Stress levels inside the Cimino homestead elevated. Then on a weekend afternoon when Cary was home, his father was standing in the kitchen when he suddenly collapsed on the floor. He had had a heart attack. He was dead.

Within days the children Cary had believed all his life were his brother and sister went away to live with their real mother, taking most of their deceased father's assets with them. This left nine-year-old Cary alone with his mother, a woman who'd never held a real job, and his little sister, Andrea, who was by now seven years old and confused about the sudden changes unfolding around her. They still had the nice Long Island house, but now they had no income save government benefits stemming from Cary's father's demise. They needed to change their way of living. Cary's mother was not prepared for this.

"I had a unique childhood. I would say that since my father's death, my mother was never the same. My mother had a very difficult time as a young widow left with debts. She lost what she knew. And I'm saying this in hindsight. It must have been so difficult for her. Just my sister Andrea and I, and it was just us left alone for an extended period of time when my mother was hospitalized."

Cary was too young to know precisely why his mother went away to a hospital, but he was quite aware that he and his sister were now all alone in their big old Oyster Bay house, a nine-year-old in charge of a seven-year old.

"We were left alone to care and feed one another," Andrea remembered. "Cary would go to the hospital and get our mother to sign the checks and then mail them out. I remember on three separate occasions hiding out and not answering the door. We knew it was some kind of social services and they might take us away and separate the two of us. I recall my mother telling me never to let them separate the two of you."

How many people on Sutton Place went through *that*? Cary was proud of the fact that he had de facto raised his younger sister by himself. They pretended as if nothing had happened. The two children stayed home alone in Oyster Bay, dressing themselves, making themselves breakfast, taking the bus to school each day, coming home and doing it all again. This went on for months. Whether the bus driver ever noticed that the Cimino kids' mother never seemed to come to the door is not known. When social service agencies showed up, the kids would hide and eventually the agency people would go away. The outside world had no idea what was going on.

"There was a lack of any supervision," Cary remembered. "We lived in an affluent neighborhood and the authorities really didn't bother us. I dressed Andrea every day and Andrea and I went to school every day."

Finally his mother felt well enough to come home, but not well enough to behave like a mother: "When my mother came out of the hospital, she signed checks and I became my mother's confidant, the male role model in the house. I helped facilitate paying bills. I filled out checks, my mother signed them. We mailed them."

Just before Cary turned thirteen, his world once again changed radically. This time his mother met a doctor she decided she'd marry. Under most circumstances, this might seem to be a positive development. The doctor was wealthy and lived in a nice house in a suburb north of New York City. Not quite. The doctor had four children of his own, and none of the four wanted anything to do with Cary or Andrea. Here was Cary, turning thirteen and moving from Long Island, away from his childhood friends, to the new and foreign suburb of Suffern. The four new kids who hated him were supposed to be his new brothers and sister. This was not something he would have wished for, but it was to be. And naturally, it got worse.

The doctor had a rule for all his kids: no TV before 6 p.m. One afternoon Cary's mother came home to see the doctor's oldest son, a teenager, watching TV before six. She told him to turn it off. He refused. A verbal exchange ensued and escalated. The teenaged kid pushed Cary's mother across the room and she fell. She broke her wrist. When the doctor learned of this, he did nothing about it. Divorce number two followed within months.

Again Cary, his sister and his mother were on their own. This time the financial pressures increased. Now they were forced to move into a lesser subdivision in Rockland County, next to Suffern. This meant Cary would see his former stepsiblings—including the one who'd assaulted his mother—in the hallways of Suffern High School pretty much every day. He would say nothing; they would say nothing. It was as if they had never known one another. For Cary, now living in reduced circumstances, humiliation became a daily event.

Once again his mother was searching for a means of support, but now she was forty years old. She found what she believed was the solution by getting pregnant and allowing the twenty-four-year-old drug-abusing father to move in with her family. The new baby was a girl named Erin, and Cary didn't get to know her. He was focused on one plan—getting away from this family as fast as possible.

"I left the house in 1978. I didn't speak to my mother for

several years. I actually took it as a breath of air to what was going on in the household. I was able to attend college by three or four methodologies. I received Social Security checks and Veterans checks because I was considered an orphan, and I used those monthly deposits. I received financial aid and I received some academic scholarships."

With a little help from the government, Cary enrolled at Boston University and majored in biology. He declared himself pre-med. Boston University was a liberating experience. He was away from the burden of family for the first time in his life, and BU in the late 1970s was a fun place to be. There were keg parties at the high-rise dorms on Commonwealth Avenue every weekend. There was all-night disco at Lucifer in Kenmore Square and an expanding punk scene at the Rat across the Square. Boston was paradise.

In college, Cary learned quickly that money impressed people. A lot of his fellow students came from wealthy Long Island families and he could talk that talk, too. With women, he started making a point of mentioning that he was pre-med. Saying you were a biology major didn't cut it. Discussing endoplasmic reticulum and photosynthesis wouldn't get you laid. The fact that he might one day be a doctor got the attention of certain women right away. In this way Cary decided money was a powerful aphrodisiac.

In fact, Cary was coming to believe that money was the defining characteristic of people. You either had it or you didn't, and if you had it, more people wanted to be around you. If you didn't have it, nobody wanted to be around you. It was as simple as that. Unfortunately for Cary, he didn't really have it quite yet. He was telling everyone he met he would one day be a doctor, but the money wasn't there to turn a boast into reality. He was spending so much time scrounging for cash just to pay his rent and phone bills and Boston University's backbreaking tuition, he didn't have time enough to complete the arduous tasks necessary to get into medical school. Now that was hard work. As graduation neared, Cary quietly dropped the medical school scheme and focused on simply getting out in one piece. In June 1982, Cary Cimino graduated Boston University and stepped into the real world, his plans for a career in medicine a childhood fantasy abandoned.

Money was what he needed, so he returned to the source—New York City. He had loans to pay off. He had people to impress. He had family to help.

Returning to New York was a complex matter. While he was far away at BU, his mother and sister had visited only once. He had pretty much pretended they didn't exist. Now that he was back in New York, just a few miles from Rockland County, he realized he'd have to accept the fact that they existed. And when he returned after four years away, he realized they were barely existing.

His mother and sister were having a tough time. Her live-in boyfriend, fifteen years her junior, was a nightmare. He was addicted to drugs and rarely around. She was trying to raise a baby and enter the workforce for the first time in her life. Cary's sister, Andrea, had also become involved with drugs and was not pleasant to be around. Cary believed that once again external forces everywhere were conspiring against him. He'd tried to escape at college but returned to find that nothing substantive had changed. His family was still his family.

He went to work as a commodity broker's assistant, got his license and began working all the time. The money was spectacular, but some always went to his mother and two sisters. There was never enough, and what did he get in return? The way Cary sometimes saw it, his mother had abandoned him and his sister when his father died. She'd chosen to do that. She let them fend for themselves while others took care of her at the hospital. And as the years passed, she continued to steal his childhood even after she came home, relying on Cary to deal with financial issues and ultimately fighting with him over money. When he was a senior in high school, she'd argued with him about Social Security and Veterans benefits he was receiving because of his father, demanding that she get a share of the money every month. Once he'd gone off to college, he'd practically had no contact with her.

But after he came back to New York and started making it on Wall Street, for some reason—he wasn't quite sure why—he changed his mind. He began supporting his mother, her youngest daughter, his half-sister, Erin, and his blood sister, Andrea, in a big way. He sent them money, bought them cars, flew them around the country on vacations. Was it guilt? Did he blame himself for their troubles? Although he was seeing a psychologist, he tried not to think about it. Instead, he wrote checks. It was a lot easier. He had figured out that money was important to his mother. She knew what he knew.

Money was what made you somebody in this nasty world.

The psychiatrists had much to say about Cary and his money, sometimes dropping into vague language that removed personal choice from the picture.

One wrote, "Earning large sums of money became an integral part of his intra-psychic reparative defense mechanism."

Translation: Cary used money to mask the fact that he couldn't relate to people.

They called this "extravagance." They listed all the things he did with his money: "He lived a lavish lifestyle, taking luxury vacations, driving expensive cars, and having brief romantic involvements with scores of women . . . He has few interests outside of maintaining a façade that will impress others with how fit or successful he is, e.g. working out in a gym to appear physically in good shape, wearing expensive clothes, sporting a healthy tan, and so on. He is a devotee of tanning salons."

Most importantly, they made it clear that no matter how

much Cary collected each week and how much time he spent in a tanning booth, it wasn't working. One claimed Cary "could never trust anyone in an intimate relationship" and noted he "has no long-term close friendships."

They had plenty to say about where this all started, and nearly every one of them attributed some of the blame to his mother. They noted how she had forced him to assume an adult role at a tender age, even after she'd returned home from the hospital: "He never again regained the parental supervision and nurturance that he had known in the past. He was his mother's confidant, baby sitter and general factotum. He was forced to assume a façade of false bravado and maturity while remaining insecure and inadequate beneath the veneer he cultivated.

"He was like a frightened little boy masquerading as a grown-up."

By 1989, the "frightened little boy" had had enough of psychiatrists. He stopped seeing the psychiatrist he'd been seeing regularly for five years. Now, two years later, his mother was dead.

She had died slowly, of many cancers, at the young age of fifty-two, wasting away on morphine down in soulless Florida, unable to get out of bed for months now. It was not a surprise, but it certainly hurt. It should have inspired in him a sudden urge to reexamine the past. What could she have done differently? What could he have done differently? Why is life so sad? Unfortunately for Cary there wasn't time for any of that.

His mother's death was not just about the past. It was also about the future, and her name was Erin.

Cary and Andrea were well aware that their bedridden mother had been trying to raise Erin all by herself down in Florida. It wasn't working out. The teenager had become a wild child whom Cary and Andrea hardly knew. Now she was about to enter their lives in a big way. They were re-

sponsible for her, by law and by agreement. Cary and Andrea were about to become parents.

Life for the devoted bachelor and his party girl sister was
over. Cary had not seen this one coming.

The day Cary and Andrea became parents by default,
Erin was a teenager who did what she wanted and listened
to no one. Her father had long ago disappeared, and Cary's
mother had been bedridden. Cary remembered, "My mother
at the time was living in Florida. I was living, obviously, in
New York, and Erin had absolutely no supervision. My
mother, the last year of her life, was bedridden and lived
on morphine. Erin was out of control. There was no, God
forgive me for describing my little sister that way, but there
was no supervision at all. My mother was incapable of even
getting out of bed."

This was not going to be easy.

As Cary and Andrea flew down to Florida for the funeral, Cary admitted he didn't really know Erin at all. When
she was two, he'd headed off to college and hadn't come
back. A simple way to put it was this: "I was thirty-one. Erin
was thirteen years old."

How would Cary fit that into his Wall Street cowboy
lifestyle? It didn't seem possible. Were his trips to Aspen
over? Was that it for the barhopping and the model hunting? Would the hours spent in the tanning booth now have
to be spent going over high school geometry homework?
He couldn't even remember half of that nonsense. Cary
Cimino—Dad. It just didn't ring true.

1994

When friends asked Cary what he thought about Wall Street,
he always answered in plain English: "You didn't go to Wall
Street to become a rabbi or a priest, all right? You went to

Wall Street to make money." When he was ultimately asked why he started taking under-the-table commissions in cash, he relied on the argle-bargle he'd picked up hanging around with psychiatrists:

"I subverted a methodology."

In the three years since his mother's death, Cary had decided that "subverting a methodology" was the only way to keep ahead of the wolf pack. The strains were enormous. Cary was paying for everything and everyone. He supported both his sisters, and he was back in a top-of-the-line apartment on the Upper East Side. The Aspen vacations, the Hamptons rental, the Mercedes, even the tanning salon visits cut into the net in a big way. There was tremendous pressure all the time, and to make that work, each day Cary looked for more money than he had earned the day before.

"I'm spending huge sums of money at this point. It's a lifestyle, a sybaritic lifestyle. Trips to Aspen two, three weeks at a time, trips to St. Bart's, trips to St. Tropez, trips to Paris, rental houses in the Hamptons, $10,000 a month for a year. Plus putting my sister Erin through high school and college. Buying my sisters automobiles. Every need that my sisters had—from medical to clothing to housing to education to vacations—I provided. My sister and I, to remind you, were bringing up a child. Erin was thirteen to twenty-one during this time, and I took the financial responsibility."

He called himself a financial adviser now. Stock promoter just didn't sound prestigious enough. It was too P.T. Barnum. Financial adviser had a ring of old money to it. And he'd achieved a kind of balance between his personal and business lives. It hadn't been easy.

First he'd first had to resolve problems that surfaced with Andrea. She'd had some addiction issues and than become involved with a guy who was involved in dealing narcotics. This had created a certain amount of intra-sibling friction, to say the least. She was now telling him she'd gone straight, but she still was unable to hold a real job for more than a few weeks. She would call him at least once a day, usually more. They had always had a strange relationship, since the time when he was ten and she was eight and he was helping her get off to school each morning in that big old empty Oyster Bay house. Now their relationship was even stranger. They were supposed be both brother and sister and also mother and father. They had shipped Erin up to New York and put her in a boarding school in a rural county as far away from the city as Cary could manage. It was a lot of work, this parenting business.

There were rewards. When Erin first arrived, she was not used to being told what to do. She got used to it, and once she had settled into school in Orange County, New York, and was learning to grow up a little bit, she made it clear that Cary was a kind of savior. They overcame age differences. He made sure she went to school and took care of herself. In one letter in which she refers to herself in the third person, she wrote, "Well aside from God, I do believe she wouldn't have turned around so glorious if it hadn't been for the care and concern of her older brother, Cary Cimino. She can thank him every day for the dedication he put towards her in having a better life and there will never be enough gratitude she can show to him. However sad this may seem, it is 100% true—he has given me more than our own mother has."

Sometimes Andrea was able to help out as well, in other ways. In the spring of 1994, Andrea took up with a new guy, an older silver-haired married guy from Brooklyn named Sal Piazza. Andrea was thirty-two; Sal was in his mid-fifties. He called himself a businessman, an owner of Document Management Network, a fax company he owned with another guy. Piazza had seen that Wall Street was beginning to rebound and he wanted to get in on that. He proposed turning Document Management Network into DMN Capital. He put it in his wife's name. He was actually quite soft-spoken and pretty savvy about business, and he and Cary got along quite well. One evening when the three were socializing, Sal mentioned a guy he knew, his new business partner, who might be interested in talking with Cary about a deal he was working up. Sal had mentioned to this guy that Cary was a registered stockbroker with plenty of connections to heavyweight investors and other stock-brokers. The guy was less interested in the investors and more interested in the stockbrokers. The guy's name was Jeffrey Pokross.

Cary couldn't believe what a small world it was indeed.

They met at the offices of DMN, in an office tower on Liberty Street in Lower Manhattan, a block or two from Wall Street. Cary was less than impressed. DMN was just unfinished office space with a couple of desks, some phones and computer monitors, and empty coffee cups strewn about the badly carpeted floor. It was, Jeffrey made clear when he greeted Cary at the door, just a start-up.

Cary hadn't seen Jeffrey in years, but he looked exactly the same. His hair was thinner and he was a little thicker at the middle, but he still had those hungry little eyes and the rodentlike mustache.

"We're going to be rich," Jeffrey said. "Let me tell you about Spaceplex."

When Cary Cimino got involved in a business deal, he liked to know all the details. When Cary Cimino walked into DMN Capital in late 1994, he definitely did not know all of the details.

He did know some. The partners included Sal Piazza, the guy who was dating his sister. Sal he knew. Jeffrey Pokross he also knew. Cary was vaguely aware that there were issues with Jeffrey, but he could live with that. He did not see Jeffrey Pokross as a man with a problematic history who could drag him into the tar pit of criminal conspiracy. He looked at Jeffrey Pokross as a solution to his many personal problems.

"Jeffrey was a bombastic, caustic, arrogant man who bullied people, who literally threatened people, bullied people and asserted himself in a methodology I didn't appreciate. But I was being substantially rewarded for bad behavior. The term is 'easy money,' and Jeffrey provided product, had contacts, and I had substantial distribution. It was, again, a meeting of the minds."

Then there was this other guy, Jimmy Labate. There was no way this guy went to the Wharton School. Jimmy was probably six feet, two fifty, a young hotheaded guy with thinning reddish hair who was built like a refrigerator with a head. He wore knee-length leather jackets. He carried rolls of bills, drove a Lincoln and was able to craft unique combinations of epithets without even trying. He would say, "Fuck you, you fucking fuck," and not even appreciate the alliteration. He was a partner in DMN.

Cary stayed away from Jimmy.

Instead, he listened to Jeffrey. Jeffrey had a plan. The company was called Spaceplex. They were going to take it public. The company's formal name was Spaceplex Amusement Centers International Ltd., and although it was certainly not international, it was fair to call it limited. Spaceplex was actually a small company in Las Vegas that owned absolutely nothing, but had obtained a contract to buy a small family amusement park on Long Island. Pokross had found Spaceplex after getting a call from an old client, a German guy named Goebel who ran the U.S. securities division for one of the biggest German banks in existence. Pokross claimed this German called him to say he had a childhood friend named Ulrich who had control of a bunch of German boiler rooms.

As Pokross remembered it, "Mr. Goebel wanted to know if I could come up with a stock in the U.S. that I can identify and handle the trading of that security and he would pump it out with his friend Ulrich at these various German boiler rooms where they were going to be paying cash bribes to the owners . . . and the stockbrokers. I started looking right away."

After a number of calls to various corrupt brokers looking for a patsy company, Pokross came up with Spaceplex. The president of the company was a guy named Manas, whom everybody called "Mr. Fingers." Jeffrey didn't bother to explain how Manas had earned such a nickname, but Cary wasn't that interested anyway. Pokross said the owner "was looking for stock promotion and to get some money in the company. He was looking for somebody to drive the price of his stock up because he was a big shareholder and he wanted to raise some additional money." If Mr. Fingers was interested in actually running an amusement park, Pokross didn't say.

Working with a corrupt broker named Andy Mann, Pokross said the scheme was to pay off other corrupt brokers and stock promoters like himself with cash and free stock from other companies Mann held in his offshore brokerage firms. He already had the boiler rooms in Germany waiting to begin pumping up Spaceplex stock. All they needed now was to go out and recruit brokers for the U.S. sales pitch. Once they got the stock where they wanted it, all the insiders would dump en masse and they'd all be rich. Pump and dump. Pokross would be paying Cary an off-the-books commission of 30 percent, which he could chop up and distribute to his brokers in whatever manner worked for him.

At the time Cary had his sit-down with Jeffrey, he didn't make it known that, as usual, he was swimming in debt. He did, however, borrow $3,000 from Jeffrey, a guy he hadn't seen in five years, and then he agreed to promote Spaceplex. He told Jeffrey he was working for Diversified Investments, which happened to be run by the president of the Upper East Side co-op where he was currently in residence. Actually he wasn't really working for Diversified; it was more that he was working with Diversified. He claimed to Jeffrey that Diversified had him on salary, that they had leased him yet another Mercedes, this time a 600 S30 (not in his name) and that he was getting cash "incentives" on the side. He told him they could use Diversified as a cover to make "incentive" payments to the other brokers they recruited.

"It made the paying of the other brokers mellifluous. It made it liquid. It made it easier. It hid the business we were doing. It hid it from every regulator. It hid it from the IRS as well. I could be making large sums of money and not paying taxes."

He was aware that he was discussing avoiding detection by legal authorities. He knew all about pump and dump. He was aware that he was involved in criminal activity. But he was also aware that so was just about everybody else he came into contact with on a daily basis in the world of Wall Street. And more importantly, it wasn't just Cary Cimino that really needed the money. Now Cary had another reason to get "flexible" with the law. He had Erin.

All the hours of headache and heartache he'd experienced as a pseudo father to his much younger half-sister had brought with it a kind of benefit he hadn't foreseen. The more he'd thought about it, the more he came to see there might be some upside to Erin. Perhaps there was something to all this altruism. There was something powerful about having a motive to earn money that was connected to someone else's well-being. If he was choosing to bend or even break rules, he was only doing it for his baby sister, and who could argue with that? He had obtained a certain lifestyle that he needed to maintain, but now he had a reason quite pure for getting and having. It wasn't just about Cary. Cary the pseudo father could say for the first time that his pursuit of wealth was now about so much more.

Of course making tons of money was not guaranteed.

While he was there, Sal Piazza stopped by and said hello. They got to talking and the subject of enforcement came up. Enforcement was a critical issue in pulling off a pump and dump scheme. In order for the scam to work, the clueless investors couldn't be allowed to sell their stock before the insiders sold theirs. Otherwise the price wouldn't rise and perhaps the whole thing would never get off the ground. In pump and dump, brokers had to keep their customers in line. And the insiders had to keep the brokers in line. Sometimes persuading the brokers to stay on program involved a certain amount of physical force. Cary knew all about this and until now had never really had to think about enforcement. Enforcement usually required the name of one of a certain group of five families.

"Not a problem," Jeffrey assured him. "I'm with a guy named Robert Lino. Everybody calls him Robert from Avenue U."

CHAPTER TWELVE

January 2, 1990

No studies have been presented to learned colleagues in vaunted journals about the amount of time the average gangster spends sitting in restaurants, but it's fair to assume it's about 50 percent of his waking hours. The gangster, of course, has no office. There's no conference room from which to transact teleconference calls with clients. There's just the corner banquette at the local diner. The day after New Year's Day on the second day of the new decade, Frank Lino and two gangster friends sat in a Middle Eastern restaurant on McDonald Avenue and Avenue N way out there in Brooklyn, waiting. It was a nasty cold night, and all the holidays were officially over. People were taking down Christmas trees and dumping the dried out skeletons on the sidewalk, the silver tinsel shivering in the wind. This was the bleak stretch of winter. The fun was over. The weeks of January and February stretched out ahead like so many miles of arctic tundra.

Frank and his pals sat in the restaurant waiting for his

cousin, Robert Lino, who was always on time. Tonight Robert from Avenue U was late.

For Frank Lino, the twentieth century—the gangster's century—hadn't been so bad. Here he was at age fifty-two, a Lafayette High School dropout by tenth grade, married at age nineteen to a girl not yet sixteen, five kids and a divorce behind him. He'd tried legitimate work, but it didn't really suit him. He was handling dice games and running sports book by the time he was a teenager, and he never looked back or thought twice about where he was headed. He did have some doubts along the way. For a time, he insisted he wouldn't carry a gun when they hijacked trucks out near Kennedy Airport. Often he thought everyone was out to get him and that the next sit-down would be his last. But he was still around. He'd been inducted into the Bonanno group in 1977 on his fortieth birthday and elevated to captain in 1983. By the second day of the last decade of the twentieth century, he was a veteran. He made a fortune from a thriving gambling operation. He dabbled in drugs and did quite well. He'd bought up pornographic videos in the 1970s when they were still called "French films" and resold them in Las Vegas for hefty profits. Now people paid him money just to use his name. As in "I'm with Frank." Everybody was happy with Frank Lino. He made money for himself and the bosses, who did not understand the concept of enough, and in this life—the life of the made man— he'd done almost no time. This had truly been the gangster's century. From a street gang in the alleyways of Lower Manhattan, an unwanted import from Sicily, the schemes had grown and grown, the power extended to the highest reaches of business. And Frank Lino was a part of all that.

Of course, Frank still had to sit in restaurants in the middle of the night waiting for things to happen that would never ever happen on time.

Usually Robert was pretty good about these things. He was Frank's star pupil. Like Frank, he'd dropped out of high school, which was good. Some of these guys who went on to college were a pain in the ass. Robert had embraced the life. He was disinclined to get a real job under any circumstances. The bosses had put him with Frank, and he was happy to be there. He was obeying his father's wishes. And he did whatever Frank wanted. He helped him track his bookmaking, collect on his shylock loans, enforce protection collection. He took messages to people. He watched Frank's back. He was an apprentice, learning the players and all their tricks. In a way, now that Bobby Senior was gone, Frank was Robert's new father.

Frank was old-school gangster. He'd survived a nasty bit of business in 1981 when he and three captains were invited to a meeting at a social club in Brooklyn and walked into a shotgun attack. The three captains were blown to pieces, and Frank—for reasons he had never quite figured out—had been allowed to leave alive and breathing. Subsequently he'd been welcomed back into the newly aligned Bonannos' loving embrace. He immediately set to ingratiating himself with the bosses by handling another nasty piece of work, the unfortunate and untimely death of Sonny Black. By 1990 Frank Lino was an established player in the family, and Robert Lino was at his side. And late.

As it happened, Frank had to cut Robert some slack. By 1990, after thirteen years as a gangster, Frank was immersed in middle age. Not retirement age, just slowing-down age. Robert was a young man. Frank was tired of tracking money he put on the street, so he put Robert in charge of that. Frank was less interested in day-to-day occurrences within his crew, so Robert helped out, letting Frank know about internal disputes petty and otherwise. Robert quietly made it his business to know everything. As 1990 arrived, Frank knew that Robert Lino was on his way to becoming a made man at a time when the Bonanno crime family was on the rise. There was, however, a bit of a speed bump. It was the reason Frank was sitting in the restaurant on McDonald Avenue.

The problem at hand was Louis Tuzzio, a low-level wannabe who someone with not very much sense had assigned the task of killing a guy named Gus Farace. Farace was a lowlife drug dealer who happened to have some Mafia friends. He was heavily involved in selling as much dope as he could and using as much as he could handle, too. He was essentially out of control, and in his drug-addled state he had made a major-league mistake. Perhaps the biggest mistake you can make. During a drug sale in Brooklyn he decided he didn't like the guy doing the buying, so he shot him to death. How could he have known that the buyer was really a Drug Enforcement Administration (DEA) undercover agent and family man? The federal government was furious. They rousted mob social clubs, letting everybody in every family know that until the shooter came forward, life would be hell for *la cosa nostra* in New York City. Gus Farace thus became marked as a dead man in every way.

The job of finding and shooting Gus Farace right away fell to the Bonanno crime group, mostly because Gus Farace was dating the daughter of a Bonanno family soldier. She was seen as the way to get to Gus. As it was told to Frank Lino, Louis Tuzzio got the job because Tuzzio knew Farace and was as close to a friend as a guy like Farace could expect. Tuzzio had set up a meeting, and Farace was supposed to show up solo. Tuzzio pulled up in a van with three other guys, to a spot in the middle of nowhere Brooklyn, and—naturally—Farace was not alone. He was with a guy named Sclafani who happened to be the son of a Gambino soldier. Louis Tuzzio decided on the spot not to call off the job. Instead, he got in a shoot-out with Gus Farace, and Farace wound up dead. Unfortunately for Louis Tuzzio, Sclafani, the son of the Gambino soldier, also ended up shot and badly wounded.

Which was why a few months later Frank Lino received word that John Gotti, imperious boss of the Gambino crime group and a guy who truly believed he was the boss of everyone, had let it be known that he was apoplectic. He wanted everybody involved in the shooting of the Sclafani kid dead. Everybody. This was his way. He frequently wanted everybody guilty of one or another perceived slight dead. Now the Bonanno group had a big John Gotti headache, and Frank Lino wound up as the guy chosen to administer the medicine. At the time, Frank was feeling somewhat vulnerable. In fact, he was constantly worrying about becoming a victim himself. He felt sure that at any time he would go to a meeting and never come back. This was due in part to his experience inside the social club when his three friends had been shotgunned to death in front of him and he'd been allowed to leave. This event cast a certain shadow over Frank's life. He needed to make things right, and the way to do that would be to resolve the big John Gotti headache. It was natural that Frank Lino would turn to his cousin Robert for help.

Gotti had demanded the deaths of the three non-made members in the van when Sclafani was shot. Members of the Bonanno family—including Frank Lino—were extremely upset about this. They felt this was unfair, given that Sclafani was only one guy and he'd survived and Gotti was saying three guys had to go. This was bad math. This was, at best, three for the price of one. The Bonanno group and Gotti came up with the usual compromise—one guy for one guy. Maybe that was what Gotti had wanted in the first place. Regardless, Louis Tuzzio, more or less by default, became the one guy.

As Frank sat in the restaurant on McDonald Avenue, the plan—his plan—was already unfolding. A Bonanno associate named Dirty Danny was childhood friends with Tuzzio. Dirty Danny was also childhood friends with Robert Lino, so the two were assigned the job of luring Tuzzio to a meeting, where he would be shot in the head adequately to kill him. Everyone involved knew this would not be a simple task. Tuzzio was in a high state of paranoia. Recently another crew tried to convince Tuzzio to show up at a lonely garage in Greenpoint, Brooklyn, owned by a guy named Patty Muscles. On the appointed day, the assigned hit man had a heart attack, so that didn't work out. Next they tried luring Tuzzio to a meeting in a residential area of Bay Ridge, but he showed up with another Bonanno soldier who was not clued in on the matter. Now here it was, the day after New Year's, and Frank Lino and two gangster friends sat in the Middle Eastern restaurant on McDonald Avenue waiting for Robert Lino, Dirty Danny and Louis Tuzzio to pull up in a Camaro.

The story they'd thought up to get Tuzzio to go along was this: Frank was going to reassure Tuzzio that the business with Gus Farace was, in fact, understandable given Gus Farace's many problems. Frank would tell Louis that he was about to get his button, to become a made member of the Bonanno crime family. This would be a great honor for Louis. In fact, it would be the biggest day of his life, the thing he'd always wanted, the dream come true. That was the story they figured would work to get a paranoid guy like Louis Tuzzio to show up for his own assassination.

And then here they were. The Camaro pulled up with Tuzzio at the wheel. Frank watched Tuzzio get out of the car, apparently relaxed, still believing he might live to collect Social Security. Tuzzio strolled into the restaurant with his childhood friend, Dirty Danny, Robert Lino, and—a surprise for Frank—another guy not on the guest list. The guy was Frank Ambrosino, a friend of Robert's since childhood. They all entered the restaurant and Tuzzio sat down with Frank. Everybody else went to a separate table.

Frank went to work with his avuncular act. He understood why Tuzzio might think that all this talk about him becoming a made guy was not real, what with the other guy with the Gambinos getting shot and all that. But Louis had to know the context. Frank reassured him that the bosses all considered Louis to be a capable guy for his work on Gus

Farace. Sure there had been a bit of mess to clean up, but it had all worked out. Law enforcement seemed far more enthusiastic about finding Farace than about finding Farace's killers, and—sure enough—after Farace was clipped, the feds backed off. Frank began instructing Tuzzio on what to expect at the induction ceremony, how it was important to pretend you didn't know what was what when they asked if you knew why you were there. He went through the list of rules that everybody knew and everybody broke on a regular basis and gave the kid Tuzzio a gentle slap to the cheek. Frank Lino told the kid everything would be fine.

"Relax," he said. "This time next week you're a man of respect."

Sure it was late and it was dark and freezing outside, but couldn't Tuzzio see he was with his best friend, Dirty Danny? His whole life was about to change. What good was fear misplaced? Frank told Tuzzio to sit with Dirty Danny and send his cousin Robert over. When Robert sat down, Frank asked quietly about the guy Robert had brought along, Ambrosino. Frank needed to know about this guy. Robert made it clear he wanted Ambrosino with him in the backup car. Robert made it plain that he'd known Ambrosino forever and trusted him like a brother. He said he and Ambrosino would carry weapons and follow the car Tuzzio was in. After the shooting they would be responsible for getting rid of the murder weapon.

Everything was ready. Events were set in motion. There was no turning back, no backing away. Soon Tuzzio would no longer be a problem for the Bonanno crime group's bosses and Robert Lino would have participated in a piece of work. That would make him eligible to be made himself, which was what Robert's father, Bobby, had wanted all along. Frank was just doing a dying man a favor here. Robert Lino Sr. would surely understand. Louis Tuzzio surely would not.

CHAPTER THIRTEEN

1981

Warrington sat in a movie theater in midtown Manhattan, waiting for the show to begin. All his friends from school were there, waiting with him. Actually they weren't there to see a movie. They were there to see Warrington—in a movie.

Warrington hadn't really made it at Villanova. He'd tried his best to pretend he actually liked economics, but they didn't call it the dry science for nothing. It was brutal. It was like learning a second language and math at the same time. He loathed every minute of it. He also had loathed the bucolic campus in middle-of-nowhere Pennsylvania. It was what his mother wanted, but not what he wanted. He had so much more to offer. He was a creative guy. In the summer after sophomore year, he'd made a decision—he was going to quit and move to New York to become what he was always meant to be—an actor.

It all made more sense than the Laffer curve and John Maynard Keynes. He had an outgoing personality, could ingratiate himself with people in power (teachers, coaches, bouncers), and was growing into his father's good looks. Hollywood beckoned, but first he had to actually learn how to act. New York City and the Strasberg Institute was the place for that.

His father—now remarried and selling real estate in Palm Beach—had helped him out. Though Warrington was now twenty-one and could certainly have gone out and gotten a real job to pay the bills, he was an artist and his father was a patron. Dad paid the rent on Warrington's Sutton Place apartment and the tuition at Strasberg. Whether his father believed any of this would amount to anything, Warrington did not know. He was just happy that his dad was contributing. He wouldn't have asked his stepfather for the money. He never liked asking him for anything. He'd come to resent spending any time at Tally Ho, feeling as though he was back at Gilman, living in a stranger's house. His father's financial help—limited though it was—was the only assistance he could bear to accept.

He really needed it to work out. It was important that he succeed, to validate his father's investment.

It wasn't easy. For two years he'd won major roles only in TV commercials. When he tried out for a part in the sequel to the hugely popular *Friday the 13th*, he'd believed it would take him to the next step. He studied for weeks, watching the first movie again and again. When it came time to read, he was stiff and awkward. He didn't understand the nuances of character. A speaking role was not to be.

But his enthusiasm showed through. He was clearly committed to working hard, and the casting director came up with an idea: why not give Warrington—who was now using the razor family name Warrington Gillette—a non-speaking role? Why not make him Jason himself?

Perhaps Jason could be his breakthrough role. Sure there wasn't a single line of dialogue, and it was difficult to recognize Warrington under all that makeup. He looked like somebody had lit a fire on his face and put it out with a rake. His hair was matted to his head and torn out in spots, the left side drooped, and his mouth hung open wide enough for a bird to fly in.

During shooting, the makeup was always driving him insane. Gobs of rubber and plastic had been glued to the left side of his face. His left eye was completely covered up, replaced by a twisted festering rubber mess that left him blind on one side. He had dentures that forced his mouth to remain open for hours at a time. He wore a skull-cap that caused him to sweat like Richard Nixon. He wore a stained plaid cotton shirt common to people who know how to gut deer and kill small animals. He looked like a lunatic, which was what he was supposed to look like. And who cared? He was in the movies.

Actually it was *Friday the 13th: Part 2*, and it was as good as he could manage in this particular moment in his acting career. It wasn't exactly Marlon Brando in *A Streetcar Named Desire*, but it would do. Warrington, after all, was a professional actor now, and he understood that you have to pay your dues.

Boy was he paying. His favorite story—one he told every model he could rope into conversation in his many nights out on the town—was the day he was supposed to crash through a window in a deserted cabin in the woods. There were always deserted cabins in these movies, and the best way for the lunatic to enter them was always to crash through the window. The day of the big scene he'd been standing all morning waiting for his big moment. He would crash through the window to slash and chop his way into the hearts and minds of teenagers and the rest of the gore-obsessed world. He hadn't eaten all morning because the idiotic makeup prevented him from taking food into his mouth. His depth perception was gone because his left eye was hidden behind the foam rubber, and he was enveloped in a fine sheen of sweat. All he needed to do was crash through the window and flail madly for a few moments. Maybe this was method acting. You got so furious at being cooped up inside this makeup that your fury became part of your role. They hadn't really mentioned that at the Strasberg Institute.

Warrington could do this. He'd immersed himself in the story of Jason. He was a lonely, tormented kid, disfigured in a fire, back to kill off his tormentors in a remote area called Crystal Lake. There was an Oedipal aspect. The boy's mother was killed in the first movie, so now Warrington's Jason had grown up but kept her head in the refrigerator. His killing orgy had purpose other than to pique the prurient interest of popcorn-munching teens. Allegedly. How did you get inside that character? Why would you want to?

Standing around waiting to crash through the fake window in the fake cabin in the real woods deep in the heart of Connecticut, Warrington had tried to become the best Jason he could be. He had to make this work. Here he was, the scion of old money, the weight of legacy pressing down upon him, living off his father's dime without a college degree to show for his troubles. It was acting or nothing.

The scene was ready. Jason was on another psycho rampage. Warrington was told to run hard and smash through the grimy window of the cabin in the woods with forearms extended and palms turned backward. The window was rigged so it wouldn't hurt. At least that was what Warrington was told. Then he would attack the actress Amy Steel, who would scream and try in vain to escape his murderous mission. Pretty simple.

The director called, "Action!" and Warrington ran as fast as he could toward the window.

He hit the window like a brick wall and bounced back, landing flat on his butt.

It was ludicrous. There he sat, in all his foam-rubber splendor, mouth agape, stupefied and humiliated. The army of worker bees around him started yelling and casting blame as quickly as possible. Some idiot had forgotten to score the window. A linebacker couldn't get through it, never mind a twenty-two-year-old Villanova dropout. They would have to shoot the scene again. The show must go on, etc.

"By the time we reached that scene," Warrington was telling his friends, "I was so sick and uncomfortable with the whole process that I really could have killed that girl."

The lights dimmed, the previews began. Finally it was time—*Friday the 13th: Part 2*. Warrington could barely contain himself when his name flashed on the screen during the opening credits.

Scene after scene unfolded. This was merely the first sequel, so the filmmakers felt compelled to offer up enough backstory that the movie actually contained plot elements. Warrington was Jason Voorhees, who supposedly drowned as a teenager at a camp for bored suburban youth called Crystal Lake. Jason's mother flipped out and hid in the woods, killing anyone who tried to reopen the camp. In the first movie, she killed eight camp counselors but was decapitated by one survivor. She did this, naturally, on Friday the thirteenth. Her partially decomposed son, Jason, showed up to avenge her death, again on—when else?—Friday the thirteenth. The counselor who killed Mom decided it would be a good idea to return to the camp two months later to face her fears about Crystal Lake. This was convenient for Jason, who burst in and stabbed her in the neck with an ice pick. Her body was never found.

Friday the 13th: Part 2 didn't end there, although the rest of the story was more or less a variation on that which had already been told. Five years later somebody else tried to reopen Camp Crystal Lake. Jason/Warrington returned and started killing people. As the movie rolled toward its inevitable bloody conclusion, yet another scantily clad counselor bimbo attacked Jason with a machete. Warrington/Jason somehow survived to escape into the woods, taking with him the promise of more sequels to come.

The credits rolled. Warrington and his friends stayed to watch his name roll by once again. They were all cheering and clapping him on the back, and in some ways it felt good. There he was, up there on the big screen, looking down on thousands of people who were willing to pay good money to watch Jason do his thing. And Warrington knew they'd all been there just to see Jason. Fame and fortune were within reach. He could taste it. He imagined himself exiting a black stretch limo at the premiere of his first star vehicle, the paparazzi braying at him as he strutted up the red carpet with a model on each arm.

Of course, his mother, father, sister, half brother and anyone else in his social circle could sit through the entire movie and not recognize Warrington up there, and in the entire film he'd uttered not a single word of English prose. The only acting involved running through woods and flailing about with a hatchet or a knife or an ice pick. An orangutan could do that. As he left the theater, he suddenly became depressed. Maybe acting wasn't for him. Standing outside the theater, the theme song of *Friday the 13th* still ringing in his head, he began to think that maybe he wasn't really cut out for the creative life. Maybe he needed to make a little cash.

Right away.

CHAPTER FOURTEEN

January 2, 1990

All the men left the restaurant and got into the Camaro. Dirty Danny agreed to drive, Louis Tuzzio got in the passenger seat. Robert Lino got in the backseat behind Tuzzio. Ambrosino and Frank got in a second car, which was to follow a ways behind. Frank's pals went off in their own direction. As far as Louis Tuzzio was concerned, he was on his way to joining the brotherhood of thieves and murderers, a life goal realized at last. The two cars pulled away from curbside and headed out into the frigid Brooklyn night.

Before this night, Robert from Avenue U had never actually pointed a gun at another man and pulled the trigger. True, he was a criminal. He had collected illegal protection payments, he'd run a sports book, he'd dug a hole for Gabe Infanti. He also had knowledge of many bad acts committed by his father and his father's cousins and friends. But to be an actual shooter—that was a different matter. You could scheme, you could extort, you could even threaten. But to actually look a man in the eye and know you were going to take it all the way—that brought you to a different place.

It was a powerful feeling, with a price. It was, like anything else, a choice. You could say you were just following orders, but in the end, you chose to follow the orders. You personally acquired the gun, inserted the clip, made sure the safety was off, sat in the backseat in the dark knowing what you were about to do. You knew that physically, all that was required was to squeeze a trigger. That was easy. But to actually point the gun at another man's head and blow out his brains—that was new to Robert of Avenue U.

What did he think about as he sat there in the darkened car, gun fully loaded, ready? Did he think of his father? His father had done things like this. He had shot his good friend, Sonny Black. Did he think of his own future? From now on he would be different from the average salary-earning dope who walked this earth. Did he think of Louis Tuzzio? Louis had a wife, a mother, maybe future kids. Did he think about what he had to gain? After, Robert would be able to say he was a capable guy. He could become a man of honor, a man of respect. He could get his button, and everybody who needed to know would know how he got it. Everybody would know that Robert of Avenue U was capable of taking another man's life. How many people who prowl the malls and buy a newspaper from the guy on the corner have taken another man's life? By the time he sat in that Camaro with Louis Tuzzio, Robert of Avenue U had known quite a few murderers. His father. His cousin Eddie. For all he knew, his cousin Frank. In a way, taking that final step, making that ultimate choice, wasn't really that surprising for Robert. In fact, you could argue, it was expected.

Dirty Danny, the driver, steered through the streets. At this time of night in this neighborhood, there was nobody around to notice two cars filled with men. Dirty Danny drove the Camaro a few blocks and then made a right instead of the left that Tuzzio had expected.

They were next to a park, known as Legends Field, right around the corner from a graveyard. It was dark and cold. The apartment buildings near the park seemed a hundred miles away. Tuzzio sat in the passenger seat. Robert Lino sat in the back, where it was very dark. Tuzzio knew right away something was wrong.

The car came to a jarring halt. A figure jumped out of the driver's side and ran away from the car, leaving the door open. This was Dirty Danny, Louis Tuzzio's childhood friend. Now the car itself was rocking back and forth, with screaming inside. A figure in the front seat was flailing madly, kicking at the windshield as if restrained from behind. Shots were fired and the car stopped its rocking. All was quiet. A few moments later, a second figure emerged, from the backseat, straightened himself up, brushed off his jacket. The two figures ran toward an approaching car and jumped in. Robert's childhood pal, Ambrosino, was at the wheel. They sped away from the scene and disappeared into the streets of New York.

A few hours later two beat cops on street patrol noticed a Camaro with the door open. There was a body sprawled across the front seat, with blood all over. The windshield had been kicked out from within. The body still had a wallet filled with bills, and the license had the name and face of one Louis Tuzzio. When the forensics team showed up, they estimated Tuzzio had five bullets inside his body, including one inside his cranium. Canvassing the neighborhood began. The shots were heard by no one. There were no suspects. The police theorized it was an organized crime hit because of the professional nature of the killing and the fact that no money was taken. And they mentioned that Tuzzio had certain associates who were known figures in the underworld. The cops loved to talk like this. They'd seen all the movies. They knew the lines. What they didn't know was who killed Louis Tuzzio.

Robert from Avenue U certainly did.

* * *

Mafia induction ceremony etiquette is subject to interpretation. Not everyone agrees on the correct way to swear allegiance to a secret society of murderers, extortionists, etc. There is no Emily Post of *la cosa nostra* to straighten things out. The rules are somewhat vague. The ceremony itself must take place away from the prying eyes of the government. It can't be held at Red Lobster, for example, or Olive Garden. The location is supposed to be known only to a select few, and made known to the inductees only at the last minute. Usually all of corporate management shows up: the boss, the underboss, the consigliere and as many of the captains as they can fit in the basement of a split-level ranch with faux wood paneling and wet bar. Those who are incarcerated are excused. Inductees are brought in one by one by their respective sponsors. Almost everybody does the business with pricking the trigger finger that's become quite popular on television shows and in movies that portray organized crime as a fun-loving group of miscreants similar to Long John Silver and his band of merry pirates. A made guy—sometimes it's the sponsor, sometimes the consigliere—uses a pin to prick the index finger of the inductee to draw a little blood, which is then smeared on a small card depicting a saint. Sometimes it's Saint Anthony. Never is it Saint Jude. The saint card with the blood is placed in the open palm of the inductee and lit. As it burns, the inductee must repeat something along the lines of "If I ever give up the secrets of this organization may I burn like this saint." Most everybody has a gun and knife present on the table to symbolize the tools of the trade. Inductees are asked if they know why they're there, and they're supposed to say no, even though without exception they all know. A list of rules is read, and everybody locks up—a circle of men holding hands, symbolizing either unity or the eternal fear that the guy next to you will turn informant and the whole house of cards will come tumbling down.

In early 1991, this was more or less what Robert Lino was expecting as he headed with his cousin, Frank, to the pigeon club owned by Anthony Spero on Bath Avenue in Gravesend. On the roof of this three-story Brooklyn apartment building were a number of pigeon coops. In the basement was a group of men, waiting for Robert Lino and another young man, who were about to participate in a ceremony they were supposed to know nothing about. For more than seventy years this ceremony had been going on in the basements and backrooms of Gravesend, Bay Ridge, Bensonhurst, Midwood, Red Hook and Elizabeth, New Jersey. In the Bonanno group, the ceremonies could be held just about anyplace. Robert's father, Bobby Senior, had been inducted in an upstairs room of a company called J&S Cake that was really just a social club. Now it was Robert's turn.

At the pigeon club Frank Lino brought Robert into a waiting room on the first floor to sit and sweat with his fellow inductee, a guy everybody called Richie Shellac Head, a supervising pressman at the *New York Post* who was known as an earner, not a tough guy. Robert from Avenue U knew he was there under different circumstances. He was a capable guy. Everyone in the room downstairs knew he'd helped with the Tuzzio problem.

This was a point of contention for some gangsters. John Gotti, for instance, favored capable guys. He didn't want to induct anybody into the family unless they had been involved in a piece of work, just like him. He and a number of the old-timers preferred tough guys to earners. Earners were like Shellac Head. He operated a major-league bookie ring at the *New York Post*, so he kicked up plenty of money. This was why he was being inducted. Not Robert Lino. Although he was extremely helpful in supporting his cousin, Frank, who was now his sponsor, he was also known as a capable guy.

Since the Tuzzio hit he'd been called upon to repeat his performance. This was the New Robert from Avenue U. From now on, he would be expected to do more than roll a guy up inside a rug. When a marijuana-dealing Bonanno associate complained that some mope had come into his home, tied him up and threatened to kill his family unless he came up with cash, Robert Lino was put on the case. The marijuana dealer paid Robert $25,000 to kill Fat Sally, the mope he believed had terrorized his family. Robert and a friend found Fat Sally at his body shop in Brooklyn, but Fat Sally saw them coming and—despite his girth—managed to hide behind a tree. Lino took some shots but failed to hit his intended target, although he definitely hit the tree. Then it turned out Fat Sally wasn't involved in the home invasion after all, so now Robert had to go after another guy whose name he didn't know but who was the new suspect in the home invasion. Robert from Avenue U tried to kill him, too, but this guy wore a bulletproof vest. So far Robert hadn't experienced a lot of luck in the business of killing people, but he had made one thing quite clear—he was a capable guy.

First Robert was called downstairs. He entered the basement and saw guys he'd known all his life. He was introduced by cousin Frank and was asked if he knew why he was there. He said no. They told him it was not a club, it was a secret society. They asked if he had any problem with any of the men in the room. He said no. They went through the burning saint and pricked trigger finger. Robert Lino was a guy who appreciated ceremony. He believed it elevated the mundane, added a certain resonance to the everyday. There was history here. Legacy. Certainly he must have been appreciative of the fact that he was there in this basement in Brooklyn participating in this ceremony to fulfill his father's dream.

The skippers went through the rules of *la cosa nostra*. Each one called out a different rule. Some made sense.

Never touch another made man without permission from the boss. Never sleep with a made man's wife or daughter. Always put your business on record with your captain. Soldiers can't talk with the administration about business; usually the consigliere deals with the captains about issues. You can't be introduced to another made man except by a made man. No stocks and bonds. That was an old rule, going back to the beginning. And so on. One rule in particular must have made Robert Lino cringe. The rule was "No drugs."

Everybody knew that Robert's father had been a major-league drug dealer, and that hadn't stopped the Bonanno crime family from welcoming him into its protective fold. Everybody knew Bobby Lino sold drugs that had nearly destroyed his own flesh and blood. He'd lost a son to drugs. His daughter was locked within the claustrophobic world of addiction. And here stood Robert Lino, nodding as a skipper said with a straight face, "No drugs," and everybody else in the room nodded in agreement, especially the guys who'd built second homes and bought nice cars and boats based on the income from narcotics.

In a world of criminals, how seriously could anyone take these rules? In this world, rules weren't really rules. They were more like guidelines. Suggestions. If you found a good reason to chuck them in the dustbin, if it was good for business or even just good for you, so be it. But you had to have rules. If you didn't, there was nothing but chaos and anarchy. You had to have rules and recite them so everybody knew what was what. When the reading of the rules was finished, all the men stood in a circle—the newly inducted Robert Lino and Richie Shellac Head—and they all held hands. They swore allegiance to this family—even over their blood family—and then the ceremony was over.

As his father had dreamed, Robert Lino was now a soldier in the Bonanno organized crime family, one of the five remaining Mafia families in America. No one could touch him without permission from the bosses. No one could bother his family. He could invoke the power of the Bonanno family name and reap its benefits, both financial and otherwise. He could make a living without doing a legitimate day's work. He was part of *la famiglia*, and his timing was perfect.

As would soon be made clear, the 1990s would be very good for the Bonanno crime family. The government believed that the FBI agent pretending to be Donnie Brasco had delivered a knockout blow to the Bonanno family, so they focused their ample resources on the other four families. The plan was simple: the bosses of all the other families would soon go to prison. Most importantly, John Gotti had just been indicted again. And this time, there were all these tape recordings of the loudmouthed Gotti going on and on about killing this guy because he didn't come in when he was called and severing this guy's head just because and so on. Meanwhile the boss of the Genovese family, Vincent Gigante, was parading unshaven around Greenwich Village in a bathrobe, pretending to be a lunatic to avoid incarceration. This was hardly a way for a boss to behave. The Colombo family was shooting at each other in the streets, split down the middle by a disagreement over who should run the family while the boss, Carmine Persico, served a life term. And the Lucchese family was pretty much on its last legs, forced underground by its decision to try and kill the sister of an informant. Until the day they went after the sister, family members were off-limits. This constellation of events presented the Bonanno crime family with certain unique opportunities, and Robert Lino was in a perfect spot to benefit. The family had, in fact, survived the Brasco fiasco, and in truth, the FBI agent had not succeeded in bringing the family down. It was a temporary setback. With all the other families jammed up and the family boss, Joseph

Massino, ready to step out of jail, the Bonanno family—
once kicked off the Mafia's commission for dealing drugs
openly—was preparing for a big second act.

January 1991

When the decision comes down from corporate headquarters to clip somebody, it's important that the victim stay
dead. Ideally that means burying a body so that the authorities never again find even a scrap of the deceased. Bodies
provide clues. Clues lead to prosecutions. Prosecutions lead
to informants and then it all falls apart. Robert Lino knew
that the ideal situation was to make sure the bodies stayed
buried. Lately that had been a bit of a problem.

In recent months, the FBI had dredged up numerous
missing persons. Sonny Black had floated to the surface in
Staten Island. Sonny Red popped up in Queens. A former
deputy commissioner at the city's Marine and Aviation Department showed up in the trunk of a car. A Sicilian hit man
was found chopped up and stuffed inside several steel drums
in New Jersey. Louis Tuzzio lay there inside the Camaro
right on the streets of Brooklyn for the cops to find. Another
guy turned up wrapped in a rug and left in the rear seat of
his own truck parked at John F. Kennedy International Airport. There wasn't anything anybody could do about Sonny
Black, or the Sicilian hit man, or Louis Tuzzio, or any of the
rest of them. They were already government exhibit whatever. But there were others out there still.

For instance, there was Gabe Infanti, the guy who'd
fallen out of favor and wound up in that weed-choked lot off
Arthur Kill Road in Staten Island. So far Gabe had stayed
dead. Nobody had turned informant and brought him back
to life. That is until Tommy Karate—a guy who had spent a
lot of time digging holes in Staten Island in the middle of the
night—got himself indicted.

No indictment scared the Bonanno family like that of Tommy Karate. Here was a guy involved in who knows how many pieces of work. Usually he personally did the shooting or stabbing or strangling, plus disposal in the bathtub. But he always did it because somebody told him to. Therefore he was a font of information for the FBI, and he'd been indicted on numerous murders and faced the death penalty. The Bonanno family immediately expected he'd turn informant, and then many a ship would be sunk. But if Tommy Karate told the FBI a body was buried at a certain spot and it wasn't, then the body didn't really exist, and Tommy might be seen not just as a sadistic killer but, even worse for the FBI, as a manipulative liar. Suddenly in the days after Tommy Karate's arrest, there were groups of gangsters with shovels gathered in remote sections of Brooklyn, Queens and especially Staten Island, digging furiously in the dark, trying to turn Tommy Karate into a liar.

For Robert Lino, this meant another frigid night on Arthur Kill Road. There he was again in January 1991, in the middle of bleak nowhere, Staten Island, by the fence company, looking for poor Gabe Infanti in the frozen weeds.

This time Robert Lino was a made man, a soldier in the Bonanno crime family. He now had his own crew of soldiers and reported to his cousin Frank. He was handling most of Frank's sports book and loan-shark collection, which provided a pretty steady stream of cash. Mostly he was interested in keeping a low profile. That was the most important thing. Look what was happening with Gotti. Here was a guy who openly taunted law enforcement, holding meetings with his crews right there on Mulberry Street, having dinner with actors, making the federal government and the city of New York look stupid with his fireworks out in Howard Beach. He liked being high-profile, and now he was in jail, indicted yet again, this time charged with killing his former boss, Paul Castellano. Sure he'd beaten three previous cases, but this one seemed different. This time there was a bug placed inside the guy's inner sanctum. This time it looked like John Gotti, the self-proclaimed boss of bosses, was on his way out.

That probably wasn't such a bad thing. The boss of the Bonanno family, Joseph Massino, had openly courted Gotti's support. Everybody knew Massino had met with Gotti the day before Castellano was shot dead outside Sparks Steak House on that chilly December evening in 1985. But now Gotti was likely to spend the rest of his life in jail, and the Bonanno family was in a position to take advantage of the expected void left behind.

That was the plan anyway, and it required an extremely low-profile approach. Most of the crew meetings had been stopped, and hardly anybody went to see the boss in prison while he served out his sentence. He would be out in three years and then the Bonanno family would probably be the only family in New York with a real boss—not an acting boss—on the street. Then they could come into their own.

Meanwhile, Robert Lino had to make sure the past—specifically Gabe Infanti—did not return to harm the plan. Tonight he was prepared. No more standing around in the frigid cold with buckets of lye and shovels. This time Robert Lino had brought along heavy machinery.

Actually it wasn't his. It belonged to a distant relative of the Lino family named Jimmy Labate. Labate was a heavy-set redheaded guy with limited memory bank and a stunned expression who happened to have married to one of Robert Lino's cousins. It was tough to be friends with Jimmy. He had a bad reputation for borrowing money and then forgetting to pay it back. He fancied himself a tough guy. He wore knee-length leather jackets and carried a .38. He was a rugged-looking character with the face of a failed pugilist. His dad had been in construction and close to the Gambino family, so now Jimmy was put with a Gambino soldier named Johnny Gammarano—Johnny G. This Gambino soldier was a nasty guy who treated Jimmy poorly, so Jimmy was looking to jump to the Bonanno family. Robert was trying to help him with the transfer, but to date, Jimmy hadn't really ingratiated himself with the people who had the power to make that happen.

When Bobby Lino Sr. was alive, Jimmy Labate borrowed money from Bobby's partner in the pizza place, the Colombo gangster Nicky Black. He and Bobby had been partners forever, and it wasn't right for a relative of the Lino family to owe Nicky Black all this money. Jimmy, of course, was sure he'd be paying it back at any moment. He had grand plans. He was going to put some of it out on the street and pump the rest into the Staten Island construction business he'd inherited from his father. But construction in the late 1980s had fallen off, and Labate liked to gamble and got behind in his payments. It is one thing to get behind in your payments to Chase Manhattan Bank. They will cut off your credit and try to seize your house. But to stiff Nicky Black would be to willfully invite physical harm upon yourself. Robert's father, Bobby, became responsible for collecting the debt, bit by bit, from Jimmy and bringing the money to Nicky Black. This was how Robert Lino got to know Jimmy Labate, debtor extraordinaire.

On this night, Jimmy was making up for all his sins. He could handle heavy machinery, and he was doing a competent job with a bulldozer, chipping away at the frozen Staten Island dirt in the frantic search for the late Gabe Infanti. Robert and cousin Frank had pulled up twenty minutes into the job and now sat inside a sedan with the heater on full blast watching as scoop by scoop of potential Gabe was dumped into the back of a dump truck.

One of the guys who was there the night they first buried Gabe had returned to the scene of the crime. It was Ronnie, and he was supposed to help remember where they'd planted Gabe. Ronnie couldn't remember. Nobody could remember. It had been years, and the actual digging and dumping had occurred in the middle of the night. It wasn't like somebody had some sort of Treasure Island map with a big X to mark Gabe. Everything looked the same and everything looked different. Gabe could be anywhere. Some of the landmarks that were familiar the night they buried Gabe—abandoned cars in the weeds, some Jersey barriers—were gone. It was possible they were completely turned around and digging yards away from where Gabe lurked. The guy Ronnie scanned the dirt like a scout, looking for who knows what. Gabe's bones? Gabe's Rolex? Who knew what would be left of poor Gabe four years later with the lye and everything.

Sitting in the car watching all this, cousin Frank made it clear he was unhappy to see Jimmy Labate and another guy nobody knew with the truck. Robert admitted he didn't really know the guy with the truck either, but he told Frank he was pretty sure the guy had no clue about what was really going on here. Cousin Frank had to wonder about this. What did the guy think they were doing out here in the middle of the night?

"Why did you bring this guy Labate?" Frank asked. He did not like Jimmy, mostly because of the Nicky Black problem but also because of Jimmy's tough guy attitude. Frank felt Jimmy was a loudmouth, among other things.

"He knows how to run the machine," Robert said, and left it at that. He wasn't crazy about Jimmy Labate either.

This went on for a while, until Ronnie came over and Robert rolled down the window.

"Nothing," he said.

Labate rolled the backhoe onto a flatbed, and he and the guy with the truck pulled out. Tonight the late Gabe Infanti would rest undisturbed. Tonight Gabe Infanti would stay dead. Hopefully Tommy Karate would get confused about Gabe and mix him up with the platoon of other guys he'd clipped and scattered all over New York.

CHAPTER FIFTEEN

December 30, 1995

A day before New Year's Eve, Gustavia Harbor was a bowlful of envy. Snug in the leeward side of St. Bart's on the northeastern edge of the Caribbean, it was no place to be if you weren't comfortable with the limitations of your personal wealth. During the tourist season, from the week before Christmas through April, the tiny little harbor was almost completely filled with enormous yachts. Each was more outrageous than its neighbor: an 84-foot Hatteras next to a 100-foot Denison next to a 118-foot Tri-deck passenger yacht next to a 140 foot Picchiotti. The staterooms contained giant-screen TVs, the galleys Sub-Zero refrigerators and restaurant-quality stoves. Inside were built-in hot tubs, queen-size beds, bidets. Their owners were Saudi Arabian princes, sugar heiresses, real estate tycoons, CEOs, assorted old money types. The yachts spent the summer in Greece or the French Rivera, the winter in Gustavia. They were hotels that float, accommodating up to forty-two passengers, plus a full crew with captain, cook and entertainment director. The teak and brass were so shiny it made your eyes hurt from squinting. Bunched together all in one claustrophobic little harbor, the display of opulence was enough to make your head spin.

Warrington and his model girlfriend, Martina, first noticed the spectacle of yachts when they checked in at the villa he was renting at the top of the volcanic hill Gustavia rested against. From up there, the biggest town in St. Bart's appeared below, a beautiful little Caribbean locale. There was a stone fort at the harbor entrance and narrow streets snaking up the hill past wooden shacks painted pink, turquoise, orange and green. It was the typical progeny of imperialistic football, "discovered" by Christopher Columbus four years after he "discovered" America, and named after his brother, Bartholomew. Over the years it belonged to everybody—first the French, then the Swedes, then the Brits, then back to the French. Its streets bore evidence of all three conquering kingdoms. The town itself was named after a Swedish king, while the streets bore names like Rue Victor Hugo and Rue des Normands. The stone Catholic church at the center of town was the tallest structure and dated back to the seventeenth century. Until the early 1980s, St. Bart's had been a sleepy little place. Then rich people and their celebrity friends discovered that it was one of only a handful of islands with absolutely no high-rise hotels, no clanging casinos and no cruise ship armies descending at noon. It was the Caribbean of old, and they decided to own it.

By New Year's Eve 1995, St. Bart's was the place to be for the social register set, which was precisely why Warrington had rented a villa up the hill in Gustavia. From his room, he and Martina looked down on the harbor and its armada of excess. He tried to figure out which one was the yacht owned by Coco Chanel, where he'd been invited to spend New Year's Eve, but he couldn't see from this far away.

After unpacking, he and Martina wandered down the

hill into town and strolled to the stone quay, taking in the yachts one at a time. Most still had Christmas trees and lights mounted on their aft decks, and there was hardly any room for more. Every spot dockside was full, and most of the moorings were taken up as well. This was the week to be in St. Bart's. Warrington found the Chanel yacht and was impressed. Its crew in matching whites could be seen aboard, scrubbing and polishing in anticipation of the big party the next night. Warrington couldn't wait.

A few years back, when he was a struggling actor forced to live off his father's income, he couldn't stand the idea of spending the night amid all that money. Now he could handle it, and the reason was simple—now he finally had enough of his own not to feel left out. He was not intimidated by a Chanel yacht or any other yacht. It actually seemed to him something that should be part of his life, now that he was a success.

For a few more years, he had tried in vain to make it as an actor. He trudged from audition to audition and landed cheesy TV commercial gigs. He slogged through one more feature, a B-list sci-fi number called *Time Walker* that was destined for predawn TV. In the end, he realized he wasn't meant for the thespian life. His ego couldn't take it. If he was going to be famous, he needed to be famous quickly, and without too much effort. He abandoned the pursuit of fame and embraced a new crusade—the unfettered pursuit of money. He became a stock picker.

He hadn't graduated Villanova, but he studied hard for his Series 7, the test required to become a broker. His scores weren't great, but he passed and set out to find a job. It was the early 1990s, and the market was a more sober world than during the 1980s. He landed a spot at Gruntal, a one-hundred-year-old midsize firm with a sterling reputation, by touting his investor contacts in the Maryland equestrian set. Use what you know. He made himself a man in demand and, more importantly, a man of his own destiny. For the first time in his entire adult life, he wasn't taking a red cent from his father.

He was there for his clients. He returned their calls quickly. He bet conservatively, rarely shorted, let his clients—especially his institutional clients overseas—know exactly what he was up to. He made them feel comfortable. He earned their trust, and he believed that trust was the thing that would make him wealthy. Without it, you could make good money—but only short-term. He was in this for the long haul, and he was sure he could succeed in ways that would make his philandering father in Palm Springs proud, or at least a little envious.

That was a liberating feeling, not having to rely on your parents. Warrington was done with the frivolous twenties and working his way toward the end of his thirties, so he needed that feeling of independence. He figured he was bringing in $250,000 worth of business to Gruntal a month, impressive by any standard. On his trip to St. Bart's, he'd decided it was okay for him to spend a little on himself.

Already he'd bought himself a red Ferrari. He'd landed a studio on Central Park South with a stunning view of the park, and he was living the Manhattan high life every night of the week. He had learned all the tricks of living large—tip the hostesses, drop the names of his family's old-money friends, discreetly mention his own blood relation to the Post cereal fortune and those United States senators. Talk horses—that always worked. Before long, he'd figured out a trick with models. Hot new Manhattan restaurants liked having lots of models sitting around looking gorgeous, so Warrington would go out of his way to find a gaggle of them and waltz into whatever trendy spot he'd read about in *New York*. He'd tell the women they'd get a free meal, and the restaurants always complied. They liked having him and his harem around. It was like investing in the décor.

He'd kept Martina interested longer than most by lavishing her with gifts and attention. Not that he wanted to settle down. He was beginning to think his father's "First I look at the purse" advice about beauty and money was pretty sound. Martina arrived with a surfeit of beauty but a deficit of cash. So while she was accompanying him solo to St. Bart's for the party of the year, he was not limiting his options. If some other beautiful blonde happened to cross his path, he would surely succumb to her temporary charms. And it helped when they thought you were rolling in it.

He and Martina wandered in from quayside to the town, stopping at one designer shop after another. This was a town that knew its constituency. He watched Martina spend his money at the high-end shops, acquiring brand names to display like military insignia. Levi's and the Gap made you a private or a corporal or a sergeant; Ralph Lauren and Tommy Hilfiger took you up through the ranks. Louis Vuitton and Versace made you a general. Strolling through this little town, Warrington felt content. He felt no envy. He could afford this. Jason was far behind him now.

New Year's Eve 1995

The hour of midnight was fast approaching and the breeze carried the scent of vanilla and jasmine. All along the dock the parties roared; Madonna was alleged to be aboard one yacht, Jimmy Buffet on the next. Generators working overtime, liquor flowing like a cataract. On the Coco Chanel yacht, Warrington soaked it all in.

Most of those present were just rich, but rumors occasionally surfaced of celebrity sightings. Puff Daddy was aboard. Bill Cosby had been seen. Sting was taking a leak in the aft head. With plenty of top-shelf whiskey swirling around inside him, Warrington was laughing along with the crowd when one of his New York stockbroker pals, a fellow master of the universe named Lance, introduced him to a guy he said might be helpful.

"Warrington," Lance said. "This is Cary Cimino. Cary, Warrington."

The guy kind of stood out. Most of these people on this crowded boat carried with them a sense of entitlement mixed with a desire for decorum. They disdained loud talk and bad manners; they ridiculed poor grammar, and looked down upon 98 percent of the world's population. Cary Cimino would definitely be a target for their derision. He possessed an unnatural George Hamilton–like tan, laughed too loud, and cursed like a longshoreman. He was sitting at the bar, his extremely expensive Rolex off his wrist and placed prominently next to his drink to be noticed. He shook Warrington's hand and offered a smile filled with white teeth. Warrington could tell Martina didn't like the guy at all. Warrington wasn't sure what to make of him.

They began the usual Wall Street dance, each trying to discern if the other had something to offer. In no time at all, Cary had mentioned he was once a partner at Bear Stearns and had gone out on his own. He was vague with details. He dropped that he had an MBA from Stanford, and mentioned that he worked out every day for two hours. Warrington was beginning to drift, watching the beautiful blondes with tan lines float by in a dream, when Cary suddenly got his attention.

"I've got blocks of stock with a 40 percent discount," he said.

Warrington was aware of the ramifications of a 40 percent discount. He'd heard stories of brokers getting stock at a discount, usually 10 or 15 percent, which was really just a bribe. The broker would sometimes split the discount with his customer, or sometimes not mention it at all. It depended on what kind of guy you were. At that time, Warrington was the kind of guy who had nothing to do with discounts, but 40 percent certainly caught his attention.

"What are you taking home right now as a broker?" Cary asked.

"One hundred fifty a month," Warrington said, not sure if that was good or bad.

"What's your net?"

"It's three fifty net."

"That's shit," Cary said.

That let the wind out of Warrington's sales. He'd thought he was doing great. He was a top producer at Gruntal; he was able to buy pretty much whatever he needed and never had to ask his father or, worse yet, his stepfather for help. He said nothing in reply.

"I can show you how to gross one million dollars a month," Cary went on. "You're buying big board stocks; you're wasting your time. I'll show you how to make some serious green."

He pulled out a roll of $40,000 wrapped in a plain rubber band. Although he was drinking someone else's top-shelf liquor on a multimillion-dollar yacht, amidst people who possessed stock portfolios that could single-handedly pull certain small Latin American countries out of debt, Warrington could not take his eyes off that roll of bills. It was so real. It was naked money.

He leaned forward to hear Cary Cimino better. He didn't want to miss a word.

CHAPTER SIXTEEN

By now, Jeffrey Pokross was a stockbroker himself. He'd taken the seventy-five-minute Series 63 exam to become a securities agent, a low-level requirement for anyone assisting a registered broker. He'd scored an impressive 92. Then he'd taken the six-hour Series 7 required of all registered stockbrokers. This allowed him to solicit investors and buy and sell just about every type of security imaginable. He scored a reputable 88. Here was a guy who'd lived his entire life in New Jersey and Queens and for the first time he was entering the high-stakes, high-finance world of Wall Street. The car leasing operation had collapsed in a mountain of debt. Here was the new tabula rasa Jeffrey Pokross, stockbroker.

Actually he was still the old Jeffrey Pokross. The fact that he had actually been handed a license to handle other people's money was remarkable indeed. That meant he had undergone a background check by the National Association of Securities Dealers. If they had taken a close look, they would have had quite a bit to jot down in their little notebooks.

On his U4, the form filled out by all prospective brokers, Jeffrey had mentioned a few civil matters, most of which arose during his adventures in car leasing. Most were lawsuits filed against Jeffrey and his company, Three Star, by irate customers. They were usually filed under the heading "Unpaid consumer credit obligations." All were noted as being settled, with Jeffrey agreeing to pay off what he owed a bit at a time from "future earnings." In explaining himself to the NASD, he'd minimized his culpability, insisting in some cases that he was merely covering the obligations of others. Others he couldn't pay because, he would explain, "I did not want to go into bankruptcy and decided to attempt to make payments rather than default to creditors." He owed the state of New Jersey $10,400 in back taxes and fines, and he hadn't even bothered to pay off the $2,397 he still owed in college loans.

Pokross did not bother to mention (and the NASD apparently didn't know) that he was also being sued by the U.S. government. The Resolution Trust Corp., which was sorting out the savings and loan mess, had discovered Jeffrey and his car leasing company had skipped out on numerous loans in their effort to keep their car-lease Ponzi scheme afloat. By 1993, the year he took the Series 7 and 63, his car leasing scam had racked up $1 million in debt.

Nevertheless he got his license, and immediately went to work breaking laws and regulations as fast as he could.

He started at Barrington Capital. This was, in the parlance of the day, an upscale boiler room, a roomful of brokers—some of whom had actual licenses, others who would pretend to be the guy with the actual license who cold-called investors around the country pitching specific stocks. Usually they targeted senior citizens and people who lived in the Midwest. The operating assumption was that if you lived in the Midwest, you were a drooling rube who might be a genius about cow breeding methods but was surely dumb as a fence post about securities. The other operating assumption was if you were a senior citizen you had plenty of time on your hands, might be a little lonely and thus would actually stay on the phone and listen to another human voice for a few minutes, even if that voice was owned by a felon. You were, in effect, a perfect target for people like Jeffrey Pokross.

In 1993 and 1994, Pokross and the other brokers at Barrington were hyping their own version of "house stocks," barely traded securities that Barrington was being paid to take public. Most of the company's stock was, in fact, owned by the brokers—at discount rates. The brokers were paid a commission based on how much stock they sold. Sometimes the company bribed them outright by giving them free stock or even cash in envelopes. The idea was to call up the retired postal supervisor in Moon Pie, Missouri, and go to work on the guy. On and on the broker would blather about how Company X was about to go public and if you acted now you could get in on the ground floor at bargain basement prices; once it went public, all bets were off. A key element was to intimidate the yokel into believing that he was, in fact, a yokel if he didn't jump on this deal right away. Questioning the customer's manhood often did the trick. Most boiler room brokers preferred to deal with men because women would commit to buying and then change their minds. Men were easier to buffalo.

And buffalo Jeffrey did. He would eventually admit it all, and even testify in court about it. His description was terse but candid: "I made baseless and unrealistic predictions on where I thought the stocks would go to push it out, push the stocks out to the customers to get more commission."

In other words, he lied to line his pockets. This did not always work in his favor.

Months after landing the Barrington job, the firm pushed him to purchase a particular stock at $40. "A couple of days after I put the stock out to my customers—a lot of stock— the stock went down by more than 50 or 60 percent within a few days. Well, anytime that you sell a stock as a stockbroker and the customer doesn't pay for the stock, the broker gets the bill for the difference. It caused me a great amount of difficulty to continue to do business at Barrington, and the firm was looking to collect $40,000 in losses for their recommendation."

It was time for another job. This time Jeffrey set his sights on a relatively big-time firm, Gruntal & Co. At that time, Gruntal was the fourteenth largest brokerage firm in America. It had been around since 1880, survived the Crash of '29, gone public in the 1980s and was now a world-wide concern with two thousand employees in thirty offices. By June 1994, Jeffrey Pokross had peaked in his career as a stockbroker by landing a job at Gruntal.

At Gruntal, Pokross was forced to deal with real rules and real oversight. He had to sell stock in real companies regulated by the New York Stock Exchange. No more "house stocks." It was more complicated dancing around the rules at Gruntal, but Jeffrey found a way. Some customers require that a broker tell them before they either buy or sell a stock. Jeffrey Pokross decided to skip that requirement for a number of customers. At first, this wasn't a problem. But ultimately when they got their statements and found he had used their money to buy stock in a company that promptly tanked, they were a tad miffed. One customer even called him up and recorded the call. In the call Jeffrey promised to cover the loss as long as the customer didn't mention this little matter to his boss. The customer got off the phone and promptly sent the tape to the compliance officer at Gruntal. Soon, Jeffrey had some explaining to do.

"I got fired immediately. It virtually eliminated me getting a normal job, because when you get hired, you have what's called a securities license. When you get fired, there is a form called a U5, which is an electronic computerized record of the brokerage license. Any type of black mark where you get fired for doing an unauthorized trade, it's a very bad thing and practically no firm would hire you after that."

As more and more customer complaints filtered in about Jeffrey Pokross, he slunk out the back door of Gruntal and returned to the underworld of the boiler room. This time, without a license, he recast himself as a stock promoter and took a job at a firm known as La Jolla Capital.

In the early 1990s, as Wall Street began again to show signs of life after the 1980s debacle, more and more brokerages like La Jolla began showing up in the over-the-counter market. These operations were 100 percent devoted twenty-four and seven to the fine art of removing money from their customers' pockets by any means necessary. Jeffrey Pokross fit right in. At La Jolla, Pokross and thirty other unlicensed brokers sat in a shabby office on John Street a few blocks north of Wall and pitched stocks using the name of a registered broker, Robert Grinberg. That meant at any one time, more than thirty Robert Grinbergs could be making simultaneous phone pitches to various victims across the country. Pokross started taking cash bribes to hype house stocks, but he also learned other interesting lessons: "For La Jolla Capital, it was incredibly profitable . . . I learned the means and methods of getting ahold of a very inexpensive piece of stock, manipulate it, control the trading on it and make a ton of money by bribing brokers."

Manipulation of stock was a nice way of saying La Jolla lied to investors each and every day about what they were doing with their money. At La Jolla, Jeffrey Pokross learned that manipulation really meant pump and dump.

By the mid-1990s pump and dump was a growing phenomenon on Wall Street. Before a company went public, secret partners bought stock at ridiculously discounted rates or were simply gifted stock for free. The company itself usually existed on paper or in overseas bank accounts. When the company went public, stock promoters like Jeffrey Pokross were paid cash bribes to hype the stock and pump up its value. Real licensed brokers were also paid cash bribes to pump the stock, but also to make sure the customers didn't get cold feet and try to sell. If a customer put in a sell order, these brokers would frequently ignore them or try to convince them to stay put. If that didn't work, the broker was responsible for finding another customer to replace the seller.

Brokers would say practically anything to hook the customer and keep him. Take the selling of Jutland Enterprises. Here was a company that had acquired the rights to (but not the property of) a sandwich shop with two stores called Yellow Submarine. That was it: two delis. Why would any right-thinking, marginally intelligent citizen of the United States invest even one cent of their hard-earned paycheck in such a company? Because they were told lies. Jutland was the "next McDonald's." Jutland was planning to expand its operations to compete with Starbucks. Jutland stock would rise 100 percent. Jutland was going to be bought out by another company. You were selling an idea, a possibility. You weren't really selling anything real. It was all nonsense.

Soon Jutland's total market value was $68 million, despite the fact that it had never turned a profit, had suffered loss after loss, and was, after all, just a couple of delis. Investors lost tens of thousands when the insiders dumped their stock.

At some point when the secret partners felt the time was provident, they'd dump all their stock at once. The resulting sell-off would cause the value to plummet, and those that still owned would take it on the chin. In effect, the partners used unsuspecting investors to create the illusion that a bogus company was really a rising star, just long enough to make a killing and get out.

Jeffrey was well schooled in the ways of Wall Street. He had a quick mind for numbers, knew the jargon up and down. He also had larceny in his heart. Pokross was the perfect guy for this game.

December 1995

It was that time of year once again. Outside the Exchange, a secular institution if ever there was one, they'd hung pine boughs and twinkling white lights in a gesture of goodwill. "God Rest Ye Merry Gentlemen" and "Rockin' Around the Christmas Tree" drifted from stores. End-of-the-year bonus checks were in the mail, and the holiday parties—"bacchanalian" as a description didn't do them justice. Money was rolling in on the new technology stock wave. Dot-com mania had set in. There was irrational exuberance to burn. Down at Joseph's Restaurant, a few blocks from Wall Street, the bar was jammed on a Friday after a long week and Jeffrey Pokross was happy to be alive.

Tonight was a big night. His wife—who almost never came into the city from their suburban paradise in New Jersey—had decided to fling caution to the wind and see what there was to see. She sat at a bar stool in the middle of the roar and din that was a holiday party thrown by his newest firm, Monitor Investments. A few months into his time at La Jolla, he'd been lured away to what he believed was unlimited opportunity at Monitor. The place was packed with brokers and stock promoters of all types. The firm's big clients were all invited to drink up the open bar as fast as they could, and most were happy to oblige. Pokross and his wife sat next to each other at the bar, where he could command a view of the people he needed to talk to and the people he needed to avoid.

In the middle of all this some obnoxious guy decided it would be a good idea to lean across the bar between husband and wife and begin to hit on wife.

At first, Jeffrey wasn't sure this was really going on. Then it became obvious. Jeffrey would tell people, "I'm not a tough guy. I never purported to walk around and say I would do personally things of that nature, personally." But Jeffrey had to do something. Something had to be done. He poked the guy in the chest and waved his arms about. The guy was quite a bit larger than Jeffrey but out of shape. And Jeffrey could make himself seem bigger than he actually was.

A scene ensued.

In a minute four of the guys from Monitor were all over this guy. They pulled him away from the bar and offered up a little threatening body language. The guy sat down with his pals, one of whom happened to be a big Monitor client nobody wanted to offend. But the obnoxious guy—Jeffrey soon learned the guy's name was Mitch—he kept up. Now it was commentary about short guys and how he'd like to fuck that guy's wife, etc. This type of commentary was not encouraging a healthy group dynamic.

One of the Monitor guys, Vinny, a guy from the neighborhood, said to Jeffrey, "You want I should take him outside and give him a beating and put him in a trunk?"

Jeffrey said no, Vinny, that would not be a good idea at this time. Meanwhile Jeffrey's wife was very upset and wanted to go home to New Jersey right away. Jeffrey was in the middle. He could just leave and then live with this guy's voice in his head for weeks on end. Or he could do something.

When the guy was facing away, Jeffrey walked up behind and grabbed him by the back of the shirt. This time he threw the guy, Mitch, onto the floor as hard as he could.

The place erupted. The bartender and the owner of

Joseph's came running over and started yelling at the guy, Mitch, telling him to get the hell out. He and his pals left, making the usual threats.

A few weeks later, the big client who was friends with Mitch showed up at Monitor's office. He said his friend Mitch wanted $50,000 right now or he would press charges. Jeffrey told the client to fuck himself. Jimmy Labate heard the whole thing.

"Jimmy, he offered me the opportunity that he would go there or send somebody up there and put Mitch in the hospital for real," Pokross said. "I told Jimmy, 'No, no, no.'" Jeffrey had a better idea. He called up a lawyer and made all the arrangements. He figured if the guy was threatening to sue him, he might as well sue the guy first.

CHAPTER SEVENTEEN

March 25, 1996

It was possible that some of the guests arriving at the Box Tree Hotel on this chilly spring evening came by Lexington Avenue subway, but it was highly unlikely. Most showed up in limousines, a few by shiny black livery cabs. They exited in formal wear or long glittering gowns, the women with their hair, jewelry and cleavage arranged for show. The men headed straight for the bar. Nearly everyone stopped to shake the hand of the man of the hour, Francis Warrington Gillet III, who stood at the door with the smile of a man who knows he is the center of the world.

This was a big night for Warrington. He was to be married, and this dinner at the Box Tree was to provide the stage for his public transformation from suave bachelor-about-town to regular ordinary married guy.

As hotels go, the Box Tree was an unusual spot, even by New York standards. It consisted of only nine rooms and four penthouse suites fit inside two adjacent town houses in a quiet street of the Upper East Side. Its lobby featured stained glass windows by Louis Comfort Tiffany and a sweeping four-story art nouveau staircase. Some of its rooms looked like Versailles, some looked like Japanese tea gardens. It was located in the heart of the Upper East Side, a unique neighborhood in a city of ever changing ethnic mix.

The Upper East Side was an exception to the rule in New York, a city that is not really a city but a collection of insular villages. There is Italian Brooklyn in Bay Ridge and Bensonhurst; there is the Caribbean in Brooklyn's Crown Heights and Jamaica in Queens. The citizens of Puerto Rico are well represented throughout the Bronx, while the Irish inhabit Woodside in Queens and Norwood in the Bronx. Almost all of the city's neighborhoods, from the border of Long Island to the edge of Staten Island to the Yonkers line, are an ever-shifting mosaic of humanity, with one ethnic group morphing into another from generation to generation. Everywhere, that is, except the Upper East Side.

There longevity is at a premium. Some of the families who've lived there forever date back to the *Mayflower*. They are the wealthy progeny of the robber barons: the Vanderbilts, the Rockefellers, the Morgans, the Astors. This is the social register neighborhood, the silk stocking district. Here are all the WASP totems that imply seriousness and sophistication: the Waldorf Astoria, upper Madison Avenue, Park Avenue duplexes, Bobby Short at the Carlysle, the King Cole Bar at the Hotel Saint Regis, Museum Mile, dowagers doing lunch, actual French poodles, and of course, the Box Tree.

At the Box Tree, Warrington watched as one hundred and fifty of his closest friends entered the elegant dining room to celebrate him. And, of course, his new wife-to-be, Martina.

The wedding was to be a few nights away at the Swedish Church, also on the Upper East Side. His fiancée, of course, was Swedish. The Box Tree was hosting a sort of pre-wedding reception for Warrington and Martina. On this delicate March evening some of the biggest money in America sat at round tables with white linen and polished silver and impeccable crystal and toasted the beautiful new couple and the boundless life of happiness that awaited them.

Mary Lou Whitney was there, along with Joseph Cornacchia, who owned one horse that was a favorite in the upcoming Preakness and another that had won the Kentucky Derby two years back. Warrington's real father, Francis Junior, was there with his new bride, another heiress from Palm Beach. His real mother was there with his stepfather, Schapiro, and his half-brother and real sister. His good friend Cary Cimino sat at a table talking his talk to an executive from a major construction firm. Although this was purely a personal affair, it would be unreasonable to expect that Cary wouldn't have conducted a bit of business by the time the last dance was danced. He could be excused.

In fact, Warrington owed much to Cary. In some ways, without Cary the wedding itself wouldn't have been happening at all.

When Martina first told Warrington she was pregnant, he'd practically run for the hills. This was life-changing news to a guy who's biggest worry was whether the maitre d' knew him well enough to comp him and his table full of models. Now he was being told that he was going to be a father. He was going to have to take care of someone other than himself. The *New York Times* had recently mentioned Warrington in a column about the city's most eligible bachelors. There was no mention of Martina or the little Warry the Fourth in her belly. The all-day, all-night party of the former Jason of *Friday the 13th* was about to morph into a life of changing diapers and warming bottles. It was enough to make any guy with a trust fund and no responsibilities run screaming into the night.

He sought advice. His father was useless. This was a

man who had told him to marry for money, not beauty. Dad was a full-time philanderer who viewed monogamy with contempt. He had nothing to offer. Instead, Warrington turned to his friend Cary Cimino.

Since the New Year's Eve party on Coco Chanel's yacht in Gustavia Harbor, Warrington had come to trust Cary in matters beyond mere business. Of course the foundation of their relationship was mutual benefit derived from the buying and selling of stock. In the last year, Warrington had done the Spaceplex deal, first while he was still at Gruntal, then when he jumped to Baird Patrick, and now at his new job as a registered stockbroker working out of the Philadelphia-based Monitor Investment Group. When Spaceplex was over, Cary had found another company, Beachport, and now Warrington was working on that.

Of course, working with Cary was a bit unusual. The first time Warrington had gone to Monitor to meet Cary's friends Sal and Jeffrey and Jimmy face-to-face, he was a bit surprised. Monitor itself looked like every brokerage he'd ever seen: oak-paneled walls, guys in shirts and ties sitting at desks working phones, tapping at computer screens, hard at work at the business of money. He could see that most of the people there were just like everybody else he'd met on Wall Street. They'd attended prep school, they'd acquired degrees from prestigious colleges, they knew all the best spots in New York before they wound up in a *New York* magazine best-of list, and they knew to stay away from those places once they made the list.

Somehow Jeffrey and Sal and Jimmy didn't really fit in with that scene.

From Warrington's genteel perspective, Jeffrey Pokross was short and loud and mightily impressed with himself. He talked with a Brooklyn accent, though Warrington knew he was from Kentucky. Jeffrey had a tendency to lecture rather than converse. Neither Warrington nor Cary really liked the guy, but he often had new deals going and he was the guy behind Monitor. Then there was Sal Piazza. He was quiet and seemed to know what he was talking about, but he was clearly not from the Dalton School. He wore jogging suits to work and lived on Staten Island. He owned a boat called the *Second Office*, moored at the World Financial Center, and made distinctions between capable guys and knock-around guys and legit guys. He talked about the Hawaiian Moonlighters Club in Little Italy and the Veterans and Friends social club in Bensonhurst. Warrington had no idea what the guy was talking about. He couldn't have located Bensonhurst on a map.

And then there was Jimmy Labate. Forget Jimmy. He was about as far from the Gilman School as you could get. If the guy finished sixth grade, Warrington would have been shocked. He was barely literate. Trying to explain a reverse merger to Jimmy would be like trying to describe the theory of relativity to a ten-year-old. But Cary loved the guy. He was always repeating Jimmy's stories about beating up guys with golf clubs and the like. Warrington didn't understand Cary's fascination with Jimmy.

Cary, on the other hand, he could relate to. Cary was a college graduate. Warrington knew he'd gone to Boston University and just laughed it off as a Cary-ism his friend's occasional claim of being a Stanford grad. That was just Cary. He tended to exaggerate. Warrington liked him anyway. Sure he visited a tanning booth each week. Sure he'd had certain injections and surgeries to keep himself looking young. Warrington could relate to that. He and Cary were about the same age, heading into their mid-thirties together.

Cary was down to earth enough to hang out with Jimmy but also smooth enough to charm Warrington's horse country friends. Even Martina. She'd hated him at first, but now even she thought he was amusing. That was his way. The longer you knew him, the more you liked him. He often talked nonsense, but it was always charming nonsense.

In a way, Warrington saw himself as Cary's escort into the world of horse farms and debutantes and all the rest. He was kind of an older brother. He and Cary had recently flown to Europe for a business/pleasure trip. The stated purpose was for Warrington to meet with overseas clients in Milan. They decided to stretch the trip out a bit, starting in Paris. Warrington had been to Paris dozens of times, beginning when he was a child. Cary had never been. Cary had also never been to a Euro horse race, so Warrington took him to the Arc de Triomphe at Longchamp the first weekend in October. It was a totally different scene, far more sophisticated. All traces of Damon Runyon had been erased. Cary was a bit out of his element. Somebody like Jimmy Labate wouldn't have known what to do at Longchamps. Here Warrington was king.

They bet heavily on a favorite. They won.

The ebullience overflowed. Warrington left Cary in Paris to meet with one client and was riding high as he flew to Milan to meet with another. He was feeling so good, he bought himself a red Ferrari and had it shipped back to the States. He could afford it. With Cary and Monitor he was making more money than ever before.

Now, as his wedding reception at the Box Tree unfolded, Warrington could see that Cary fit right in. He was charming everyone at his table. He was tan and fit and wore the right clothes. He said the right things. He laughed at just the right moments. Sure, he was a bit rough around the edges, but that was part of his charm. A little taste of Brooklyn was refreshing for this crowd. And he was like them in another way—he rarely made a distinction between a social setting and a business opportunity. As he chatted away, Warrington imagined that Cary was probably lining up a deal. That was important, to always have a new deal on the horizon. Now that Warrington was about to become a married man with a kid on the way, it was even more important to pay attention to the bottom line.

That was something even his Palm Beach father would appreciate. His father hadn't said much when he told him about getting married to Martina, but he'd certainly been mightily impressed by his new red Ferrari.

It was Friday, and Warrington once again stood in line at the Marine Midland Bank branch in Lower Manhattan, around the corner from Monitor Investment Group's office. He held in his hand a check for $9,750 written on a Monitor account and made out to one Johnny Casablanca. In front of him snaked a line of Monitor brokers, all waiting patiently to cash their own version of that check. All amounts came in just under $10,000, the amount that requires a bank to report the transaction to federal authorities. This was a weekly event, this line.

In the middle of 1996, Warrington Gillet was invisible to the eyes of law enforcement. His rap sheet consisted of a handful of traffic violations in the state of New York. In one incident, he'd drifted through a stop sign. In another, he'd driven a tad too fast. He was hit with a summons that described him as a wanton violator of New York state laws governing the use of motor vehicles on the common byways. That, more or less, was the full extent of nefarious behavior known to the authorities regarding Francis Warrington Gillet III.

Sure, he'd probably lied to his friends and family about certain matters. He'd probably cheated at checkers once or twice. He might have glanced at a fellow student's test answers in algebra II. He'd certainly lied to his father about how much money he was making as a stockbroker. But these were white lies, good lies. Like his grandfather's lie about being eighteen to get into the Canadian Air Force. These were the kinds of lies people told every day to make their lives a little easier. They hurt no one. Sometimes he told people he was thirty-six, sometimes he told them thirty-seven. Who really cared? During his so-called acting career, he'd lied about his age whenever possible. Everybody in that business did, too.

That was the toughest part about knowing whether it was actually and factually right or wrong to take envelopes of cash or checks made out to fictional characters to push Spaceplex stock to his customers. He couldn't really tell, because everybody else at Monitor—whether they were registered stockbrokers or just stock promoters—was doing it, too.

"I was expecting to walk into a legitimate-looking brokerage house or a businessman's office. I didn't expect to walk into a town house full of gangsters. I never knew people from Brooklyn. I never knew people with diamond pinkie rings and polished crocodile shoes. The money is so good you overlook these unusual character traits . . . You knew you were doing something wrong when you looked at Pokross and Labate and Piazza. You said, Oh shit. Go look at this office, this tiny office with Labate, Pokross and Piazza in a one-room office, look at what they're wearing, look at the pinkie rings, look at their polished nails, listen to their anecdotes—come on! But the fact that they're handing you all these checks?

"You learn to live with it."

His first trade was a hundred thousand shares of Spaceplex for the Bank of Monaco. He made the trade, and they almost had collective heart failure. He assured Jeffrey and Sal and Jimmy that those shares wouldn't be going anywhere. He was cutting the banker in on his commission, so the banker would do as he was told. When he met Cary Cimino at the bar at the Rigas Regal Hotel, Cary handed him an envelope. Inside was $25,000 cash.

"Then you knew something was wrong. That was the time you should have gone to the U.S. attorney, gone to your manager and said, 'I did something wrong.' It was like the politicians in the Abscam trials. You were tainted by the money. And that overrode your judgment."

The line at Marine Midland inched forward. Here stood Warrington with his check made out to Johnny Casablanca, headed to the same teller he saw every week. Sometimes he'd sign off on a check made out to Warrington Gillet, and sometimes the check would be made out to Mr. Casablanca. The teller didn't care. The teller also didn't seem to care that every broker that stepped up to her window was cashing checks that came in just under the $10,000 red flag. That was the way it was. Everybody knew what was going on, but no one had a real incentive to make it stop. The bank benefited from the Monitor brokers who opened accounts there. Warrington could have brought in a check made out to Jason from *Friday the 13th*. Marine Midland would have cashed it, no questions asked.

Sometimes he deposited the money into secret accounts in Switzerland.

Did he know this was wrong? Perhaps. But there were ways to explain it away until it seemed legal and right. Cary Cimino was expert at this.

The way Cary explained things there was every justification for their actions. It all started with the investors themselves. Investors by nature were willfully naïve. They just wanted easy money. The skepticism required of any competent investor was sometimes overwhelmed by the sight of high-percentage immediate turnaround profit. They saw the market going crazy, so they went crazy. The profits were beyond the pale and would disappear at any moment. They were distorting people's faculties, but the distortion was deliberate. Cary insisted that the investors—the Wilmas and Chesters out there in Moosebreath, Indiana, the AARP members with their mall-walking sneakers and Sansabelt pastel pants, they knew damn well what they were doing. They had the same information everybody else did. They didn't have to stay on the phone. They could hang up when they wanted to. Maybe the cold-callers at Monitor took advantage of the fact that some of these people were lonely, but too bad. They were grown-ups. It was their decision to buy the stock and theirs alone.

Cary logic dictated: the investor is greedy, so all you're doing is capitalizing on that greed.

Plus, you had no choice. Just about everyone else out there was doing exactly the same thing, so you'd better do it or be left behind in the dust. The legitimate firms like Bear Stearns, where Cary once was partner (as he dropped into conversation practically every day), they did more or less the same thing. They promoted house stock in companies whose IPOs they were quietly underwriting. Full disclosure was a joke, and besides, what was the difference, as long as the customer was making a profit?

The first time Warrington was handed that envelope of $25,000 cash, he'd wondered if it was right to keep it. Would his father have done it? Certainly. Would his grandfather the flying ace of World War I have done it? Probably not. Warrington decided it was okay, as long as he reported it to the Internal Revenue Service and didn't take any more. But then he was handed another envelope. Did he return it in disgust? Feign outrage that Cary would try to bribe him and question his integrity as a registered broker who'd sworn total allegiance to the customer? Certainly not. He took that envelope, and then another and so on. He took them and spent the money.

He spent some at nightclubs. He bought a nice suit. He put some of the money into buying Thoroughbred horses. The red Ferrari was paid for with Spaceplex bribe money. He spent it because it was his money. It wasn't just a bribe. Somehow Warrington pictured a bribe as dirty money

Cary Cimino, stock promoter, leaves Manhattan Federal Court after sentencing is postponed.
Corey Sipkin, *New York Daily News*

Frank Lino, Bonanno captain, walking out of Manhattan Federal Court.
Mark Bonifacio, *New York Daily News*

James Labate, Gambino family associate and DMN partner.
U.S. government exhibit.

Salvatore Piazza, Bonanno crime family associate and DMN partner, outside Manhattan Federal Court with unidentified woman.
Andrew Savulich, *New York Daily News*

Staten Island garage where Robert Perrino was buried.
New York Daily News

The cluttered interior of the garage.
New York Daily News

Frank Lino.
U.S. government exhibit.

Robert Lino.
U.S. government exhibit.

Police examine the body of Louis Tuzzio on January 3, 1990. He was slain by Robert Lino. Ken Murray, *New York Daily News*

handed to someone to do nothing. This wasn't true at Monitor. He'd earned his bribe. He'd spent months cultivating high-maintenance complaint-filled customers. He'd had to overcome the reluctance of his overseas banker friend who managed institutional accounts worth millions, by splitting his bribe. He'd worked hard to hold up his end, convincing customers to hold on to Spaceplex long after they should have dumped every cent they owned.

Cary was right. Those customers really just wanted the same things Warrington desired—enough money to live comfortably. If they lost out on Spaceplex, no problem. There were so many opportunities now, they'd make money elsewhere. Warrington could still help them with that. Jeffrey and Sal and Jimmy didn't care about the rest of his customers' portfolios, as long as they left the Spaceplex in place until the game was over.

In fact, most of his customers were doing well regardless of Spaceplex, because in these wildly bullish conditions on Wall Street, everybody was doing well. It was like surfing. You didn't just go down to the beach and sit there until the waves were right. When the waves were right, you got your board down to the beach. The waves of Wall Street were as right as they'd ever be.

And Warrington really had no interest in getting caught. Not getting caught, of course, involved another level of deception. That was the reasoning behind checks made out to Johnny Casablanca and other ridiculous noms de guerre. And the overseas accounts. If you were going to make the money, you might as well keep it. Only fools handed it over to the tax man. Warrington saw the numbers and dollar signs and wanted to keep them all for his own.

He stepped up to the Marine Midland window and smiled at the bank teller, exchanged the usual pleasantries. She was probably making about $30,000 a year. He could almost make that with one of Cary's fat envelopes. There was no way a girl like this was going to rock the boat. She knew how the system works. He signed his name, Johnny Casablanca, with a little flourish on the final "a."

She smiled and asked, "Fifties and twenties?"

The fifth race at Aqueduct featured a Najinsky colt named Glory of Fun. He'd been purchased at auction from a Saudi prince. His bloodline was strong, but this was his first race. His owners included Francis Warrington Gillet III and an old Gillet family friend, Joseph Cornacchia, a major-league name in the world of Thoroughbred horse racing. Cornacchia was a printer from Queens who'd transformed himself into a multimillionaire man-about–Palm Beach with money he made printing up a little game nobody ever heard of called Trivial Pursuit. Cornacchia owned dozens of famous horses. In 1994 his Go for Gin won the Kentucky Derby. Two years later his Louis Quatorze won the Preakness. He'd bought into Glory of Fun because of Warrington's relationship with his father. It was likely Cornacchia had no clue about the third partner on Glory of Fun, Salvatore Piazza.

After Warrington started talking up Glory of Fun at the Monitor office, Sal had come around asking questions. Warrington was not entirely clear on what exactly Sal Piazza was all about. By now, he'd become aware of a certain influence at Monitor. The influence seemed to involve guys from Staten Island and Brooklyn in jogging suits and gold jewelry and manicures floating in an out with no apparent vocation. Every Friday, a guy everybody called Robert from Avenue U showed up, went into Jeffrey Pokross's office for a while and then left. Warrington never actually heard the guy say a word, but he could tell that everybody at Monitor would have listened if he did.

Sal Piazza was a slightly different version of Robert from Avenue U. He was a congenial silver-haired guy in an aquamarine nylon jogging suit who knew something about buying and selling stocks. And now he wanted a piece of Glory of Fun. This was something of a dilemma for Warrington. Sal Piazza was surely affiliated with organized crime. It wasn't as if Sal had told Warrington anything like that. It didn't say "Bonanno crime family" on his business card. But Warrington just knew there was more to Sal Piazza than a passing knowledge of the stock market and an ever-changing set of jogging suits. So when Sal Piazza asked to become a partner in Glory of Fun, Warrington knew that Sal wasn't really asking.

Sal wrote checks to Warrington under a business called Chateau Margot. Warrington didn't ask about this. Warrington didn't ask about anything. He just made sure the checks cleared, which they did. Now there were three partners attached to Glory of Fun: Francis Warrington Gillet III of Maryland horse country; Joseph Cornacchia of upstate Saratoga County, New York, and Palm Beach; and Salvatore Piazza of the Bonanno crime family.

At Aqueduct Glory of Fun was running five to one. Sal Piazza had shown up with Warrington to watch, and he'd brought his entire family. His wife, his mother, his kids, his friends from the social club—everyone. It was like a scene from *Goodfellas*, with Warrington the odd man out. Warrington was very popular with this crowd because he could talk Thoroughbred horses all day and not get bored. He knew what he was talking about. Other than that, he had absolutely nothing in common with Sal Piazza and his entire Staten Island clan.

At post time it was like a scene from a Rodney Dangerfield movie. The Piazzas were hollering like crazy, waving cigars and slapping each other on the back. As the horses sprinted out of the gates, Warrington was torn about the outcome.

Sal had put big money down and it was a $50,000 race. He was trying to impress his family. If Glory of Fun lost, Sal would lose all his money and possibly be mad at

Warrington. But he might also be soured by the experience of owning a horse, which usually consisted of dumping piles of money into a burning pyre to watch it turn into smoke. If Glory of Fun took the fun out of owning horses, maybe Sal Piazza would call it a day, and Warrington's father's old friend, Joseph Cornacchia, would never have to know he was business partners with a gangster.

On the other hand, if Glory of Fun won, Sal would probably be delirious and want to invest even more. Then what would Warrington tell Cornacchia, the big-name owner of a Kentucky Derby winner?

The horses rounded the turn and headed into the final stretch. The crowd began its usual roar.

In a minute, the race was over, and Glory of Fun won it all.

Sal and his entire family jumped in the air cheering and hollering. Warrington began thinking of a way to get either Sal Piazza or Cornacchia out of Glory of Fun as soon as possible.

CHAPTER EIGHTEEN

Spring 1995

The stockbroker lay sprawled on the floor of the conference room, his tie askew, his eyes shut tight, not a sign of
movement in him. Jeffrey Pokross couldn't tell if the guy
was alive or dead. Jeffrey was furious.

The offices of DMN Capital were supposed to sparkle
with legitimacy. That's how Jeffrey wanted it. If the NASD
guys came sniffing around, they'd find nothing but law-abiding
citizens going about their business, contributing to the economy. No sign of criminality anywhere. The brokers all wore
shirts and ties; the support staff dressed professionally. An
investigator buzzed past the three secure doors into the office would see brokers diligently filling customers in on the
latest bargains, phones ringing cheerfully, computer screens
blinking with the latest market updates. This was no typical
Mafia Wall Street rodeo. This was legit.

Jeffrey knew all about the rodeos. There were some
boiler rooms downtown that had more in common with the
World Wrestling Federation than the New York Stock Exchange. There was one where there were fewer phones and

desks than there were "brokers," so whoever got there first in the morning got the phones. If you got there late, you could always try to beat the hell out of some guy who was already at a phone. It was dog-eat-dog, with guys parading around in full Staten Island regalia—nylon sweat suits, gold chains, the works. There were holes in the plasterboard at this place. A biker guy built like a mountain range stood by the trading window. If a broker showed up with a sell order, he'd grab the guy by the neck and shout, "Somebody show this guy how to run his business!" Not at DMN Capital.

Except, of course, for the stockbroker sprawled on the carpet in the conference room.

It was the guy's own fault, of course. The number one rule at DMN was simple and easy to understand—no sales, period. This guy, this broker they were bribing to the tune of $25,000 a hit, had gone and violated that rule. They hadn't noticed it at first, but when they found out, Jeffrey knew they had to do something about it. So he called up Jimmy Labate and had him come into the DMN office and wait in the conference room. Then he'd summoned the broker by telling him there was a staff meeting.

The idea was just to scare the guy. The guy walked in, and Jimmy got up from his chair, walked over and hit the guy as hard as he could square in the forehead. The guy had gone down like a piece of frozen meat falling off the back of a truck. And now, unfortunately for all concerned, he wasn't moving.

"Get a rug," Jimmy said. He said it the way you say, "Pass the salt" or "What time is it?" Jeffrey didn't know what he was talking about. All he knew was that he had a dead guy lying in the conference room of a company that had his name on its letterhead. The aroma of legitimacy was seeping out the windows like air from a punctured balloon.

"To wrap him up," Jimmy explained.

"Oh. Right."

They started scrambling around, considered ripping up

the rug from one of the rooms, but figured there'd be all these little carpet tack things flying everywhere and that would just add to the mess.

Suddenly the guy sat up.

Labate was furious at the guy for so many reasons. First he was furious for the sell orders. Then he was furious for having to hit him in the forehead. Then he was furious for him not being dead, but instead getting everybody all worked up. He grabbed the guy and ripped his shirt and started hollering. It appeared he believed that the guy was wearing a wire. The guy looked like he'd awoken in the middle of some bad science fiction movie, the ending of which was surely not pleasant. He put the pieces of his shirt back on and scurried out of the office. He promised he'd never sell another stock as long as he lived.

Before he began working for DMN, Cary Cimino hadn't spent much time hanging around gangsters. In fact, he hadn't met any. He watched movies, of course. Like any other American he knew the *Godfather* lines: "Make him an offer," "sleeps with the fishes," "take the cannolis," etc. Having grown up in New York, he knew what "connected" meant, but that was about as far as it went. He wasn't really into that world, didn't really understand it. He certainly had not sought out business with these guys. Perhaps if he'd thought about it more, he might have walked away from that first meeting with Jeffrey before it was too late. If only he had known certain facts related to this relationship. Legitimate guys who do business with the mob always end up on the losing end. It is a fact. No matter how charming they may appear, gangsters ultimately are looking out only for themselves. And legitimate guys are considered weak links, like extra baggage on a too-small life raft. They're the first to go overboard.

When Cary first heard about the incident at the office of

his new employer, he had one of those sea change moments. Here were certain facts presented and certain decisions required. A broker had been beaten senseless inside a respectable office on Wall Street. He realized he was no longer working at Bear Stearns or Oppenheimer. This was unfamiliar territory.

There were different ways to view the incident. One was to see that this was not a good thing and it was time to go. The other was to figure that maybe it wasn't going to be such a problem. He'd known Sal Piazza for several years and he'd never seen him act unreasonably. Sure he considered Jimmy Labate a thug, but Jeffrey and Sal seemed to have the guy under control. At this time Cary made a choice. He would pick ambition over sagacity. Or was it just greed? How could you tell the difference between ambition and greed? No matter what you called it, the money was fantastic. Cary experienced a thought adjustment, explaining it in his own unique manner:

"Jimmy was an absolute thug, but the financial remuneration that I was receiving? And Jimmy wasn't threatening me. At this point in time, he wasn't. I mean later in the future he does. And I was dealing directly with Jeffrey. Jeffrey was paying me. They were paying and I had had a long-term established relationship with Sal, who to me, never appeared as a thug, who I never knew had crime family ties as Jeffrey alleges. I really want to delineate the difference of how I perceived Sal and how I perceived Jimmy. I perceived Sal as a nice guy that my sister had a long-term relationship with, that I socialized with, that I went out to dinner with and double-dated with I never saw Sal act violent or raise his voice in any manner. Unlike Jimmy, who was inarticulate, prone to rages, and who Jeffrey manipulated."

Cary's thought adjustment had to do with math. For the first time in quite a long time, Cary was wallowing in money. Cash payments flowed to the point where he could now take a supermodel to a top-end restaurant in Soho and not worry about picking up the tab. DMN was taking care of his car payments, so that was no longer a sword hanging over his head. And besides, Cary felt he was being paid well because he deserved it. He had brought in maybe 90 percent of the corrupt brokers needed to make Spaceplex take off. His new friend, Warrington, was using his overseas contacts to make six-figure buys. Sal and Jeffrey were ecstatic. Cary could do no wrong. Cary had brought in a dozen brokers and was getting 35 percent commission on all sales. The math was this: organized crime was not getting in the way of Cary's net profit. Cary could live with organized crime.

For Jeffrey Pokross, the gangster presence at DMN Capital was both a blessing and a curse. Mostly the curse involved Jimmy Labate, who had evolved into somewhat of a problem. On the one hand, Jeffrey needed the guy around. Now that the Spaceplex campaign was up and running, enforcement of the no-sell rule was always an issue, and Jimmy was quite good at scaring the hell out of the brokers and stock promoters in the office. He kept a .38 in his waistband and loved to talk loudly about how useful a golf club had been while beating some guy bloody in Staten Island. That same kind of talk, however, added a certain edge to the proceedings and made keeping the place looking legit more complex. Jimmy was a gangster on display. He looked like a gangster, he walked like a gangster, he talked like a gangster. He didn't hide it from anyone.

With difficulty, Jeffrey came to realize that for the scheme to work, he would have to live with his decision about Jimmy. He really needed Jimmy around. Jimmy's ties to Robert Lino were crucial. Without this, morons from other families would ultimately come knocking on the door demanding their percentage. On the other hand, Jeffrey was increasingly aware that Jimmy needed him as well. Jimmy's construction business was failing, so he needed the income provided by DMN. Jeffrey knew well how to turn someone else's lousy situation to his advantage. He'd made Labate an actual partner in DMN and thus Labate was, in a way, indebted to him. And everybody was clear about his role. Labate wasn't there to draft analysis on the futures market or make buy and sell recommendations to investors. His role, Jeffrey made clear, was simple:

"He would continue to find mobbed up brokers that could put out our stocks. We bribe and hold on to it. In addition Mr. Labate would enforce the no-sale policy through threats of violence."

The effort to keep DMN looking legitimate was a never-ending high-wire performance. The idea was to keep the threats of violence (and the actual violence) to a minimum. The beating of the stockbroker had been a fairly drastic example. Usually all Jimmy had to do was walk up, open his knee-length leather coat, show off his gun and check the computer for sell orders. It was a delicate job, choreographing this friction between Wall Street and the streets of South Brooklyn. Now that Spaceplex was starting up, Jeffrey would have to see if his marriage to the mob was going to make him rich or dead.

In March 1995, the Spaceplex pump and dump was a going concern. Mostly it was a Jeffrey Pokross production. Maybe he hadn't gone to the Wharton School and maybe Illinois State College wasn't quite the London School of Economics, but Jeffrey Pokross was quite creative when it came to making money work for him—especially when it came to finding ways to conceal what he was doing from the NASD and Securities and Exchange Commission.

First they had to get control of the majority of shares in the company, which was already trading for pennies in the over-the-counter market. They did a reverse split, which shrunk the number of shares, then the company issued a number of free or absurdly discounted shares to Pokross and Piazza. "That would control the amount of shares that were allowed to trade in the market that weren't friendly or that we would have no control over." That meant they couldn't control the rest of the shares, the so-called public pool, but the pool was much smaller now.

Next the corrupt brokers pocketing bribes would contact market makers, that is, other brokers representing institutional investors, and get them to buy big gobs of shares in Spaceplex. That would drive up the price. The institutional investors had no real incentive to do this and weren't getting bribes. Instead, they were told by DMN's troops that they would be guaranteed against a loss. This was completely illegal, but it got the job done.

Pokross described it this way: "I would call him on the phone and say, let's say the stock was bid at one, offered at one and a quarter. I would say, Hey Johnny, why don't you move the stock up, why don't you take out the one and a quarter and move it up to one and three quarters?" I would make a call a half hour later, Hey Johnny, why don't you move the stock up to two and offer it out at three. I would guarantee them against a loss and give them a small profit."

Now with the price on the rise, the retail brokers could go to work. Cold-calling victims all over America, they pointed out Spaceplex's remarkable stock performance in recent days. They'd then launch into a dog and pony show, claiming Spaceplex was going to be the next Six Flags when, in fact, it was just a creaky little amusement park in suburban Long Island with a handful of crappy rides and games no one could win. It was a joke, but it worked.

This was supposed to happen on two fronts—in America and in Germany. Here is where DMN had to switch tactics.

"I had done my job," Pokross recalled. "I had found the stock, the price of the stock went up and we were waiting for the Germans to start buying it. The Germans didn't buy it. So we found U.S. brokers and promoters to go buy it and bribe the stockbrokers here in the U.S."

It was a delicate little dance. As usual, the biggest pressure was to keep the customer from trying to sell before it was time. This was the trickiest aspect of pump and dump. You didn't want a furious investor whining to the NASD that his broker wouldn't sell stock when he was told to. So if a customer insisted, DMN had a solution that put the pressure back on the broker. Sell the stock, but find a buyer.

Pokross called this "crossing the stock": "In other words, if a broker has got client A that wants to sell the stock and that's demanding to sell the stock, that broker couldn't go and give it to the trader and say sell it. That broker had to find customer B. So effectively he had to sell it from Customer A to Customer B directly."

The effect of this was to make it appear as if Spaceplex was a hot commodity, a must-buy. And it worked. They started lining up with buy orders. There were amateurs and pros, big money and small. Even some institutional investors jumped on Spaceplex. They came from all over. There was Carmen Campisi of Howard Beach, Queens, and Astaire & Partners Ltd. of Queen Street, London. A firm in Germany invested $300,000; another in Switzerland committed $500,000. An Italian invested $482,000; a wealthy guy from Pueblo, Colorado, dumped in $221,000. Warrington got the Bank of Monaco to put in another $285,000. All told in 1995, more than two hundred investors sunk $3.5 million into Spaceplex. It's probably a safe bet that none of these investors had seen the Spaceplex Family Amusement Center in Garden City, Long Island. If they had they might have thought twice.

While this was going on, Cary Cimino and his band of corrupt stockbrokers did no good but did quite well. Jeffrey was writing Cary checks for 35 percent commission and expecting him to chop up 20 percent for the brokers. These payments were straight-ahead bribes; none were disclosed to investors. Sometimes they were by check, sometimes by wire transfer to an overseas account, sometimes by cash. The checks were always made out for less than $10,000, the amount that requires banks to report transactions to oversight authorities looking for money laundering.

Most importantly for Cary Cimino, the checks cleared. Investors actually believed the nonsense the brokers were saying about Spaceplex. And this was why Cary didn't feel so bad about it. Warrington at first expressed some reservations and dabbled in guilt, but soon he, too, embraced Cary's credo that investors were just as greedy as the rest of us. They bought the craziness about "the next Six Flags" or "the next McDonald's" or "the next Starbucks" because they *wanted* to buy it. Their choice to buy was not bovine inspiration. It was a choice. They listened, they chose to stay on the phone and not slam it down in disgust. They authorized a stranger to spend their money. So if they got burned, that was their problem, not yours.

As it happened, DMN principals Pokross, Labate and Piazza made a killing. The suckers out there in the hinterlands lost out big-time: $3.5 million—pretty much everything they put in.

May 1995

On some Friday afternoons, Cary would stop by DMN Capital and spend hours sitting and listening to Jimmy Labate. It was better than TV. The nicknames: Patty Muscles, Joey Goggles, Frankie the Bug, Scooch. And the local color—the El Caribe in Brooklyn, the social club on McDonald Avenue, some abandoned lot in Staten Island where some bodies might be buried. Cary had no idea what was truth and what was fiction. He didn't care. After months of working with DMN, Cary had taken to calling the place "the circus," but it was clear he loved being part of the act.

He was now dropping gangster language into his conversation. Some of the models liked that. Everybody used language for their own purposes, of course. He'd been using the euphemisms of psychology for years with his "methodology" and "process" references. Jeffrey used business language to show how smart he was, dropping in "reverse splits" and "yield burning" whenever he could. Of course, Pokross—who was born in Kentucky and grew up in New Jersey—also had taken to dropping into mob-speak. It was infectious.

Cary learned quickly that for a group that was about breaking the law, there were a lot of rules in the mob. A soldier couldn't speak to another crew's captain. His own captain had to do that. The captains weren't supposed to bring disputes directly to the boss or underboss, but could reach out to the consigliere. A made guy could only be introduced as a made guy to another made guy by a made guy. It was worse than Robert's Rules of Order. But Jimmy made it sound kind of fun. And there was also the added benefit that if people knew you were with one family or another, they couldn't try to play games with you. You were a man of respect. Fear had that effect on people. It was probably inevitable, then, that Cary began to think that he himself was a gangster. He'd grown up in suburbia and even started well-heeled, but time and circumstance can do pretty much anything.

He started using terms like "whack" as in "whack a guy" or "bounce" as in "go out bouncing." It was kind of ridiculous. Here was a guy who had a weekly appointment at a tanning salon and who injected himself with growth hormones to keep looking fit talking about "the vig." But there it was, and thus did Cary come up with a solution to a problem that he must have found in the pages of a Mario Puzzo novel.

The problem was a guy named Herman. Cary had known

Herman for years. He and Herman, a fellow stockbroker turned stock promoter, had traveled the country doing dog and pony shows on different companies their firms were plugging. At one show in Orlando, Cary remembered how he and Herman—both avid *Star Trek* fans—paid some guy a couple thousand so that they could be part of a *Star Trek* episode as extras. Herman was one of the brokers Cary had paid to hype stock before he came to DMN. Herman always insisted on cash, and that turned into a big headache for all concerned.

Cary believed that Herman owed him $40,000. Herman insisted he did not. Cary claimed that he had paid Herman the cash bribe when he sold two hundred thousand shares of a company Cary was promoting. Unfortunately, the customer had five days to actually pay for the sale, and during that time, the stock tanked. Thus the customer refused to pay, and Cary was stuck with the fact that he'd paid his good *Star Trek* buddy Herman $40,000 in untraceable bills for absolutely nothing.

Cary was, understandably, furious. After Cary moved on to DMN, Herman stopped returning his calls. Cary tried to look at the situation reasonably: "I don't believe that Herman's efforts were to just take the $40,000 and run, because I had an established relationship with Herman . . . [But] Herman was, based on the rules of the game, based on the established parameters that we worked within, Herman was responsible, solely responsible."

Then out of the blue, in the middle of the Spaceplex scheme, after dodging Cary's phone calls for months, Herman suddenly called Cary looking for product to push. Herman suggested he could make amends for the $40,000 by buying a hundred thousand shares of Spaceplex. Only just for now, he needed to do it on credit. It's not entirely clear who was most offended by this arrangement—Cary or Jeffrey Pokross. Both insist it was the other's idea to call

Herman for a meeting at J.D.'s, a respectable restaurant in Midtown Manhattan frequented by brokers and lawyers and office workers.

When Herman showed up at J.D.'s, he found Cary and Jeffrey Pokross sitting at a crowded bar, two well-dressed stockbroker types sipping Scotch and blending right in with the crowd of professionals. He didn't at first notice the two other guys with them, mostly because they looked so different. One was a big, square guy with reddish close-cropped hair who looked kind of like a psychotic version of Curly of the Three Stooges. The other was a heavyset dark-haired guy with tinted glasses who looked like he spent a lot of time at Belmont Raceway. He didn't know it yet, but Herman was getting his first introduction to Jimmy Labate and one of Jimmy's pals, a guy named Bobby. Neither had business cards, but if they had, Jimmy's would have said, "Associate, Gambino Crime Family," and Bobby's would have said, "Associate, Genovese Crime Family."

Herman and Cary exchanged banalities, and Cary introduced Jeffrey. Later Cary would claim Jeffrey laced into Herman about moneys owed, while Jeffrey would say Cary was the screamer. Either way, after a few minutes of furious rhetoric, Herman was told he was going to take a walk outside J.D.'s with two gentlemen whose names he was not provided.

The bar happened to be at a window looking out onto the street, so Cary and Jeffrey could observe what was occurring as if they were watching a TV show. Jimmy and Bobby were standing very close to Herman on the street, one on each side. Jimmy was gesticulating and hollering in Herman's face, while Bobby stood right behind Herman like a backstop, silent. Herman looked like he was going to puke; the crowd of New Yorkers passing by acted as if the three men did not exist, going about their business, eyes averted.

Jimmy and Bobby began slapping Herman right there on the crowded sidewalk in the middle fifties in Manhattan.

From inside the bar, Cary and Jeffrey watched as Herman crumpled to the ground and Jimmy shouted something down at him. Then they picked him back up, brushed off his suit, and escorted Herman—the side of his face a bright red from the slap—back into J.D.'s to continue their civilized conversation over a Scotch. Pokross realized right away that the whole incident had been a mistake.

"Why did you do this?" Herman whined to Cary, never looking directly at Jimmy or Bobby. "I don't owe you money."

"You didn't hold it like you were supposed to. You know your obligation."

"I paid for some plastic surgery for you," Herman said. "I really don't owe you money."

The mood shifted.

Plastic surgery? Associates of New York's Mafia were hanging around with a guy who got plastic surgery? Jimmy and Jeffrey were looking at Cary, waiting for an explanation. Cary kept insisting the guy owed him money, but it didn't sound right. Pokross said, "The meeting ended with Bobby and Labate being nice to Herman. They were looking at Cary like, 'Why did we do this when this guy really didn't owe the money?'"

It was a bad move all around. It wasn't that Jimmy felt bad about beating on Herman the *Star Trek* fan in the middle of the sidewalk. He would do it again on the weekend if asked. It was just that doing things like that brought attention, and Jeffrey was trying to keep a low profile at DMN.

A few weeks later when Bobby came to Labate and Pokross to say Cary had another Herman-like problem and was requesting a Herman-like solution. Jeffrey was not pleased. Cary wanted Jimmy to enforce the no-sale policy on another deal Cary was doing outside DMN. Even Jimmy Labate thought that was a bad idea.

"You're not going to be running around being the John Gotti of Wall Street," he said, and Bobby did nothing more.

To make the point clear to Cary that they preferred he act like a stockbroker and not like a wannabe gangster, Jeffrey and Sal and Jimmy hired Herman to work with him on other jobs. Cary thought that was hilarious.

"Herman gets slapped and then works for Jeffrey and Jimmy," he said. "Herman works for these guys in a happy-go-lucky fashion."

Business is business. Cary shut his mouth, went back to work. What could he say, as long as those checks kept clearing and the envelopes of cash showed up on his desk?

CHAPTER NINETEEN

May 1992

The historians will one day acknowledge that the guys from the neighborhood did not figure out the lesson of John Gotti right away. Here was a guy who taunted the FBI every day to come and get him. He'd whacked a boss on a crowded Manhattan sidewalk, in front of civilians buying Christmas presents, and strutted around Little Italy like Macbeth, making a public display of his power. He'd required his captains to meet with him regularly, guaranteeing that each and every one would wind up in an FBI photo album. Everybody but the janitor was in there: his underboss, his consigliere, and all the captains and soldiers and hangers-on. There were crowds of them on the Mulberry Street sidewalk, milling about with the tourists passing by. It was a wiseguy convention, and it was very bad for business. It was obvious that this was more than a bunch of guys from the neighborhood getting together to play casino. Hours of video had played out in federal court, along with the hours of tape-recorded conversations inside an apartment above the club, and together with the sudden transformation of the second-in-command, Gravano, from sociopath to the federal government's employee of the month, Gotti had been convicted the month previous and now faced the likelihood of dying inside a federal facility. One might have thought that the brilliant tacticians of New York City gangland would thus have second thoughts about the parade in and out of social clubs and institute an immediate ban on going anywhere near these places. Not a chance. The meetings continued, the walk-talks went on as if nothing had changed. It was always the same thing: they won't catch me because I'm smarter than they are.

Robert Lino had a different idea about all of this. Robert from Avenue U stayed the hell away from Avenue U, and from all of Brooklyn for that matter. John Gotti's loss of Teflon sobered him right up. The streets of Gravesend and Bensonhurst and Bay Ridge and Maspeth were crawling with federal agents, guys with cameras sitting inside vans for hours at a time, day and night, never going home to see their families. This was not a convenient arrangement for meeting your crew. If you dropped by social clubs near McDonald Avenue or anywhere else in that part of Brooklyn, it was almost guaranteed you'd show up on some videotape that would later be used against you in a court of law. Robert Lino figured the best place to be was in a place nobody would think to go—across the East River in an innocuous Manhattan neighborhood known as Murray Hill.

Murray Hill was a middle-class high-rise neighborhood with little flower stalls and barbershops somewhere between the Upper and Lower East Side. It was neither here nor there. In fact, it wasn't really a neighborhood. It had no real personality. There were no Italian cafes or bocce courts or social clubs with ridiculous names like the Bergen Hunt and Fish Club or the Hawaiian Friends Society. It was banal. It was a perfect little rabbit hole into which Robert Lino from Avenue U could disappear.

His choice of venue was a Murray Hill restaurant called

Katrina's owned by a childhood friend, Frankie Ambrosino. Despite the ownership's family history, the restaurant served only Polish food. It was ideal. Robert from Avenue U could come and go without being observed. Katrina's was not on the federal radar. Robert's friend Frankie had long ago made it clear that he didn't want anything to do with the gangster life. He didn't mind Robert and his crew hanging out in the back room of his restaurant, but that was as close as he was willing to get. He was quite straightforward about it. He never wanted to become a gangster, just a gangster's friend. Therefore not only were the feds unaware of Katrina's, they were also unaware of its owner.

Operating out of Katrina's was a sound idea. Robert Lino favored the notion that a secret society of organized criminals should endeavor to remain secret. In the old days, that had been much easier. People who signed up for the program stayed in the program and never strayed. Over forty years, there had only been a handful of exceptions. Joe Valacci. Fish Cafarro. Jimmy the Weasel. These were guys who'd decided that, for whatever reason, informing on your friends and family was worth the risk that someday while walking alone along the streets of Phoenix or Seattle some guy might come up behind you and put five in your cranium. That was when becoming an informant was highly unusual. The shame of being labeled a rat was powerful. Now something had changed. Now there was Gravano, a top boss of the most powerful Mafia family in America, an allegedly stand-up guy, who had one day awakened to discover that it was time to become a friend of the United States government.

Robert from Avenue U was the kind of guy who believed in the whole movie script, that when you swore an oath you swore an oath, that there really were men of honor, that the concept of *omerta* was to be taken seriously. Guys like Robert Lino were at a loss to explain why Sammy the Bull had flipped over to the government's team. That was why Robert truly favored the notion of spending his days in anonymous old Murray Hill. To have this Gravano turn rat, that was a profoundly disturbing moment for a society of criminals who'd long clung to the ancient notion that telling on your friends was worse than killing them. Once somebody that high up went over to the other side, the whole contraption was on shaky ground.

In fact, the Gravano defection was beginning to look like a virus. A month after Gravano turned, Little Al D'Arco, acting boss of the Lucchese family, walked into the FBI even before he was asked. And the federal government's pursuit of Gotti had ramifications for all the five families, especially those who were videotaped meeting with Gotti and his crew. Only those who stayed away preserved the ability to survive the storm caused by Gotti. The bad habits of the self-proclaimed boss of bosses were not going to be mimicked by Robert Lino and the Bonanno family.

In the back room of Katrina's, Robert's associates dropped by weekly with envelopes and complaints. He would count money first, then listen to complaints. That was what soldiers did. They collected as much money as they could from as many sources as possible—loan-sharking debtors, gambling debtors, protection debtors—and kicked up a percentage to the skipper, in Robert's case his cousin Frank Lino. In turn Frank kicked up a percentage to the hierarchy. Each week Robert with the sixth-grade education carefully chopped the money up. This was math he could handle. Some weeks were good, some weeks weren't so good.

As for complaints, he spent too much time on those. If there was a dispute with another family, he would take it to his skipper. Sometimes Frank would deal with the issue. Sometimes he'd let Robert handle it himself. On this day, Frank showed up at Katrina's with an issue they both would have to deal with. As always, Frank kept things vague.

He had been at a funeral parlor in Queens for some

wiseguy's wake and Sal Vitale, another captain in the Bonanno crime family and the brother-in-law to Massino the boss, had approached Frank with a problem that needed repair. Frank's job was to first find a place to eliminate the problem and then find a different place to dispose of the problem. During the entire conversation at the wake, Sal had made a point not to mention the name of the problem. Frank liked to know the names of his problems, so he'd asked around and soon learned from another source the problem's name—Robert Perrino.

Perrino was married to the daughter of a former Bonanno underboss named Nicky Glasses. He was a superintendent of delivery at the tabloid newspaper, the *New York Post*. There he ran a lucrative bookmaking operation, kicking back a percentage to the Bonanno crime family. He also had a leadership position in the union representing the drivers who dropped newspapers off every morning across New York City. Organized crime liked unions like this because they existed more or less to provide jobs to gangsters who didn't actually have to show up and as a weapon to extort payments for the promise of "labor peace." Newspapers, after all, couldn't exist if the drivers couldn't get them to newsstands on time. Perrino was the Bonanno family's go-to guy at the *Post*, and now the rumor was there was an active investigation of his activities there.

The issue that turned Perrino into a problem was that he was not considered to be a tough guy. It was felt that if he were indicted, he would right away forget all his friends in the Bonanno crime family and realize that the government was his new friend. Especially, it was believed, he would be a problem for Sal Vitale, the Bonanno capo to whom he reported. And now he was Robert Lino's problem.

Frank let it be known that Robert would not have to be the shooter. Frank himself had never done such a thing, always relying on others in his employ. He wasn't interested in making Bobby Lino's son pull the trigger again. All Robert Lino had to do was find a place to get the job done and then a place to get rid of the aftermath. No heavy lifting. Somebody else had already dreamed up a story to get Perrino where they needed him. Perrino would be told he was meeting with Sal Vitale to let him know about the investigation at the *Post* and work it out so he could go on an extended vacation to Florida for a while, until things quieted down. That was the story Perrino would be told to get him to whatever spot Robert Lino would pick.

Robert Lino decided it was time to visit with Anthony Basile, a friend of his who owned a social club on the second floor above his sister's nail salon in a building at 86th Street in Bay Ridge, Brooklyn. That would be perfect for disposing of the Perrino problem. Robert had another idea for the disposal issue. Jimmy Labate had a beat-up garage in Staten Island where he stored construction equipment. The lot was in a highly residential neighborhood, with three-family homes right next door where they left the Christmas lights on all year. The garage was perfect. Jimmy could be called upon to get things ready by digging a hole in the floor inside the garage. No one would see what was going on in the middle of the night. Jimmy was desperate to ingratiate himself with the leadership of the Bonanno family, so he undoubtedly would be happy to help out.

At Katrina's, the cousins Lino agreed the plan was perfect.

Robert Lino sat with his childhood pal, Frankie Ambrosino, in a restaurant a few blocks from the Brooklyn social club over the nail salon, near the 20th Street BMT subway stop he'd picked. He was waiting to fulfill the final task related to the resolution of the problem named Robert Perrino. Apparently picking the spots was not good enough. He also had to participate in something called cleanup. Cleanup was usually not a job you wanted to do. Usually there was a big mess, and sometimes you had to make the item in need of disposal more disposable. This could involve the use of saws and knives, and usually took quite a while. Unlike Tommy Karate, a specialist at this who enjoyed it, Robert Lino did not, and so when the pay phone in the restaurant rang and the restaurant owner told him the caller was looking for him, he took the call with some apprehension in his gut. It was a guy he knew called Mikey Bats.

Mikey said, "We're ready" and hung up.

Robert called his cousin, Frank, who was sitting in another restaurant down the street, to let him know it was time. Robert and Frank left their respective restaurants and headed down the street.

The plan was simple: Robert and Frankie would enter the club, wrap Perrino in a rug, then walk the package downstairs and around the corner to a car parked and waiting with the key in the ignition. It was a little tricky because the stairs hit the sidewalk very close to a subway exit, and it would likely be somewhat complicated to explain to passing commuters what precisely was going on if they happened upon two guys carrying a rug in the middle of the night. However, cousin Frank was going to watch the entrance and signal when the coast was clear.

Simple. Choreographed in every way. Someone else would actually pull the trigger, and when the cleanup crew arrived, that guy would already be gone. That way fewer people knew who did what. It was important—no, essential—that things go smoothly, because the cops had discovered the body of a guy named Sammy in the trunk of a car in Queens just six weeks earlier, so the FBI was watching the Bonanno family closely. Failure was not an option. Expectations were high.

Robert and Frankie passed the 20th Street subway exit, the green globe shining in the warm May night. It was a perfect night for people to be out. Large groups could emerge from the mouth of the underground at any minute. The two men walked up the stairs and opened the door of the club.

They practically tripped over the body on the floor. There were a bunch of guys standing around looking at the body. It lay right by the entrance, facing the bar. It was obvious the guy had been shot the minute he'd stepped inside. Blood was oozing from his head. The gun that had been used to shoot him lay next to the body. And there was one more little detail that caught Robert Lino off guard. The guy lying on the floor was still alive. He was breathing and then moaning and twitching.

One of the guys in the room had an ice pick in his hand. He jammed it in the moaning guy's ear and the guy stopped twitching and breathing. The ice pick guy took the gun and put it in his pocket.

Frank Lino left to watch the subway exit. Robert Lino, Frankie Ambrosino, the ice pick guy and the guy who owned the club, Anthony Basile, went to work. Basile produced a rug, and they all rolled the dead guy's body inside, trying not to get blood on their clothes. Then Robert Lino and Frankie and the ice pick guy picked up the body and stood by the door. They looked outside and Frank Lino signaled for them to move. They heaved the body all the way down the stairs and past the subway exit and put it in the back of the car waiting around the corner. They slammed the trunk and everyone breathed a little easier. No one had yet emerged from the subway. Robert Lino and Frankie Ambrosino got in the car and turned the key.

Nothing happened.

Chaos ensued. Now they had to open the trunk, drag the guy in the rug out into the open again, haul him out of there right away. Should they pull another car up next to the one that wouldn't start? Should they just walk the guy in the rug down the middle of the street and hope a bowling team didn't emerge from the mouth of the subway in

time to witness this bizarre tableau? First they decided
which of the other stolen cars on the scene would make the
best vehicle to transport the guy in the rug. Then they went
with option one, pulling that car up next to the dead car
and quickly transferring the bulky rolled up rug and all its
contents into the trunk of the second car. During the entire
frantic procedure, no one stepped out of the subway, proving once again that timing is everything.

Cousin Frank followed in a second car as they drove
over the Verrazano Bridge into Staten Island. They paid the
toll and headed toward the property owned by Jimmy Labate. As they entered the neighborhood, the lead car pulled
over and Frank Lino followed. Jimmy Labate was waiting
at the chain-link gate and waved them inside. They backed
the car up to the garage and heaved the body out and onto
the garage floor. In the back corner of the garage the concrete floor had been broken up and there was a big hole in
the dirt underneath. Jimmy had a fresh batch of concrete
ready to go.

Basile left to go back to his club to clean up the mess.
The rest of them—Robert, Frankie, the ice pick guy and
Jimmy Labate—stuffed the body inside a fifty-five-gallon
steel drum and Jimmy poured concrete on top to seal it.
They then lowered the container into the big hole in the
corner of the garage. Jimmy had already set up a rectangle
of wooden planks all around the hole to hold the cement in
place. He dumped some dirt on top of the hole, leveled it
off, and poured concrete on top of the whole affair. Robert
Lino and Frank Ambrosino left as Jimmy began smooth-
ing out the top to make it look like this slab of concrete in
the corner of the garage actually belonged there.

Robert Lino had never actually met Robert Perrino.
Robert did not know his wife and children, had never discussed the Knicks with the guy, had no idea whether Perrino would, in the end, turn into a rat or remain a stand-up
guy. At this moment, it didn't really matter. Robert was part

of Perrino's end, and also knew the precise location in the city of New York of Perrino's final resting place. Perrino would now be with Robert Lino forever, along with Louis Tuzzio and Gabe Infanti.

Robert Lino sat in yet another restaurant, this one in midtown Manhattan, waiting for Jimmy Labate. By now, Robert was making good money in a number of ventures and didn't need this aggravation. He was a floor manager at a strip club called Wiggles in Queens where cash flowed like rain in Seattle. He was overseeing the bookmaking operation for the Bonanno group's boss, Massino, whom he never referred to by name but instead tugged on his left ear to let everybody know without really knowing who he was discussing. He had a driver, Angelo, who accompanied him everywhere and opened the door for him when he pulled up to the curb. Mostly things were going good for Robert, with a few exceptions. Jimmy Labate was one of those exceptions.

Today in the restaurant Robert from Avenue U once again found himself addressing a Jimmy Labate situation. Lino sat across the table from a contractor who had a dispute with Jimmy. He was sure that Jimmy was in the wrong, as he was so often, but he had to hear the story from both sides. Of course, it didn't help matters that Jimmy was supposedly "with" him and that he was also late for the meeting.

Being a soldier in an organized crime family was sometimes like being the principal of an unruly high school. Today's Jimmy Labate dispute centered on Jimmy Labate's interpretation of certain rules that Jimmy insisted existed. Jimmy was always looking to get paid, so he decided to put some of his guys in no-show jobs on a hotel renovation in Manhattan. One day he decided to show up at the hotel and make his position clear. He pulled up in his Lincoln with four guys and strutted in, ordering the contractor to put all four guys on the payroll or there'd be problems. The four guys started knocking things over, making a big mess. The contractor said okay, okay, I can't afford four guys but I'll take two. That seemed reasonable. Most guys would think it was reasonable. Even Jimmy—who was only reasonable on occasion—agreed. The two guys went on the payroll, and that was that.

Only it wasn't. Instead, Jimmy showed up a few days later with the other two guys and said you have to put them on anyway. The contractor was furious, so he decided to go straight over Jimmy's head and take his situation to Robert Lino. Everyone told him Robert was reasonable and fair, which was why the contractor now sat across the table in the restaurant in Midtown, waiting for Jimmy Labate.

This was not the first time Robert had had problems with Jimmy. His cousin Frank, who was also his skipper, was always complaining about Jimmy. A few weeks after the bit of business with Perrino from the *Post* and the car not starting and all, Jimmy had shown up at a bar and announced to Frank that he'd put his role in helping bury Perrino on record with Johnny G, a Gambino family soldier who mistreated him but with whom Jimmy hoped to make a name for himself in organized crime. Jimmy was trying to impress Johnny G, but the true effect of this little bit of sycophancy was to let the Gambino family know all about the Bonanno family's business. The way Frank saw it, what happened to Perrino from the *Post* was nobody's business. Frank had come to believe that Jimmy Labate was a loudmouth and stupid, a combination that works fine for Department of Motor Vehicles employees but is not good for gangsters.

Such were the problems Robert Lino was always dealing with. Anybody who was put with him was there for a reason. Usually the reason was money. The guy had a healthy sports book or shylock operation. The guy had his hooks into a union. The guy owned a strip club or a nightclub or any business that involved lots of cash. The guy had something to offer. Robert, in return, let them use his name and the power of the Bonanno crime family if disputes arose with other Mafia families or any other form of criminal fraternal organization. That was his end. Also he had to show up and settle the dispute.

Usually this was an arrangement that worked out in Robert's favor. Take, for instance, the situation with another guy who reported to Robert: Jeffrey Pokross. Here was an earner. He had been running car lease schemes for years and had not once visited the inside of a jail cell, but had consistently kicked up significant amounts of money to Robert Lino and the Bonanno crime family. In recent weeks, Jeffrey Pokross had encountered a problem with a Gambino associate named Billy. Billy was a large guy, probably six foot four. Jeffrey was a small guy who was good with numbers and quietly robbing people blind but wouldn't know how to give somebody a beating if his life depended on it. Billy had been involved with one of Jeffrey's insurance scams, where the driver, in this case Billy, pretended to have a car accident. Jeffrey's friend, another Bonanno associate named Patty Muscles, would use his auto body shop as a cover to generate fake bills, and the insurance companies would pay out. Jeffrey, Billy and Patty Muscles all split the amount evenly. Only Billy had decided Jeffrey had stolen some of his share. Billy didn't have any real proof of this, just the fact that he was huge and Jeffrey was not. He called Jeffrey on the phone and screamed that he was going to kill him and his children's children if he didn't cough up some cash. Jeffrey hung up and called Robert Lino. Robert told him to let Billy know that if he had a problem, he should call Robert from Avenue U. Jeffrey did as he was told, and that was the last time Billy bothered him.

In return Jeffrey got Robert a car and sent him a nice fat envelope at Christmas. That was the way it should be: make a phone call, get a car. Then Pokross said he might be able to get Robert a salary. This guy Pokross claimed to have a stockbroker's license and was going to start up a brokerage house that almost sounded legitimate. He was going to call it DMN Capital, and he'd rented out an office a few blocks from Wall Street. Pokross let it be known that he felt the stock market was about to go through the roof, and he wanted Robert from Avenue U to be part of that.

Robert didn't really understand how it all worked, but he could tell it was easy money. It wasn't hijacking trucks or collecting shylock loans or chasing down degenerate gamblers for the vig. With this crowd it was highly unlikely there would be a need for a beat-down, and the amount of money this Pokross was promising was fantastic for doing practically nothing. Pokross had told him he would only be needed if other mob families figured out what was going on down on Wall Street; then Robert would step in and smooth the way.

It all seemed simple enough, although Robert was well aware there was a specific rule in *la cosa nostra* forbidding involvement in the stock market. That rule, of course, was like most rules in the world of gangsters—it was nonsense. The glory days of *la cosa nostra* were finished. The FBI was cracking down on all the traditional money sources: the garbage carters, the fish market, the unions. Wall Street was simply a new opportunity, and if you missed out you were nothing but a fool. For a guy with a sixth-grade education who had trouble signing his name, this kind of arrangement sounded pretty good.

It was never this easy with Jimmy Labate, who had finally entered the restaurant and sat down next to Robert. He stared at the contractor like he would like nothing better than to pour a pot of boiling coffee on the guy's lap.

The contractor explained the situation. He didn't want to put anyone on the payroll, but out of respect to Robert Lino of Avenue U, he allowed for two guys. He made it clear he couldn't afford four guys on the payroll, and Jimmy had agreed that two guys—not four—would suffice. Robert asked Jimmy if it was true that he'd agreed to two guys, not four. Jimmy admitted that it was true.

Robert slapped Jimmy in the face.

"You shook hands with this man and then reneged on the deal?"

Robert made it clear how this would work. Jimmy, who was also making a salary at Jeffrey Pokross's Wall Street operation, DMN, would now deliver a portion of his salary every week to the contractor until the guy was compensated. It was a win-win situation for Robert Lino. The contractor was now his best friend, and Jimmy would learn a lesson about restraint. Maybe. Sometimes being a soldier in an organized crime family was a big pain in the ass.

Mid 1995

Usually Robert Lino didn't stop down to DMN Capital more than once a week. The narrow streets around Broad and Wall were not exactly familiar territory for Robert from Avenue U. There he looked more like a janitor than a man of respect, with all these college guys in suits and ties and the whole attitude of exclusivity that hung in the money-driven air. Usually he'd drop in just once a week, on Thursday afternoon, make a little small talk, see how things were going, pick up the envelope of $1,500 cash. Sometimes he'd check up on the people he'd recommended for jobs there. There were some brokers he knew of through other members of the Bonanno family who were working there at his recommendation, and he needed to know that they were holding up their end. Usually a visit to DMN was an uneventful affair, a session of listening to Jeffrey's list of minor complaints and applying common sense to resolve them.

Until now Wall Street had been nothing but money for

Robert Lino. The disputes were tiny. A broker claims he hasn't been paid by a stock promoter. A promoter claims a broker isn't holding up his end by pushing the bogus stock they're trying to pump up. That sort of thing happened every day down there. It was no big deal. The big deal would be some guy from another one of the families laying claim to specific brokers or stock promoters, or another family screwing around with the schemes of DMN by manipulating the stock DMN was trying to manipulate for its own ends. So far Robert had had only a few interactions with members of other organized crime families, and all had resulted in solutions both sides could live with.

Now that was changing. Until now only a handful of wiseguys out there had figured out what Wall Street had to offer, and that had been good for DMN and Robert Lino. Most wiseguys really weren't cut out for it anyway. Most had barely made it halfway through high school before dropping out, and they were usually overwhelmed when confronted with quarterly reports and understanding when a company was overleveraged or undervalued. Robert Lino himself had made it only through sixth grade; he hadn't come close to basic algebra and was nowhere near the calculus required of an MBA.

Recently, however, Robert had become aware that there were other guys from the neighborhood out there who did understand the numbers game. In fact, more and more of these guys were showing up.

It started with Philly Abramo. He was a captain in the wannabe family from New Jersey, the DeCavalcante group. He claimed to be the father of the pump and dump scam, which was nonsense but sounded impressive. Pump and dump had actually been around since the 1980s, when a handful of gangsters made some money hyping bogus stock. Regardless, practically everyone in the underworld knew that Philly Abramo had mastered the art of keeping pump and dump below the radar. That, of course, was the key. You didn't actually have to know everything about Wall Street to play the game. You just had to appear to know what you were talking about. It was the magician's trick—misdirection. Make the audience pay attention to your left hand while your right hand is robbing them blind. Philly Abramo was the Harry Houdini of Mafia Wall Street.

And now he wasn't alone. It had long been rumored he was making millions—not thousands, not tens of thousands, not hundreds of thousands. Millions, all on Wall Street. And he didn't have to pull out a gun, shove in a knife, chop up a body, pour in the concrete—none of that messy business. He surrounded himself with guys who could do that, but even they rarely had to make a guy disappear. Mostly the scheme worked with a mere threat, and that was easy. These Wall Street guys—even the corrupt ones—were pushovers. Just talk about putting them inside a fifty-five-gallon drum and they'd do whatever you wanted. Fear without blood. That was a good deal. And now everybody had heard of Philly Abramo and his millions and it was clear that Philly Abramo was no longer going to be the only gangster on Wall Street.

As a result of Philly Abramo and his reputation for pulling down millions, Robert Lino had received a telephone call from Pokross about a guy showing up at DMN's office on Liberty Street who didn't belong there. This wouldn't have been a problem if the guy was just another stock promoter, but this guy was claiming to be with the Lucchese crime family and had announced that DMN was now going to be his.

Robert Lino did not need this aggravation. Here he was, a married man now, his wife a college-educated administrative assistant for a big corporation in New Jersey (and the daughter of a gangster). They were planning on having children. This was the new Robert Lino: family man. Unfortunately the old Robert Lino, Robert of Avenue U, had to surface occasionally to ensure the provider could provide.

Today's problem was the Padulo brothers, Vito and Vinnie. The two were registered stockbrokers in their late thirties who'd bounced from one boiler room to another and were now pushing stock for DMN. Jeffrey Pokross had invited them in to push a couple of new stocks DMN was selling, and was paying them bribes to do it. The two companies were called Beachport Entertainment, which allegedly put on ice shows, and International Nursing, which owned a couple of nursing homes on Long Island but was pretending to be a multimillion-dollar operation caring for seniors coast to coast. For weeks Jeffrey wrote checks to the Padulo brothers to hype both Beachport and International Nursing. As far as he knew the Padulo brothers were not affiliated with any particular crime family. Jeffrey was wrong. He realized his mistake the morning a guy with glasses called Joe Baudanza showed up at the offices of DMN along with ten of his own personal brokers without a legitimate license between them. Baudanza announced that they were setting up shop at DMN, as the Padulo brothers had requested.

A broker named Robert Gallo was there when it happened and he called Jeffrey Pokross, who right away called Robert Lino. Robert Gallo knew this Joey Baudanza from the neighborhood. He called him "the kid with the glasses."

"This kid with the glasses, he's up there with a whole crew," he told Pokross. "What's he doing up there? It's Robert's place."

Now Robert Lino was forced to drive over to DMN, and it wasn't even a Thursday. He went into Pokross's office and took this guy, Baudanza, with him. They came out a few minutes later and Lino went into another room with Pokross.

"How could you let this happen?" he said. Robert said he'd take care of it, and when he left, he wasn't smiling.

This was a big problem. It was like one group of pirates coming upon another group right after they'd opened the

map and saw the big "X" in the middle. It meant the Bonanno family would have to sit down with the Lucchese
family and figure out a way to divide up the spoils without
seeming weak. This did not seem right considering that the
spoils had been created by the Bonanno family in the first
place. And it raised questions about the loyalty of the Padulo
brothers. Who, precisely, had told them bringing in another
Mafia family to DMN was a good idea in the first place?

A few days later Baudanza, the kid with the glasses with
the Lucchese group, was out of DMN. That took care of the
Lucchese group. Then the Colombo group showed up. This
time it was the Padulo brothers again, whining about money.
They had a different math than Jeffrey Pokross. They claimed
DMN owed them $160,000 more in retroactive bribes, and
they wanted it because they were out the door and headed for
a boiler room operated by the Colombo family. Again Pokross called Robert Lino; again Robert Lino had yet another
sit-down, this time with the Colombo family. Again he prevailed, and DMN didn't have to pay the Padulo brothers a
cent. Out the door they went, leaving Robert from Avenue U
with a bad feeling about Wall Street.

CHAPTER TWENTY

January 19, 1996

By seven thirty in the morning, the crusaders of Wall Street marched toward the New York Stock Exchange, resolute in their pursuit of the Grail. The streets of Lower Manhattan were alive with the bustle of ambition: Broad Street, Wall Street, Beaver Street, Exchange Place, Maiden Lane. Each teemed with crusaders assigned their mission. These knights were called stockbrokers, investment bankers, financial analysts, each the product of years of training. Instead of learning the skills of archery or fencing or hand-to-hand combat, these knights had immersed themselves in the principals of accounting, the language of economists, the calculus of profit. None wore a steel mail leotard or cast-iron helmet. They wore Burberry topcoats, Brooks Brothers suits, crisp white shirts, silk ties. None carried a broadsword or lance or shield. They wielded shiny leather suitcases with gold monogrammed initials, stuffed with earnings reports and 10-Qs. Their noble steed amounted to the Seventh Avenue IRT subway line.

In the crowd one soldier of fortune pressed forward,

wrapped in winter coat and scarf, head bowed against the January wind. His name was Robert Grant, stock picker, and he pressed forth with the purpose of one who believed he would surely be richer by day's end. He was headed for his job at the Monitor Investment Group, and he didn't want to be late. When you're on a crusade, being late is simply not an option.

Like most crusaders, Robert Grant had trained for years to get to this place. He'd completed undergraduate studies and then obtained a master's in business administration. He believed he knew what he was doing. He could have gone to law school or med school or run a restaurant, but he chose Wall Street because that was where you made the most amount of money the fastest. Unlike for the knights of yore, this Grail was within reach, if you knew how to get it.

This was the time of year when everybody was done with the business of Christmas and Hanukah. This was January, that bleak series of dark days before the February trip to St. Bart's. The big fir in front of the Exchange was gone, and the statue of George Washington a block away at the old Federal Hall looked particularly frozen. The idea was to get from the subway into your office as quickly as possible, even if all you had to look forward to the first thing in the morning was yet another wretched meeting. That was Robert Grant's mission this morning. He'd been told to be on time.

Robert Grant was one of the new recruits at Monitor Investment Group's new office at 30 Broad Street, just a block from the Exchange. Here was the heart of moneymaking in America, and as 1996 dawned, boy was there money to be made.

The Street was hot. The tech-stock boom was creating an atmosphere of adventure. When the wild 1980s came screeching to a halt in the Crash of '87, Wall Street was seen as a volatile game of roulette, a kind of casino run by blue bloods. Now everybody had forgotten about that. Now Wall Street was the place to be. Innovation was rampant. All the way down in Mississippi Bernie Ebbers's World-Com was buying up little phone companies created by the breakup of AT&T at a pace fast enough that Bernie got himself on the front page of *Fortune* dressed like a cowboy. Ken Lay of Enron made the front page as a visionary, his new Houston-based company that bought and sold energy touted as the company of the next century. CEOs were celebrities.

And once again, stockbrokers were kings. The old masters of the universe from the eighties were now much cooler, mostly because everybody had become an investor. Not just old money capital but new money capital: the guy who owned the bagel store. The owner of the nail salon. The retired postal supervisor. The Kmart stock clerk. Cable TV was devoting entire channels just to stock market gyration, and people were watching. In barbershops, on the rows of TVs at the mall retail stores, at the airports. Forget baseball. Forget politics. Forget what's happening in Afghanistan.

Money was the new Crusade.

It all seemed so easy. It was practically guaranteed that if you paid attention, you could make 1,000 percent profit overnight. The returns were astonishing. You just had to act quickly. Your neighbor the hairstylist just made in one week $10,000 betting on Amazon. How could you ignore that? And in order to make real money you had to risk real money. Why not take a chance on a margin account? Sure, they could call it at any time, but what was the risk when the market was so bullish? If your neighbor the hairstylist could do it, so could you.

But for the troops out there slogging in the trenches along Broad Street and Wall Street and Exchange Place, the actual making of money, the job itself—it could be so profoundly tedious. Especially during meetings. This was what Robert Grant had to look forward to: a roomful of guys bored out of their skulls trying to stay awake through the latest pitch, the newest shtick, the most up-to-date patter. Each new strategy was supposed to produce more customers willing to buy product, which was supposed to mean more commissions. But mostly the newest pitch was just a warmed up version of the previous pitch. It was all pretty much the same. Keep the customers moving. Keep them believing that they must act fast. Momentum was the key. Never get too specific with numbers. Most of the material Grant had been given about the companies he pushed was pretty vague anyway. There wasn't a whole lot of detail about assets. It was hard to tell from the prospectuses whether any of the companies had any real track records to speak of. But from the perspective of the broker working the customer, it really didn't matter. Just keep the monologue going. Overwhelm them with the urge to make money fast. Robert Grant didn't need a meeting to tell him that. All he needed to do was get on the phone with a potential client and throw that slider over the plate.

The big push at Monitor the past few weeks was a company called Reclaim, which allegedly recycled roofing shingles. Environmental spin was always effective. Somehow it was easier to sell the idea of profiting while saving the planet. There were dozens of companies like this one out there. Monitor was pushing Reclaim under the symbol ROOF. Grant's job was to cold-call, often to seniors, usually in the Midwest. He was handed a list of names. He didn't ask where they got it. He didn't really think that these people could be his own grandparents. He just made the calls and performed the pitch.

By the time he arrived on the scene, Monitor had already paid off the market makers to drive up the price, guaranteeing them against a loss. The Monitor insiders were buying Reclaim at 25 cents a share, buying them up through offshore shells, knowing they could sell after forty days. The market makers drove the price up to $2.50, then Grant and the other brokers at Monitor went to work in the retail market. The brokers were paid by cash or check to pump it up further. This was going on in New York and overseas. There were rumors that suitcases filled with cash were coming and going from Germany. When they got it to $6, everybody on the inside was going to dump as fast as they could.

So far as he knew, Robert Grant was holding up his end, snagging customers across the nation. The only warning sign he'd experienced was the repeated admonition not to let his customers unload their Reclaim. Not yet. If they insisted, Robert had to find somebody to sell it to. It was as simple as that.

Robert Grant and another broker, a sometime friend named Eric, arrived at Monitor around 7:45 a.m., right on time. Both were told to report to the conference room immediately. They hustled in even before they had their coffee.

The minute he opened the door to the room, Grant realized this was not the usual pitch meeting. Mostly he realized this because once he stepped into the conference room, he was immediately whacked in the face with an office chair.

Robert Grant went down on the carpet and curled up in a fetal position. The guy with the chair was named Bobby Gallo.

Robert Grant knew Bobby Gallo only as some creep from Brooklyn who seemed to hang around the office. The guy didn't actually work, as far as anyone could see. He was from a different world than Robert Grant. He hadn't bothered with the abstract knowledge of the MBA. He hadn't spent any time in school at all. His knowledge came from the streets of Brooklyn. While Robert Grant was learning about the Laffer curve, Bobby Gallo was learning how to coldcock a guy so he couldn't get up. Robert Grant used a calculator; Bobby Gallo used fists. The rumor was Bobby Gallo had actually passed his Series 7 exam, but Robert Grant couldn't believe such a thing was possible. He could believe that Bobby Gallo was now hitting him about the face and back with an office chair.

As he flailed away, Gallo kept screaming something about taking money from a man's family. Then he'd swing again with the chair. He was also kicking Robert Grant in the sides, in the back, in the legs, wherever he could. He seemed to be enjoying himself. Grant could see that a couple of other guys built more or less like Gallo were also kicking at Eric, who was also on the carpet, writhing and howling in pain.

Robert Grant managed to slide himself under the conference table and come up on the other side. Maybe it would have been better if he had learned archery or swordsmanship or hand-to-hand combat like a real knight, but here he was, slinking his way out of the conference room and into the women's bathroom.

He slammed the door behind him. There he lay, bleeding, his chest heaving, his face bruised, his sides and back racked with searing pain.

It had all happened so fast.

He remembered screaming, "What the hell are you doing?" over and over, but couldn't remember what Gallo and the other guys were yammering on and on about as they went to work on Robert and Eric. Something about trying to take customers away from Monitor to jump to another firm. He had no idea what they were talking about.

This kind of behavior was not something he'd expected to find on Wall Street. He didn't remember the use of office chairs being discussed in business school. He didn't know guys like Gallo were part of this world. He'd been told Wall Street was all college guys, lots of preppies, plenty of fraternity brothers. But this? This was a version of *Animal House* he hadn't thought existed.

Lying on the floor of the women's bathroom, Robert Grant figured a guy like Bobby Gallo hadn't thought up the idea of busting up his morning himself, so he decided to make a plan. He'd get the hell out of Monitor, go directly to Beekman Hospital and make sure they took some good photos of his injuries. Then he'd make three phone calls.

First he called his boss.

Then he called the cops.

Then he called a good lawyer.

CHAPTER TWENTY-ONE

Warrington sat in his cubicle at Monitor, watching the ticker for signs of Spaceplex. The market makers had already gone to work and now they were out in the retail market, driving the numbers higher. All the brokers at Monitor's three offices were on the case, and there was a serious competition to see who could sell the most in one day. Jimmy Labate walked up to Warrington's cubicle and slapped a set of car keys on his desk.

"Sell fifty thousand shares in the next fifteen minutes, and this is yours," he said, pointing at the keys. Warrington could see the Mercedes logo on the key chain.

"What color is it?" he asked.

"Green," Labate answered, and then he stood there, waiting.

Warrington didn't really like Jimmy Labate. He usually avoided him. They were from different worlds. Warrington was a guy who'd pay somebody to fix his clogged up sink. Jimmy would just fix it. Warrington had a prep school education and almost four years of college, and a Series 7 broker's license. He was a man of reason. Jimmy probably didn't make it out of high school, and when he approached things, he relied exclusively on the threat of physical harm to get what he needed. Frankly Warrington considered Labate to be a moron. He was also just a little afraid of the guy. Jimmy and his like were clearly at Monitor for one reason—to enforce the no-sale policy. He'd heard rumors regarding how this was accomplished. There was the story about the broker who'd tried to jump to another firm who was beaten bloody with an office chair. There was the broker who was punched in the nose so hard they thought he was dead, and when he woke up, Jimmy threw him out on the street.

Then there was the little misunderstanding. Warrington had been told by several sources that Jimmy carried a weapon. He'd never actually seen it, but Jimmy often wore his knee-length leather jacket into the office, so who knew? A few weeks back, Warrington had looked up from his computer to see Jimmy standing just inches away, barking at him to open up his trading history. Now! Warrington had looked up at Jimmy and then down at his waistband, which was a few inches away. He could clearly make out the grip of a pistol tucked inside. He opened up his computer and showed that he hadn't made any trades in the last hour. Clearly Jimmy had thought he had violated the no-sale policy. Jimmy smiled and patted Warrington on the back. Warrington smiled, but only with his mouth. He hoped his eyes weren't revealing his mixed sense of fear and relief.

Mostly Jimmy was always in a lousy mood. He seemed to dislike just about everyone at Monitor except Cary Cimino. He certainly didn't like Jeffrey Pokross, who openly manipulated Jimmy whenever possible. And he was seriously paranoid. He would often be seen whispering to his pals in the hallway and stopping the conversation when Warrington walked by. He probably disliked Warrington, but at that moment, with those car keys sitting in front of him, Warrington decided that Jimmy's challenge was just business, nothing personal, and he went to work.

He began calling customers until he found one who was around. It was his friend at the Bank of Monaco. He made his usual pitch. He made it clear this would be a fast turn-around, but that his friend had to act quickly. He didn't guarantee the stock against a loss, but he did offer the guy substantial discount shares for his own personal use that amounted to a bribe. Naturally the guy—who was overseeing institutional money, which somehow was less personal than an individual's money—accepted.

Warrington filled out the buy ticket as Jimmy Labate watched. He hit the send button, and in minutes, the Bank of Monaco had purchased not 50,000, not 75,000, but 100,000 shares of Spaceplex, the next Disney World that was really just an amusement park on Long Island.

Jimmy Labate smiled and walked away, leaving the keys right where they were.

At lunch, Warrington walked downstairs and over to a spot in a parking garage down the street. In the corner sat a sea green Mercedes 580SL, brand-new. Warrington sat in the car and turned the ignition. It made a nice quiet sound that implied power and affluence, and it all belonged to Warrington.

The name of the company was Discovery Studios Inc. The idea went like this: create a chain of storefronts in malls across America to recruit potential models. It was to be a kind of *Star Search* for the next "it" girl, with aspirants paying fees to get their photos taken and sent off to a big name agency. The storefronts would also market Discovery Studios cosmetics and other beauty products, and would offer the Discovery Studios advice of "beauty consultants." Finalists would win contracts with big-league agencies in New York City.

It was all Warrington's idea. Warrington was still doing well with Cary and Jeffrey on new stock deals, but he felt it was time to personally branch out. It was time to be an entrepreneur.

This would surely be Warrington's way out of the office grind. By now he was officially a father, and he wanted to actually act like one. Francis Warrington Gillet IV was all of two months old. He'd been born May 21, 1996. Warrington was thirty-seven years old. It was time to get serious. No more fooling around. He wasn't going to be like his own father and hit the road for Palm Beach once the responsibilities of parenthood kicked in. He was going to do it right. That was his promise to little Warry the Fourth and to Warry's mother.

Discovery Studios was the key. He'd already scared up some big-money investors through Gillet family connections. He'd persuaded Cornacchia the Trivial Pursuit guy to dump some money into Discovery, and he'd convinced socialite Mary Lou Whitney, the doyenne of the Saratoga Springs set and former actress, to join his "beauty advisory committee." He also claimed to have two actual princesses—Bea Auersberg of Austria and Loretta Wittgenstein of Germany—signed up to help market Discovery Studios' beauty products overseas. Already it glittered with legitimacy.

He was also borrowing a page from the Jeffrey Pokross playbook; he was going to reverse merge the thing into another shell company, then pay off his former Monitor broker buddies to push it in the retail market. Cary Cimino had been very helpful with that, even recommending a new guy from a company called Thorcon Capital inside the World Trade Center.

The guy's name was Nick Vito, and he was very helpful. He had overseas customers and he was happy to promote Discovery, knowing full well it had no real assets and was not much more than a dream inside Warrington's imagination. All Nick wanted in return was some discount shares, preferably wired to certain bank accounts overseas. Warrington also offered to gift Nick free shares of restricted stock in Discovery equal to the number of shares Nick could convince his clients to buy. This provided Nick with an enormous incentive to convince his clients to buy stock in Discovery. If the clients bought a hundred thousand shares, Nick Vito would get a hundred thousand free shares in Discovery. Of course, Nick would not be mentioning anything about free shares to clients.

On a sweltering afternoon in July 1996, Warrington made his way downtown to Thorcon's office the World Trade Center. When he arrived, Warrington made it clear to Nick that it was time to move on the Discovery stock. He said several other broker dealers were getting ready to make a market for the stock, and that it was now or never for Nick Vito to jump on board.

"What's in it for me?" Nick asked.

"This is a gray area," Warrington replied. "I know I'm not supposed to be giving you cash or stocks. Do you have an overseas account?"

The plan was simple. Warrington arranged for a Swiss banker he knew to wire money into Nick Vito's brokerage account in the Bahamas after Nick got his clients to buy Discovery stock. Back and forth they went about precisely how to do this, and after all the dancing around, Warrington suddenly started speaking in plain, declarative sentences whose intentions were clear. The payment would be worth 30 percent of the value of however much Discovery stock Nick convinced his clients to buy.

Warrington preferred that it be in cash. Thirty percent was the best he could do because he owed a percentage to Cary.

Nick was very helpful. He suggested that the Swiss bank could set up a consulting agreement with him to justify the

payment. Warrington said no way. Instead he promised that
the Swiss bank would transfer the money from a bank in the
Bahamas to Nick's account in the Bahamas one day after
the Discovery stock purchases were settled. And he brought
up the free restricted stock idea, making sure to remind
Nick not to mention this little side arrangement to the National Association of Securities Dealers. They had already
been giving Warrington headaches about the Discovery Studios stock offerings, and headaches he didn't need. He made
sure to add that it would probably be best if they didn't mention the free stock to their mutual acquaintance, the guy
who'd introduced them.

Nick agreed. Warrington's foray into the world of the
entrepreneur was under way. In no time at all, girls across
America would be signing up at their local malls to become the next big discovery. It was Warrington's way of
spreading around the wealth and fame. It was his little gift
to America.

Spring 1996

The morning Accessible Software went public, it opened at
$1, about twice what the wives of DMN's partners had paid.
This did not make the front page of the *Wall Street Journal.* Accessible Software of New Jersey was not exactly a
household name, but the word on the over-the-counter bulletin boards was that it was hot. The company as presented
seemed like a brilliant idea. It claimed to have designed and
developed large computer application systems that acted as
management software for companies. Run your business by
computer program. DMN had arranged a private placement
deal that allowed certain qualifying insiders—close relatives—to acquire 1 million shares of Accessible without a
holding period. Most of the stock was purchased by the

wives of DMN's partners. Now Jeffrey Pokross just needed somebody to make a market for Accessible and sell the stuff.

Until now Pokross had traipsed from corrupt brokerage to corrupt brokerage, searching for enthusiastic stockbrokers and stock promoters willing to hype whatever nonsensical company was put in front of them for exorbitant hidden fees, otherwise known as bribes. This was becoming tedious and dangerous. Every time you did this you ran into a new crime family. It was getting like the garbage business out there. Jeffrey decided it was time for a new approach. It was no time to take over a brokerage house and make it DMN Capital's own, and Jeffrey even had the perfect candidate in mind—a small boutique outfit in Philadelphia called Monitor Investments.

Always the opportunist, Jeffrey had run into the owner of Monitor, William Palla, who'd told him he was very interested in opening an office in New York City. Nothing was that simple. Palla informed Jeffrey that he'd heard that to make a good living in the world of pump and dump, you required certain friends. Jeffrey agreed that this was true and said he might be able to help out. Pokross then met with Robert Lino, and it was agreed that grabbing on to Monitor and squeezing it like a grapefruit was the best possible option. It was decided that the newly acquired Monitor would get its feet wet hyping Accessible Software's initial public offering.

Within minutes of opening, Accessible began to take off. By the close of business, it was selling at $9 a share. The wives quickly sold 120,000 shares to retail customers and made a fortune. The brokers at Monitor who did the heavy lifting pocketed huge undisclosed commissions. In one twenty-four-hour period, the three DMN partners— Jeffrey Pokross, James Labate, and Salvatore Piazza— cleared $500,000 in profit. They still had a lot of stock left over when regulators halted trading of Accessible.

When it resumed trading, they stopped the manipulation and went legit. The gamble paid off. The regulators walked away and the stock held around $7. DMN and Monitor were a marriage made in Wall Street heaven. Robert Lino and the Bonanno crime family got their share and everyone was happy, but there was a little problem. When Jeffrey and Robert had decided to take over Monitor, they did not know that—once again—one of the principals already had a relationship with another crime family, a guy named Ron.

Ron was somehow related to a guy who knew a guy in the Gambino family. At least that was how it was explained to Robert Lino when his presence was requested at a sit-down with a Gambino soldier named Johnny R. This guy Ron claimed Robert had stolen $75,000 from Monitor and a solution had to be reached. When the time came for the meeting, Robert Lino showed, along with Jeffrey Pokross and Jimmy Labate and Jimmy's friend in the Gambino family, Johnny R, showed as well, but Ron did not. He'd changed his mind and relocated to Florida.

This did not please the Gambino family. This absence of complainant made them look bad, which in turn made them feel bad. They left the meeting in a huff, then later reached out to Jimmy Labate and demanded he come to yet another meeting, a proposition that made Jimmy quite nervous. The Gambino family was insistent, and also insisted that Robert Lino be present as well to put the dispute on record with the Bonanno group. This time they met in Manhattan. Lino sat down with a soft-spoken captain in the Gambino family named Mikey Scars DiLeonardo, who was said to be quite close to the Gotti family and was believed to be a fan of compromise. Although Gotti had been convicted and was slowly dying in prison, he still ran the family and had to be recognized.

During the meeting with Mikey Scars, Robert Lino admitted right away that he had, in fact, taken over Monitor and that he wasn't about to walk away. DiLeonardo insisted that Lino owed $75,000 to the Gambino family. Lino admitted taking all the money and sending it on to the Bonanno crime family. But he didn't see it as "stealing," at least not from the Gambino family. He offered, as a token of "respect," to pay the Gambino family $17,000 and have them walk away.

"That is an insult," said Mikey Scars.

He was flexible. He offered more reasons why the Bonanno family needed to pay the Gambino family money, as soon as possible. Jimmy Labate, who was supposedly associated with a Gambino soldier, had neglected to forward anything to his boss when the guy went away to prison. This was considered an extreme breach of etiquette, and DiLeonardo, a man of reason, suggested that Labate could be the conduit for a $20,000 payment to the Gambino family come Christmas. All of this talk was businesslike, like a company merger, or two money managers discussing bonds versus derivatives. Robert Lino and Mikey Scars were nothing like Jimmy Labate. They both believed that reason and accommodation worked well, as long as everybody looked good and nobody walked away with an empty wallet. On this day, their approach prevailed. Monitor became an asset for both Robert Lino and Mikey Scars.

CHAPTER TWENTY-TWO

May 1996

Bill Palla sat in Jeffrey Pokross's wood-paneled office at DMN Capital with the Illinois State University diploma on the wall. Palla was the CEO of Monitor Investment Group, but he was anything but in charge. He was the front man, the guy installed by the guy, the name on the paperwork. He was sitting before his real bosses, Jeffrey Pokross, Salvatore Piazza, and Jimmy Labate, and he was holding several certified letters, all of which were sent personally to him but none of which had he bothered to answer.

He was explaining to Jeffrey and Jimmy and Sal that the letters were from the National Association of Securities Dealers (NASD) enforcement unit.

"They want me to come in for an interview," Palla said.

"Maybe you should find out what they want instead of ignoring five certified letters," said Jeffrey, clearly not amused.

The morning Palla showed up at DMN, Monitor Investment Group was the company the investing public dealt with without realizing it was really dealing with DMN. To the investing public, DMN did not exist. Investors saw

Monitor letterhead, Monitor monthly statements, Monitor telephone help lines. As far as they could see, Monitor appeared as a multimillion-dollar Wall Street success story. In reality, Monitor was one big fraud concealing another.

For Jeffrey, Sal, Jimmy and the bosses of the Bonanno crime family, Monitor was perfect. Jeffrey had long sought an unrestricted brokerage outside the New York area that he could call his own. He wanted something off the regulatory radar screen where he could hire his own brokers and promoters, where he could run the show from behind a legitimate front.

So far, it had worked well. During the months DMN secretly controlled Monitor, Pokross, Piazza and Labate had made millions of dollars off of a handful of bogus stocks—Accessible Software, Spaceplex, Reclaim, Beachport and any number of assorted and sundry capers Jeffrey could dream up. DMN had made $1.2 million on Reclaim alone. At its peak, Monitor had one hundred brokers (some licensed, some not) and three offices in New York City. It was a symphony of schemes, with brokers pumping up stock in unison. Pokross was even able to get his sister, Jody, a job at Monitor as an executive assistant. In less than a year, Monitor had helped make DMN a growing business.

Much of the reason for Monitor's success could be laid at the feet of Cary Cimino. For a year he'd worked his tail off for Jeffrey and Sal and Jimmy, hustling up legitimate brokers who were willing to take bribes to hype house stock. For a year he'd made Jeffrey and Sal and Jimmy a lot of money. He gave himself much of the credit for this. He estimated that he himself was the top earner at DMN, and he believed that without him, Monitor and DMN would never have existed in the first place.

As Cary saw it, he was the man behind the millions. It was he who'd introduced Jeffrey Pokross to Todd Nejaime, who in turn introduced Jeffrey to the guy who owned Monitor down in Pennsylvania. It was he who'd produced

Warrington Gillet, the rich WASP stockbroker he'd found in St. Bart's on New Year's Eve. In the year Warrington did business with Cary, he'd brought in major investors who routinely bought huge chunks of stock. He had his Maryland horse country pals and their blue-blooded cash, but he also had contacts with overseas bankers who were always willing to help out—for a fee.

Cary figured that between Todd and Warrington, the partners at DMN Capital would make millions this year.

He figured they owed him big-time.

"It was a stock promoter's dream—an unrestricted broker/dealer based outside of the scrutiny of New York City," Cary remembered. "Albeit the company had no sales force, but since it was unrestricted, it could grow as fast as Jeffrey could fill it up with his friends. They could make an enormous amount of money with a sales force who came from firms known to make markets in high-commission, low-quality stocks called chop stocks. Brokers from these firms could be expected to be more interested in chop stocks than a broker from an NYSE firm. Once fully operational, with a sales force, Pokross could supply his friends with large amounts of shares, many of which he owned directly or indirectly, with high commissions."

But of course, it couldn't last.

A few weeks after the certified letters from NASD showed up, the phone call came from the NASD. Somehow despite Jeffrey Pokross's best efforts to keep it off the radar screen, the NASD had noticed Reclaim and Accessible and Spaceplex and all the rest, and connected the up-and-down pattern to Monitor. The phone call was notification of a formal NASD challenge.

Monitor had a choice. They could fight the challenge, and subject themselves to scrutiny with document production and depositions and all the rest. Or they could fold their cards and go away. The choice was obvious. By the end of the business day, Monitor had notified the NASD that it would voluntarily cease trading and market-making operations immediately.

The plug was pulled on Monitor.

"On the surface Monitor showed all the signs of legitimacy," Cary recalled, "but in the background, it was a scam."

Still, DMN stayed out of the sun, and Jeffrey Pokross—as always—had a new plan. Days after Monitor shut down on June 12, 1996, Jeffrey flew to Florida to meet with the head of another brokerage he was all excited about—Meyers Pollack. They were up and running with a whole stable of corrupt brokers ready to push the next stock, Innovative Medical Services. It was easy money—a San Diego company that purported to sell water filtration devices for pharmacies. They intended to raise $4 million. Monitor was just starting to work that one when the NASD spoiled the party. No matter. Meyers Pollock could handle it.

When Innovative Medical Services began trading in August 1996 under the symbol PURE, it opened at $4. By day's end, the brokers of Meyers Pollock had done what the brokers of Monitor could no longer do—they had driven the price up to $7 per share.

Monitor's demise was but a speed bump on the autobahn to instant affluence.

October 10, 1996

Jeffrey Pokross emerged from the PATH train into the station deep inside the World Trade Center concourse. He was just one of the millions of salary-earners streaming out of New Jersey into the New York City morning to earn their daily bread. The place was, as usual, like a cattle yard, a sea of hardworking humanity fueled by caffeine and driven by the desire to make money. The commodities exchange was here. Numerous brokerage houses were up in the twin towers. Wall Street was just a few blocks away. Jeffrey Pokross, like the rest of the crowd, trudged along, the latest stock DMN was pushing weighing heavily on his mind.

The stock was called Crystal Broadcasting. He'd gotten the deal from a soldier in the Bonanno crime family who'd been referred over by Robert Lino. The guy wanted a 50/50 split, and that wasn't a problem. The stock wasn't really a problem either. Anything even resembling communications was selling these days. Pokross's biggest pressure was assembling an army of corrupt brokers to push Crystal on the unsuspecting investing public.

After a few false starts, everything seemed to be going as planned. True, Monitor had imploded and Meyers Pollock hadn't worked out. There was some dispute with the Genovese crime family over who got to run the place and Jeffrey had been forced out the door. But he and Sal and Jimmy were now working on taking over another brokerage, also in the Philadelphia area, this one called First Liberty. Forget about the WASPy names. This one even had a taste of the Founding Fathers thrown in.

Also they still had some of the old high-producers from Monitor like Cary Cimino and Todd Nejaime and Warrington Gillet. But the best news was a new prospect that seemed quite promising named Jeff Morrison, working out of One World Trade Center. His firm was called Thorcon Capital, which was where Jeffrey was headed now.

Morrison had come to DMN a few months back, recommended by Cary Cimino. He'd made it clear what he was willing to do.

"He said he was looking for some stocks that he can put out to some wealthy clients that he has and he can hold on to those stocks for an extended period of time," Pokross recalled. "And for doing that, he was looking to get a bribe. I thought it was great. We ended up constructing a deal on this Crystal Broadcasting where he would put out the stock to his wealthy clients, he wouldn't disclose that he was getting a bribe, and we sent him some stock in Crystal Broadcasting in advance—anticipating that he would do a lot more business. We sent him some stock that he can just hold on to that he can just pay the bribe, pay himself the bribe as he continued to book more stock to his customers."

So far DMN had sent Morrison nine thousand shares of Crystal, trading around $5 through something called a depository trust company. Morrison had sold off about two thousand of those shares. Jeffrey looked at the business he was doing with Thorcon as an investment of sorts. He believed that Jeff Morrison would be ready to do more deals when Crystal Broadcasting was over, which was one of the subjects he hoped to broach when he arrived at Thorcon's offices.

As he emerged from the PATH station into the concourse itself, he noticed Jeff Morrison walking toward him with another guy he didn't know. The concourse was a maddening place, with people streaming in every direction simultaneously, so Jeffrey couldn't even be sure the guy was with Morrison. That's why it didn't seem strange when Morrison walked right up to him smiling. What did seem strange was that the guy walking next to Morrison was holding a gold badge out in front of him.

"Jeffrey Pokross?" the guy asked, and Pokross didn't respond. "I'm Special Agent True Brown of the FBI. This is Special Agent Joe Yastremski."

The guy with the badge was pointing right at Jeff Morrison of Thorcon Capital when he said this, and Jeffrey Pokross suddenly understood everything.

December 1996

The holding cell next to the fifth-floor magistrate's courtroom in the Southern District of New York is a pretty antiseptic place. There are no windows. The walls are pale gray-blue concrete and there's about enough room for one dozen defendants. That's what you are when you're in that room—a defendant. You might be a drug dealer from the projects, a terrorist from the slums of Egypt, a lawyer gone bad or—as was the case this morning—a busted stock-broker. It didn't matter. You were a defendant. At least you weren't an inmate, yet. That was still only a possibility because when you sat outside the magistrate's courtroom, waiting for your turn, you were still considered merely charged with a crime. Not convicted. Just charged.

This distinction was on Cary Cimino's mind when he saw Jeffrey Pokross sitting at the other end of the cell. It was a pretty unusual sight, seeing Jeffrey there under these circumstances. It made it seem more real, tougher to ignore. The whole scene didn't seem right. Cary always pictured jail cells full of people like Snoop Dog or Humphrey Bogart or Jimmy Labate. Tough guys. Not like this, a cell full of stockbrokers. A cell where your cellmate is named Jeffrey Pokross.

"This is your fault," Jeffrey hissed, and the two of them began screaming at each other until a marshal came and told them to shut up.

Cary decided merely to glower at Jeffrey, who glowered back approximately the same amount.

As far as Cary could tell, the charges filed against him seemed somewhat vague. It appeared he had violated some specific provisions of the United States Criminal Code regarding securities fraud. Specifically he had bribed brokers to hype stock, and received bribes in the form of hidden commissions. Cary couldn't decide whether this was serious or not. He certainly did not enjoy sitting in the holding cell inside federal court, but the complaint he'd been shown seemed laughable, as if they were charging him with having too many parking tickets. What they were charging him with was as common a practice in the over-the-counter market as any.

Cary also tried unsuccessfully to remember who'd introduced him to Jeffrey Morrison of Thorcon Capital. Cary was aware that he was the one who had put Thorcon with DMN, but he couldn't really blame himself. Thorcon seemed so real. Jeff Morrison talked the talk. How was Cary supposed to know the guy was FBI?

That was certainly his reaction when the FBI had first knocked on his door at 6:30 a.m. that morning. At first he couldn't figure which broker turned him in, but the more he thought about it the more Thorcon seemed the likely suspect. It was too perfect. Jeff Morrison was too willing to help out. If only Cary had hesitated, but then why would he? The guy was just another broker with a deal. That was the way Wall Street worked, wasn't it?

Jeffrey was led out of the cell first for his appearance before the magistrate, and then it was Cary's turn. As he stepped out into the courtroom, he was confused.

Usually the uniforms of life make it easy to tell who is who and where you are in the food chain. You can tell the real estate broker selling the house is the woman with the floppy hat and clipboard. The manager at the Kmart wears the short-sleeve button-down shirt and clip-on tie, while his minions wear ludicrous matching smocks emblazoned with the Kmart logo. Here in the courtroom, some distinctions were obvious. The judge wore a black robe and sat above everyone else, letting everybody know who was in charge. There was one guy dressed in a pale blue jumpsuit with laceless rubber-soled shoes. His hands were cuffed behind him and he had two big guys in suits sitting next to him. Cary guessed that he was a real criminal and the guys next to him were marshals. Beyond these two, it was tough to tell who was who.

Specifically, it was tough to tell the lawyers from the clients. Most of those arrested were stockbrokers, and most had been arrested on their way to work. They still wore their suits, which made them look just like the lawyers paid to defend them. The difference was that none of the stock-brokers had ties or belts or laces in their shoes. The marshals frowned on suicide attempts while in United States custody.

Cary wasn't quite sure what to expect. His experience with the court system until this day was limited. He'd once had a beef with a guy over money owed on a parking space. He'd been parking his Mercedes there, and an attendant also let him leave his motorcycle. Then the owner started claiming he owed back rent. Cary spirited his car out of the garage, and then tried to get his motorcycle. When they guy threatened to kick his ass, Cary returned with one of Jimmy Labate's friends and a gun. The guy let him take the motorcycle and then called the cops.

That case had been settled in state court without anything going on Cary's record. This was different. This was federal. Cary calculated how much money he would have to spend on lawyers.

His lawyer, Michael Bachner, was as experienced at criminal defense as any lawyer doing regular work at the Manhattan Federal Court. He told Cary not to sweat it, and arranged with the prosecutor for his release on low bail bond—$50,000, with no cash down. He just had to get two friends or family to cosign the bond by the following week. He did have to surrender his passport and would have to ask the government's permission to travel outside the New York City area, but otherwise he was free to go. This wasn't serial murder or racketeering or even narcotics. This was obscure white collar crime, and difficult to understand at that. When he was finished filling out all the paperwork, getting his mug shot, cleaning the fingerprint ink off his fingers, Cary decided he would call up DMN first thing and make an appointment with is codefendant, Jeffrey Pokross.

Jeffrey agreed that a sit-down in a setting other than the holding cell in Manhattan Federal Court was a not a bad idea.

The two met at DMN's Hanover Square office and went over their respective complaints. Jeffrey, too, had been released on low bail. Jeffrey's lawyer was telling him the same thing Cary's was—the case is a joke. They'd fight it and win. The more they discussed the situation, the better Cary felt.

The two men tried to figure out how many people they knew of the forty-four who were picked up by the FBI in the bust. They recognized about a dozen names. That indicated to them that whatever they were allegedly doing on Wall Street was hardly unusual. Three dozen strangers were doing the same thing. Jeffrey argued that spending money on a good lawyer was a sound investment. They would surely walk away from this without any trace of criminality on their record.

Cary felt Jeffrey knew what he was talking about. He'd spent a lot of time around people who'd actually been to prison, so he could talk about strong cases and weak cases. Jeffrey said all the feds had was the FBI undercover, Morrison, and maybe some taped conversations. They'd still have to show that Cary and Jeffrey actually knew they were breaking the law when they made deals with Thorcon Capital. That wouldn't be so easy. Surely the charges would be dismissed. They just had to be. The Wall Street boom was just beginning to really take off, and Jeffrey and Cary did not want to be left behind.

Certainly not by a little arrest.

October 10, 1996

Again and again Warrington was trying to get Cary on the phone. No answer. He'd just seen a headline float by on CNBC about a bunch of brokers being busted, and though there weren't any names given, there was one troubling mention—Thorcon Capital.

The news reports were brief because the story was considered hardly worth mentioning. The reporters on TV didn't even seem to understand why anybody had been charged with a crime. It all seemed so inconsequential. And best of all from Warrington's perspective was the fact that there was no mention of people like Jimmy Labate.

Mostly Warrington was trying to remember precisely what he'd done with Nick Vito down at Thorcon Capital versus what he'd talked about doing. He couldn't really remember but he wasn't that concerned. Why should he be? He hadn't been arrested. If he'd done something truly illegal, surely they would have picked him up with the forty-four others mentioned on TV.

Finally he got through to Cary and he was surprised by how calm the guy was. Cary told him Jeffrey Pokross and Todd Nejaime and a few other guys he knew from Monitor had all been picked up in one big sweep. He described getting fingerprinted and photographed and appearing before the judge, and he made it sound like *Bill and Ted's Excellent Adventure*. There he was with all these real criminals— drug dealers, gangsters, money launderers. He was released on $50,000 bond and didn't have to put down a cent. As Cary saw it, the whole thing was ridiculous. He made it clear that after his initial shock at being arrested by an agent of the United States government, he and Jeffrey had decided there was no way any of these pathetic charges were going to stick. Cary made it clear to Warrington that he and Jeffrey were going to fight and they were both going to win.

Warrington was more than a little upset. Mostly he wanted to know all about Thorcon Capital. Was the whole thing an FBI sting? Yes, it was, Cary said. From the World Trade Center office to the receptionist answering the phones to the plastic flowers in the corner with the bug inside, the whole thing was a production of the Federal Bureau of Investigation. Everybody there was an undercover FBI agent. It had shut down the morning of the arrests. Cary had worked his deal with a guy named Jeff Morrison, who was really Special Agent Joe Yastremski.

Warrington got a sick feeling his stomach. What was Nick Vito's real name?

He couldn't figure out why Cary had been picked up and he hadn't. It must have been a different scenario, a different fact pattern. Cary's arrangements with Jeff Morrison must have been different than Warrington's deal with Nick Vito. What had he said to Nick? What had he done? The Discovery Studios deal had collapsed and Warrington had never actually wired any shares to Nick under any of the circumstances they'd discussed. Was discussing something illegal itself illegal? Or did you actually have to do something? He had no idea, but Cary told him he had nothing to worry about.

That sounded pretty good to Warrington. He decided not to give Thorcon Capital another thought.

CHAPTER TWENTY-THREE

February 12, 1997

The shiny black cars pulled into the parking lot at the pier in the far end of Brooklyn. It was dark and the wind whipped in off New York Harbor. This was miles from Little Italy. This was Canarsie, which is an Indian name, though there hadn't been too many Indians in the neighborhood for a while. Two groups of men exited the black cars and greeted each other in the parking lot before turning and heading into a restaurant called Abbraciemento's.

The restaurant was perfect for a sit-down. It was located on a pier that jutted out into the swirling mouth of New York Harbor, a no-exit cul-de-sac that allowed patrons to sit with their backs against the water and see anybody coming into the lot. It was not *A Tree Grows in Brooklyn* or *Arsenic and Old Lace* or even *Dog Day Afternoon* Brooklyn. It was a part of Brooklyn that hadn't found its way to the silver screen, and probably wouldn't anytime soon.

The receptionist at Abbraciemento's was accommodating in every possible way. Both groups of men were ushered quickly to a corner table where there was enough room for the Bonanno crime family of New York to sit across from the Genovese crime family of New York. It was time for a little gangster détente.

Robert and Frank Lino were there with a six foot four inch associate named Eugene Lombardo. They were there to represent the interests of the Bonanno group. Representing the interests of the Genovese group was Ernest Montevecchi and two of his associates. Nobody called him Ernest. Everybody called him Butch. The matter at hand was simple: who gets what on Wall Street.

When Robert Lino first showed up on Wall Street as a silent partner at DMN, Jeffrey Pokross had promised that only a handful of wiseguys knew about the money to be made there. He'd mentioned Philly Abramo and claimed the other families were clueless. That was true, as far as it went, and for a time it was one golden opportunity after another for the up-and-coming organized crime family named after the disgraced boss Joe Bonanno. It was surely a way for the only Mafia family in history to allow an FBI agent to infiltrate its ranks to recover its good name in the underworld. Wall Street was the hills of California in 1849, and it was all theirs. This was, for a time, good news for Robert Lino. Robert Lino was convinced he'd found El Dorado, and so he enthusiastically convinced his captain and cousin, Frank, to get involved in the Wall Street miracle.

But Robert was ambitious. He'd found another brokerage called Meyers Pollock Robbins through one of his second cousins, Eugene Lombardo, the six foot four inch street guy with the knee-length leather jacket. Eugene believed himself to be a man of finance. He carried at least two cell phones at all times, and was on one or both at any given moment. Lombardo was not an actual member of an organized crime family, although he yearned to be one. He was just a lowly associate, but he had found Meyers Pollock all by himself, and he saw it as a way to win himself a promotion into the Bonanno crime group. Meyers Pollock had all the trappings of a legitimate brokerage house. Headquarters on the ninety-first floor of the World Trade Center, branch offices at 100 Wall Street and in suburban New Hyde Park. It was perfect, and now the Bonanno family had two guys in two Wall Street houses, pumping and dumping to their hearts content.

It was too good to last. In months, it was clear to Robert Lino that just about every tiny brokerage house with a WASP name had a guy named Tony or Vinnie working behind the scenes. They were everywhere: Joseph Stephens, White Rock Partners, J. W. Barclay, A. R. Baron, D. H. Blair & Co. At any given moment, wiseguy brokers both licensed and otherwise would drift from one of these firms to the other, leaving when they got too many customer complaints. There were more wiseguys wandering in and out of these firms than at the Ravenite. It was clear that soon conflict would visit Meyers Pollock.

The problem with Meyers Pollock was Eugene Lombardo. Most of the time he was all bluster and blather, but he had an unfortunate habit of throwing his weight around in front of people. He seemed to believe that humiliating a subordinate was not effective if it was done in private. Lombardo became an issue when Pollock was having problems with a stockbroker named Jonathan who ran Meyers's office in New Hyde Park. Jonathan didn't seem to understand that the company he was now working for was run by gangsters. He certainly was happy to pocket the cash bribes forwarded his way, but he did not like to be lectured by guys he believed to be inferior to him. They were farther down the evolutionary scale; he was at the top. He operated under the misconception that intellectual superiority trumps physical threat. All he wanted was to be left alone to make money and keep his end of the scam running.

His job was to push a company called HealthTech, which purported to run a string of upscale workout gyms in Texas and Arizona. It traded under the symbol GYMM.

To pump up GYMM, Jonathan had recruited a number of brokers who weren't controlled by Lombardo. They far outproduced those under Lombardo's wing. He then tried to fire Lombardo's brokers. Jonathan the broker insisted that he had the "right" to fire unproductive brokers. Lombardo's response was simple. He leaned his six-foot-four frame forward in the conference room of Meyers Pollock in front of a roomful of people and slapped Jonathan the broker in the face.

Jonathan the broker did not pull out a .38 and shoot Eugene Lombardo in the forehead. He did not reach for a baseball bat or pull a shiv to avenge his compromised manhood. He sucked it up, for the moment. Eugene Lombardo was a big guy, allegedly backed up by an organized crime family. Jonathan the broker knew that. But something had to be done. He couldn't let this insult go. The solution was obvious. If a big guy smacks you, get another big guy to smack him back.

Jonathan the broker made a decision. He reached out to another guy he knew who was with the Genovese crime family. That guy's name was Butch.

Now, in a corporate setting, this would be like going over your boss's head to complain about your boss. It was a maneuver fraught with danger. But Jonathan the broker decided his manhood was worth it, and so he called upon Butch Montevecchi, a soldier in the Genovese crime family, to fix things up. A sit-down was arranged at Abbraciemento's in Canarsie.

Pleasantries were exchanged. Butch Montevecchi was an affable silver-haired guy from the West Side who was known for his connections to Russian organized crime. He was considered tough but reasonable. The Bonannos were coming into this little dispute at an advantage because they already had control of Meyers Pollock, but it was always better to have control of something nobody else knew about. And the Genovese family was not to be taken lightly.

They were considered the stealth family, run by the quietly ruthless old boss Gigante. Now that Jonathan the broker had let them know all about Meyers Pollock, the Genovese family wasn't going anywhere.

In between the plates of antipasto and gnocchi, a compromise emerged. It would be simple: both families would chop up Meyers Pollock, bleed it dry, and walk away. Jonathan the broker would think he'd received some form of retribution because Eugene Lombardo would be told to stay away from him. Now Jonathan was put with the Genovese family, who could treat him however they wished. In a way, there was even more pressure on Jonathan because he now had not one but two mob families looking to make money, which only meant that more money needed to be made.

Soon the conference at Abbraciemento's was over. Everybody shook hands all around. The Linos and Eugene Lombardo went their way, Butch and his associates went the other way. Everybody was happy. The gangsters had achieved a first—a brokerage house selling stock to unsuspecting investors across America was now attached to not one but two separate sets of organized criminals. It was just a new version of the New York/New Jersey waterfront being divided up. That was the whole reason organized crime was organized—to eliminate unnecessary conflict so everybody got his share. There was plenty for all. Wall Street was an endless supply of other people's money.

June 6, 1997

At 2:45 in the afternoon on a beautiful June day, Eugene Lombardo had one of his ubiquitous cell phones pressed to his ear. His friend, Claudio Iodice, was boiling like a teakettle down in Boca.

"Where are you now?" Lombardo asked.

"Where am I now?" Iodice screeched. "I'm in the

middle of the biggest fucking aggravation, motherfucker. We're going to Arizona. As soon as I get this guy's home address, we're on a plane to Arizona."

Eugene had heard this kind of thing before from Claudio, who was a fairly emotional guy. Claudio didn't know much about doing things in moderation. He owned a 1997 thirty-two-foot Powerplay speedboat and had made millions with a bogus consulting firm in Boca Raton called Equities Consulting Group. Pretty much anything could set him off. Eugene was considered a bit of a hothead, but compared to Claudio Iodice, he was Gandhi.

Once again Claudio was having problems with the CEO of HealthTech, a guy named Gordon Hall. Gordon was very frustrating. Eugene was pretty sure HealthTech was going to make everybody a lot of money. It was a good scheme. They were using a string of workout gyms in Texas and Arizona and Oregon to claim they were selling the next Bally's. At the time, national workout chains were burning up the market. All they had to do was overstate the assets a bit, such as by 80 percent, and soon they would all be rich. That, anyway, was the plan as imagined by Eugene Lombardo.

Meyers Pollock had handled all the brokers and promoters, cold-calling senior citizens and plastering the bulletin boards on the Internet with hyperventilation about Health-Tech. On New Year's Eve, 1997, HealthTech was selling for 87 cents per share. A day later it was selling for $1.34 per share. The trading volume had jumped 250 percent. Only a month before 642,000 shares of HealthTech were traded. In January 1997, the number blasted to the sky—2.3 million shares traded under the SIC code GYMM. In exchange, HealthTech's CEO, Gordon Hall, had transferred two hundred thousand shares of HealthTech to a fake consulting company owned by Lombardo called N.A. Promotional Services—free of charge. Another one hundred thousand shares showed up in the accounts of N.A. Promotional in

February 1997. Lombardo and Iodice, who was responsible for recruiting corrupt brokers in Florida to pump up Health-Tech, split the profits. N.A. Promotional allowed Lombardo to claim he'd been hired by HealthTech as a financial consultant, when in reality he was more an organized crime consultant.

For Lombardo, this was better than hijacking truckloads of women's bathrobes out at Kennedy Airport or milking the proceeds of Joker Poker. Between January and April, he sold all 200,000 shares of his free HealthTech stock for $430,000 in pure profit, kicking up a percentage to the Bonanno family as required. He and his partners then repeated the scam with HealthTech warrants, with Lombardo, Iodice and another co-conspirator selling off warrants they'd received for free for a breathtaking profit of $900,000.

"Let's forget everybody," Iodice was saying. "Let's go right to his house. That's it. He can't pull that stock certificate. There's no money. They got a buy in there on Wednesday. That's it. The whole game is over."

"What happened now?" Lombardo replied. "Tell me what happened."

The problem was Gordon Hall, who was sick of dealing with Claudio and Eugene and had ripped up half the certificates for the warrants he'd gifted to the two of them.

"And there's nothing you could do?"

"Forget about it," Iodice complained. "I'm gonna end up getting them thrown in jail for this today. I told the other guy, you don't find him in fifteen minutes, I said, 'Do yourself a favor. I'm on my way to Arizona. Keep yourself outta the office because even if I just see you, you're fucking getting hit."

Lombardo did his best to calm down Iodice. He was aware that this kind of behavior, this paying visits to people's houses, was sometimes necessary but almost always bad policy. And at the very least, he needed to let the Linos know what was going on before anything unusual happened out in Arizona. This would not be easy. Iodice was steaming.

"I don't really care anymore," he said. "These fucking people are not making me out to be a fucking jerkoff. I'm tired of it. I ain't no fucking jerkoff! I never was somebody's jerkoff. I'm going to Arizona. I'm not going to his office. I'm going to his family's house."

"When do you want to go?"

"I wanna go today. I want to knock on his wife's door, kick it in, and fucking hold him hostage."

"You can't do that. Relax. You're flipping . . ."

"Oh *you* can't do that. Let *me* do that . . . I'm gonna fucking knife his family. He took away something I like, I'm taking away something he likes."

"Relax. Come on, relax."

"I'll call you back in a half hour when I got my tickets. If you want to come, you come. That's where I'm going. I got the address."

"Will you please calm down?"

Iodice hung up.

Somewhere in New York, an FBI agent wrote down in a log, "Wire 5105, Tape 38A, Call 49." Participants were listed as "Eugene Lombardo and Claudio Iodice." Anything they couldn't make out was listed as "UI" for unintelligible. The log was filled with similar notations, all of them involving conversations taking place over Eugene Lombardo's busy cell phones.

The more Lombardo talked, the more the FBI listened.

CHAPTER TWENTY-FOUR

July 1996

The day Cary Cimino learned that all the charges were going to be dropped he made sure to reach out to Jeffrey. It had gone just as Jeffrey had predicted. Jeffrey had told him to stick it out, that the case was weak, and then he'd proved it. He may have been arrested, a criminal complaint with his name on it had been drafted, but now it was as if nothing had ever occurred. It was tabula rasa. Clean slate. If he was filling out some job form and they asked him if he'd ever been convicted of a crime, he could say no.

Jeffrey had gone right back to work at DMN, the day after his arrest, and he hadn't stopped since. Cary couldn't do that. He'd truly been spooked by the entire procedure with the FBI agents and the court appearances and the long conversations with his criminal defense lawyer. He was just a little gun shy. He decided to stay away from DMN and only communicate by phone. No more hanging out hearing the stories of Jimmy Labate. Now it was strictly business. If Jeffrey needed people to push a stock, he could help. No matter how optimistic Jeffrey was about the whole thing, Cary's plan was to ease his way out of DMN within a year.

Besides, Jeffrey was swimming in deals. On most days at DMN, Jimmy Labate and his Mafia pals might stop in once or twice a week. Robert Lino would drop by weekly for his envelope. Brokers Jeffrey worked with would stop by to complain or demand more money. But everybody who stopped in to DMN was just passing through. The only one who was there each and every day from before seven in the morning until after eight at night was Jeffrey Pokross, the hardest working guy in the place.

Usually he worked two phones at once. Routinely he screamed at his sister, his partners, anybody who walked into his office. That was how he did business. Never talking, always screaming. Nothing was ever going right for him. The amount of time to execute a sale, the spreadsheet information handed to him by an assistant, the presence of too much cream in his coffee—all of this made him irritable, even more so than before he was arrested.

Sure he'd walked away from the ordeal with nothing on his record. He'd told Sal and Jimmy that even if he'd been forced to plead guilty, the amount of money was low enough that the rules governing prison sentences would have allowed him to receive a sentence of probation only. He wouldn't have had to do a day in jail no matter what. But he felt the charges were bogus and demanded that they be dismissed. He'd advised Cary Cimino to do the same. Surprising nearly everyone, they prevailed. All the charges against both Jeffrey and Cary were dropped by prosecutors in the Manhattan U.S. Attorney's white collar crime unit.

The *Wall Street Journal* reporter was a young girl named Peggy something, probably straight out of journalism school. The idea she was pitching to Cary was this: there were a lot of single guys working on the Street with money to burn, and she was interested in how they were burning it.

Cary took her on a tour of his new 2,100-square-foot Upper East Side condo, the one he was renovating. He claimed he planned to spend $700,000 to fix the place up. In the living room, he pointed out that the wall fixtures were candelabra that had been wired and fitted with lights. In the dining room, he showed her his Christofle china and silver for formal settings and his Wedgwood china for informal affairs. He made sure to let her know he had a separate set for his deck, which offered a stunning view of the island of Manhattan stretching all the way to the source of his wealth, Wall Street.

In his bedroom, he pointed out the antique box that held his TV set bolted into the ceiling. He mentioned that his girlfriend "loves everything," which gave him an opportunity to drop in that he owned Pratesi sheets. He showed off the rack of Brooks Brothers suits, the drawers of crisp white shirts, the wall of silk ties with designer names easily recognized by readers of the *Wall Street Journal*. The Boston University biology major presented a tour of his art collection. Cary was comfortable with conspicuous consumption, though it was likely a phrase he did not remember from economics 101.

"No one wants to live like they did in college. We are finding ourselves in our thirties and forties, single, with the means to live well," he said as the reporter scribbled furiously. "Everything in the den is Louis the Eighteenth and Charles the Tenth."

He claimed he would soon be hiring a design consultant to give him direction on how to decorate his bachelor pad. The consultant would be given a budget and instructed to fill his apartment with even more important works of art and only top-of-the-line home furnishings. Not that this was a home. Cary hardly spent any time there. He was always out wining and dining, shepherding this model and that model from Cipriani's to Lutece to Café Des Artistes.

In the kitchen, he told the reporter, "When I do get married, I will need a full formal kitchen. Now the caterer is really the only one who uses the kitchen. I have Cap'n Crunch and coffee in there."

He mentioned he knew people in the movie business, and that he was semiretired. He was not, he emphasized, a stockbroker. He was a "private investor."

She scribbled away. He felt he looked particularly good that morning because once he'd known that the *Journal* was interested in his story, he'd timed his weekly session in the tanning booth for the day before, plus he'd just returned from a week in Aspen. He kept waiting for her to ask about the arrests.

As they walked about the apartment, it appeared she didn't know about the arrests. He would have been happy to tell her all about it, but why disturb calm waters? If she had asked, he would have admitted that in fact he had been charged with certain felonies. But he could also have said that his lawyer quickly got a commitment from the United States attorney to drop all the charges, and within thirty days of the morning he was arrested, all the charges filed against him had been completely dismissed.

By now, Cary was aware that the whole business of Thorcon Capital had been a disaster for the federal government. When it was first announced, it was a big deal. All these government lawyers and agents had stood in front of cameras and expanded on the nefarious nature of this major conspiracy. The head of the Securities and Exchange Commission's enforcement unit even talked about honor.

"Billions of dollars change hands in our markets every day. They change hands on the honor of a broker's word and the trust that is placed not only in the broker, but also in the integrity of our market systems. The people who were arrested today have abused that trust. The consequences for abusing that trust must be severe."

Now all charges had been dropped against almost all of the forty-five defendants in what the FBI had called Operation Uptick—at least those who didn't plead out immediately and decided to stand and fight. Jeffrey Pokross and Cary had made a point of calling up everybody they knew to announce that their cases had been thrown out. They'd said the whole thing was nonsense and shouldn't prevent them from coming back to DMN. When Jeffrey started talking about a new deal, however, Cary wasn't listening.

The *Wall Street Journal* reporter seemed happy with the answers Cary provided. He answered all her questions and then took her business card. She said good-bye and Cary felt confident about the whole affair. He was, of course, taking a chance. If she knew all about the arrests and was just using this bachelor pad nonsense to get an interview, he'd be screwed. So far hardly anybody he knew was even aware of his arrest. His name hadn't made it into any of the stories written in the papers.

A few days later the article appeared on page B12 in the "Home Front" section under the headline "Bachelor Pads: Men Behaving Grandly." The author was listed as "Special to the Wall Street Journal," whatever that meant. It began, "Cary Cimino didn't see any reason to wait to get married to set up his dream home."

Cary had hit a home run. The article described his apartment, leaning heavily on the brand names. It described Cary as a "personal investor who has spent 15 years working on Wall Street." It was better than Cary could have hoped. There were several financial advisers and brokers mentioned, but he was the lead example. There was mention of the fact that the consultant he'd hired charged people $30 to $60 a week to have their plants watered. There was no mention whatsoever of Cary Cimino's arrest. Apparently the "special" reporter really didn't know a thing about it.

What a remarkable world. In his years on Wall Street, Cary Cimino had gone from being a Bear Stearns partner to a vice president at Oppenheimer to struggling in boiler rooms to making millions—more than he'd ever imagined—with DMN and Jeffrey Pokross and his Mafia pals. He'd even been arrested and cleared. Now here he was, in the pages of the *Wall Street Journal*, portrayed as one of New York's most eligible bachelors.

The phrase "crime doesn't pay" was all wrong. "Stupid crime doesn't pay" was more like it. Only stupid criminals got caught. If you were smart enough, you could walk away from anything. Now Cary Cimino was sure he could do anything he set his mind to, and nothing would stand in his way.

CHAPTER TWENTY-FIVE

On the July morning when the FBI knocked on his door, Francis Warrington Gillet III did not clearly understand the difference between regret and remorse. As he stood there listening to his former business buddy turned cold-hearted FBI agent explain to him in a friendly manner that he wouldn't have to wear handcuffs as he was escorted from the building out onto Central Park South, he probably believed he was experiencing remorse. More than likely, he was merely experiencing regret.

Regret always came first. It's easier to swallow. You don't have to admit to anything. Regret shows up in many costumes: regret at having been caught, regret at having not done certain things that could have meant not getting caught. And of course, regret at hanging around with certain people—Nick Vito, for instance—who clearly should have been avoided. Regret at having sullied your own good name, the name of your family, your father, your mother, your children, your nieces and nephews. Your war hero grandfather! Of course, regret about the nefarious effect you were having on your loved ones meant only one thing—remorse was on the way.

Francis Warrington Gillet III was escorted by the FBI from his exclusive address on Central Park South at the ungodly hour of 7 a.m., past the allegedly unseeing eyes of the doorman. Warrington had no idea what lay ahead. He had expected to wake up, brush his teeth, take a quick shower, shave and begin yet another day accumulating piles of money. He was a licensed stockbroker. He was a good guy. Now he was headed to court. It might even be a public courtroom, where people drift in and out, watching the spectacle of human failure unfold. His folly would soon become fodder for idle gossip. He had to think quickly.

He was taken to a room in Lower Manhattan, a section of the city he rarely visited. It was sort of near some clubs he'd partied in, but he hadn't spent any time here. His only experience with courts until this morning was jury duty. He remembered that. You put your life on hold for a day or two, then begged and whined until they let you go home. It was annoying but essentially harmless. This was certainly not going to be jury duty.

Inside a windowless room he answered questions about his background, his family, his financial assets. He was asked if he had ever been arrested and he practically laughed out loud. He confessed that he'd once had his license suspended when he'd twice made rights after stopping at a red light in Manhattan, something that's allowed in most places but not in New York. That was the extent of his experience with the criminal justice system in his thirty-seven years on the planet. No felonies, no misdemeanors. Not even a trace of youthful folly was evident in the file of Francis Warrington Gillet III. There was no file.

He was taken to another room with a sign on the glass door, "United States Marshal," and fingerprinted and photographed for the first time in his life. He tried to imagine what the photo looked like. Did he look like John Dillinger?

John Gotti? He hadn't shaved and was barely awake before dropping in on the United States marshals, so he had to assume he looked like Keith Richards after a tough night. He shuddered to think of that mug shot running in the newspaper for his mother and father to see.

He could fight the power. That would mean pleading not guilty and keeping his mouth shut. He'd have to hire an expensive lawyer and work out a deal where you write a check to the Securities and Exchange Commission, promise never to trade securities again and go back to acting school with a student loan. That was an option. But suppose there was no deal? Suppose they made you go to trial, and you faced a jury of angry Social Security recipients furious at their lousy investments. Suppose they found you guilty of all charges—even some you weren't aware of—and the judge sent you away to prison for forty years. Visions of old prison movies came to him. *Birdman of Alcatraz*. He'd end up like that guy, talking to sparrows. He nearly retched.

There was also option two: admit to everything you've done in your life and beg the court for mercy. Immerse yourself in remorse. This was much more complex than regret. If you admitted you'd done something terrible or bad or just stupid, and you even said it out loud to yourself while taking a shower or sitting alone drinking Scotch in the dark, you'd have made enormous progress. You'd have taken a huge step. But of course much more was required. To make it official, you had to make the admission in a public place, and ultimately to people you love. You must say it out loud and with simple noun-verb syntax—"I did something wrong."

But did he? When he was having those talks with Nick Vito/D. True Brown about a possible deal, it was all just possible, wasn't it? Had he really done anything that any other normal stock picker would not have done under the very same circumstances? He could certainly admit to whatever they needed him to admit to, just to avoid jail time, but then he'd have to live with himself. Was the great-stepgrandson of Marjorie Merriweather Post really a felon? The more he thought about it, the more confused he became.

Suddenly he thought of the original Francis Warrington Gillet.

Francis Warrington Gillet III, of course, was hardly an original. His grandfather was the original Francis, followed by his father, Francis Junior, and ultimately by his son, Francis the Fourth. His name had implications. He was burdened with the legacy of it; encouraged not to bring shame upon it. It wasn't easy. His grandfather—born on a frigid November day in 1895 in the port city of Baltimore, Maryland—set the bar high.

On April Fool's Day, 1917, the original Francis signed up for the United States Air Service. He wanted to learn how to fly. At the time, the United States had successfully stayed out of the great conflict raging from England to Russia. But that conflict wasn't going so well for the Allied Powers, and the United States was finding it more and more difficult to justify staying out of the mess. German submarines were making a regular practice of shooting at anything that tried to float across the Atlantic. Still, on April Fool's Day, the United States had yet to actually declare war against Germany. That wouldn't come for another week. The original Francis could not wait. He joined up.

A graduate of the University of Virginia and a son of privilege, the original Francis tried desperately to make it into the elite world of the flying ace. It was not to be. At that time you could learn to fire a gun, don a gas mask and slog it out in the trenches at the age of twenty-one, but you could not fly. He was declared too young to be commissioned, and so he did what many other young men of his time did—he headed for Canada, not to dodge but to seek the life of the soldier. He joined the Royal Flying Corps by telling a lie. He was no longer the original Francis. Now he was Frederick Warrington Gillet.

Now a lie is a lie is a lie, but it could be argued that there is such a thing as a good lie. The original Francis clearly had nothing but good intentions when he pretended to be someone else so he could participate in the mighty battle against evil. He was committing a lie for the greater good. And as a result, he was allowed to join and learn to fly. Off he went to England to begin training as a pilot.

In the horrendous March of 1918, with General Pershing in France and headed for Chateau-Thierry, Frederick Warrington Gillet was assigned to the 79th Squadron of the Royal Flying Corps, posted to France. His machine was the legendary one-man Sopwith Dolphin, with two Vickers machine guns to score kills. And score he did. In the next eight months before the War to End All Wars came to a bloody end, he registered twenty kills. That would include 14 Fokker D VIIs, the same plane flown by the Red Baron, and three kite balloons. And he did it all as a Canadian named Frederick Warrington Gillet, of the Royal Flying Corps. He was, in truth, a hero. On November 2, 1918, exactly nine days before Armistice Day, the *London Gazette* misspelled Frederick the temporary Canadian's last name as Gillett and described a key and final battle against a German two-seater as he attempted to attack a kite balloon.

"Lieut. Gillett shot the machine down and turning to the balloon which was being rapidly hauled down he dropped two bombs at the winch and fired a drum into the balloon, which deflated but did not catch fire."

He was awarded the Distinguished Flying Cross. Three months later, he was described as "a pilot of great dash and skill" who had destroyed twelve hostile aircraft. In one September 1918 battle he attacked three Fokkers at once, driving one down "in flames." When the war finally ended two short months later, on November 11, 1918, with 10 million dead and 20 million wounded, the original Francis was still alive. He returned to his native Baltimore and began the

legacy that would haunt his grandson Francis Warrington
Gillet III for the rest of his life.

The original Francis died at his home in Glyndon, Maryland, four days before Christmas 1969, when Warrington
was just eleven. Francis Warrington Gillet III officially inherited the legacy of the man who lied to become a hero.
No matter what else he did in his life, the original Francis
would always be a war hero. He would always be the guy
with twenty kills. When all was said and done, the original
Francis was a tough guy to live up to. Even worse for Warrington III, his grandfather's life proved there was such a
thing as an admirable lie. The original Francis was proof
that there is no such thing as black and white—only gray.

Gray made everything more difficult. It was brutal, this
decision. The hardest part of moving from regret to remorse was that you had to know in your heart the difference between right and wrong. You had to know that what
you had done wasn't just some little technical violation,
some misunderstanding of complex regulations or an action taken after receiving really bad advice. It had to be
that you, personally, understood that you—as a grown-up—
made specific choices after weighing facts and came out on
the wrong side. You maliciously chose to do a wrong thing.
You acted willfully, with specific intent.

In order to understand that he'd really done something
wrong, he'd have to translate his actions into plain English.
Instead of saying he'd violated a section of a federal law that
he'd never actually seen in print, he'd have to say straight-
out that he'd wanted something so badly he was just going
to take it away from someone else. Or he hated someone so
much he had to destroy them, or at least their reputation.
Call it what you will—pride, covetousness, lust, anger, glut-
tony, envy or sloth. The Seven Capital Sins were merely explanations for the same thing—a wrongful act. An unethical
act in disobedience to a personal god.

There were whole libraries filled with books describing the nuances of sin. There were sins that cry out to heaven: willful murder, oppression of the poor, defrauding a laborer of his wages. There was the sin of the angels: pride. Some believed actions were either good, indifferent or sinful, others said there was no such thing as an indifferent act—just good or sinful. Some divided sins into categories—mortal and venial. Mortal sins were committed with conscious intent, venial were committed without the perpetrator's conscious knowledge. Where was Warrington on the spectrum of sin? Why wasn't it clear to him, even as he was brought to a room called "Pre-Trial Services" and asked questions about his brother's middle name and the year he finished junior high?

He had no idea what to do. The expression of remorse was usually enough to stop the lies you tell yourself when you get up in the morning. It was the best part of remorse, but it was difficult to remember that when the ramifications of the declaration were swirling around you like a maelstrom, pulling you and your good family name down into the abyss. People say there are good acts and bad acts. Some go so far as to say there are good people and bad people. In theory, it should be pretty simple to tell the difference.

For Francis Warrington Gillet III, discerning the difference was a difficult if not impossible task.

Warrington sat in a government-leased van with other accused criminals. Outside the window he could see they were being transported a mere three blocks to a white marble courthouse for more process and procedure. He realized this was going to take all day. He dreaded what lay ahead. He had been allowed his one phone call and called his half brother, Joseph, to get a lawyer and come down and bail him out. His brother was furious at being forced to interrupt his busy schedule. He said he'd see what he could do. Now Warrington dreaded having to look his own brother in the eye.

At the courthouse, he and his peers were herded inside a windowless room with a number of other strangers. A United States marshal wearing a suit and leather gloves closed the door. Only it wasn't a door. It was iron bars.

For the first time in history, as far as he could tell, a member of the storied Gillet family was sitting inside a prison cell looking out. The thought made his stomach quail.

The hours ticked by. At ten minutes before four in the afternoon, after he'd spent nine hours sitting in various anonymous offices, Warrington was escorted by a U.S. marshal into the magistrate's courtroom on the fifth floor of the United States District Court of the Southern District of New York. This was it. This was his public debut.

An older guy with thinning hair sat in a black robe behind a big hunk of oak. An American flag hung off a pole to his right. A young Asian guy in a blue suit with striped tie was handing up a piece of paper to the guy in the robe. A middle-aged woman announced his name, as in, "United States versus Francis Warrington Gillet III, 97 M 1278." He seemed to detect a hint of contempt in her voice, but he couldn't be sure. His lawyer, a guy he'd never met before in his life, told him to sit down. He was unbelievably nervous, but he did as he was told. He looked behind him and noticed that the courtroom seemed empty.

He tried to read the paper as fast as he could. It consisted of a series of sentences outlining one count of conspiracy to commit securities fraud. The details were somewhat vague but also somehow familiar to Warrington. He knew what they were talking about. Their arrival was not a complete mystery. The guy in the robe said he was a magistrate and asked him if he'd seen the complaint filed against him. He whispered to his lawyer that he had not, but the lawyer stood up and said, "Yes, Your Honor. We waive its reading at this time."

As the hearing progressed, Warrington began to understand that the young Asian guy was the prosecutor handling his case, Assistant United States Attorney Bruce Ohr. He and his lawyer for the day had worked out a plan so that Warrington could get out of jail that day. He would not have to return to the room with the bars on the door. He just had to scare up some cosigners for a $100,000 bail bond by the end of the next week and he'd be free and clear. They even said they'd allow him to travel abroad for work if he had to. Assistant United States Attorney Ohr waived the government's usual practice of demanding the passports of accused criminals.

And then prosecutor Ohr gave Warrington the greatest gift of all—he let him know that as he had stood there, naked in his shame to the entire world, the room had been emptied of spectators. The government had ordered the courtroom sealed. Warrington had been arrested and accused of a serious crime, and, for the most part, nobody knew.

When the hearing ended and he finished filing out more paperwork, the reason for the government's generosity became known to him. Warrington was a perfect candidate to take on one of the most important but reviled roles in the criminal justice system—the cooperating informant. The United States Attorney's Office of the Southern District of New York wanted Warrington to secretly join their team. They had kept his arrest and appearance in court a secret so they could use him to catch more criminals just like him. He was, as far as the world knew, still just Francis Warrington Gillet III, stockbroker, able to mix and mingle with potential codefendants.

Prosecutors, of course, never see just one defendant. Somebody like Warrington means more defendants might be coming soon. The sealing of the courtroom was the first step in the little seduction. In truth, they could do pretty much what they wanted with him. It was now up to Warrington to decide how to proceed.

Outside of court, Warrington's brother, Joseph, finally showed up. Warrington could tell by his brother's look of utter disgust that he was just beginning a journey of humiliation and shame. He was just beginning to examine the paradox of what would better suit his needs—regret or remorse. He had to choose. He couldn't make up his mind. He stepped out into the Manhattan afternoon, with all the people going about their business as if nothing had changed. There they were, glancing at watches, trying to beat the light at the crosswalk, cursing the idiot taxi drivers, acting as if the world was a normal place. Warrington had been just like them yesterday. Today he looked at them and thought, What the hell do they know? They're all lucky and they don't even know it. Francis Warrington Gillet III was a man transformed.

CHAPTER TWENTY-SIX

Jeffrey Pokross had learned some disturbing things about Warrington Gillet. First, there was talk that Little Warry was about to hop a plane for elsewhere. Guys like this were always a problem. Then he learned that Warrington was going to be arrested. Then Cary Cimino learned of Warrington's actual arrest and came to DMN to talk about it with Pokross. In the office, Cary mentioned the fact that Warrington's arrest was sealed. This began a series of frantic inquiries by Jeffrey and Cary. Soon they learned that Warrington had met with prosecutors, and then they learned Warrington had mentioned a specific dollar figure that Cary had made on a deal. The implication was clear. Warrington was cooperating with the FBI.

This was when Cary asked Pokross if he could assist in giving Warrington what Cary coyly called "a dirt lunch."

"You know," Cary said. "Bury him face-first in the dirt."

Pokross replied, "I don't think we're going to want to do that, and don't bring it up with Jimmy."

Pokross was aware that Jimmy Labate was not crazy

about Cary Cimino. After Cary's charges had been dismissed, Jimmy began to suspect Cary was a cooperator. Jeffrey did not believe Cary was cooperating, although he was quite sure that Warrington was. This put him in a difficult spot. The gangsters also suspected Warrington was a rat, and if they decided this was true, they might just go and put Warrington in a trunk. Pokross did what he could.

At one point, he, Sal Piazza and Jimmy Labate discussed potential harm caused by Warrington if he was cooperating. Piazza noted that Warrington knew quite a lot about Monitor and DMN. Warrington had been right in the middle of both the Spaceplex scheme and the Beachport debacle. Jimmy thought the guy with his pedigree and prep school ways was a joke. He called him "the blitherer," and said no professional member of law enforcement would take the guy seriously.

November 25, 1997

Frank Lino sat in the same fifth-floor courtroom in Lower Manhattan Warrington had recently visited, surrounded by the chaos of criminal justice in action. He leaned back in his chair, smiling broadly at the spectacle unfolding around him. He wore a purple Super Bowl jersey over his gray sweatshirt, which was generally the kind of thing you wore when you were awakened at your home by the FBI at 6:16 a.m. He folded his hands over his chest and yawned. Dozens of lawyers milled about in the well while the magistrate on his bench perused paper and courtroom personnel called out the names of Italian-Americans. The proceeding appeared to be like a large-scale Broadway revue where every single actor and actress went on stage and forgot his or her part all at the same time.

That morning Frank had joined a long list of friends and colleagues taken into custody by the federal government.

There were agents all over Brooklyn, picking up everybody involved in Meyers Pollock Robbins Inc. They picked up the broker who'd caused all the trouble between the two families, Jonathan. They got one of Frank's soldiers, Boobie Cerasani. They got Eugene Lombardo out in Las Vegas, and Claudio Iodice down in Boca. Butch Montevecchi they got upstate. Nineteen guys in all. It was a big headache for Frank, and it was also a big headache for federal magistrate's court.

The prosecutors went on about how this was the biggest example in history of the mob's infiltration of Wall Street. They were saying the infiltration was "relatively isolated" and did not "threaten the overall stability of our markets," but it demonstrated "efforts by members of organized crime and their associates to extend their unlawful activities to the federal securities markets."

Nevertheless, Frank Lino was relaxed. He sat back as if poolside, skimming the paperwork with the confidence of a man who does not see the term "life imprisonment" anywhere on the page. It was a pretty unusual piece of paper for a gangster case. There was, of course, the usual racketeering and conspiracy and extortion, but there was no gambling, no labor shakedown, no shylock charges, no allegations of murders or murder attempts or even beatings with office chairs. There were all these allegations having to do with securities fraud and wire fraud. It was almost embarrassing.

While the bureaucrats in the crowded room moved about with files and the magistrate wrote notes to himself, Frank Lino joked with Boobie Cerasani. It looked like the agents had given Boobie time to put on his best gangster ensemble when they dragged him out of bed at 6 a.m.—he wore a black turtleneck under a black suit coat and had a face like Don Rickles in a bad mood. Boobie had been one of the few guys who really spooked the FBI agent, Joe Pistone, when he pretended to be Donnie Brasco. Donnie believed Boobie had been involved in a number of murders, and had made a point of staying away from Boobie. Frank and Boobie went way back. Here they were, arrested by the FBI and sitting in court, but they could have been hanging out at the social club for all the anxiety they displayed.

The magistrate was getting the tedious job of arraignment and bail done by groups of four. The script was the same for everybody—you're escorted in, you're told you're a notorious Wall Street criminal, your lawyer argues for bail. In cases like this, everybody gets out, because there is no violence in the paperwork. This would go on into the afternoon, with codefendant after codefendant—all of whom weren't used to getting up at 6 a.m.—milling groggily about the courtroom, waving at relatives and trying to find a marshal to get them their belongings so they could go home.

When it was his turn, Frank Lino expected to be labeled a "danger to the community" and a "risk of flight." It was not to be. Today Frank was just a respectable captain in the Bonanno crime family involved in clean criminal activity on Wall Street that was clearly a danger to the community but not that kind of danger. A different kind of danger. An acceptable kind of danger, economic in nature and mostly detrimental to the senior citizens who'd invested their life savings in Meyers Pollock's many scam over-the-counter stocks. Under these circumstances, the criminal mastermind usually gets to walk out the door after promising to put up his house as collateral in case he decides to take a quick unscheduled trip.

For Frank Lino, this was quite a bit different from the time he was busted back when he was a kid, when the New York Police Department of the 1950s went after him with the lit cigarettes in the dirty basement room. This was a civilized affair. The FBI agents were polite. The bail seemed steep—$1 million—but it wasn't real bail. It was bail bond. He just had to scare up four relatives to sign over their homes and that was that. He was even free to go before they signed. His lawyer made a point of telling the judge that

Frank was a hardworking telephone company salesman with nine grandchildren, but the bail didn't budge. The prosecutor stopped his argument, Frank's lawyer stopped his, and they all filed out to the clerk's office to sign papers and turn in Frank's passport. It was all quite amazing, what with all the "with all due respects" and "if it pleases the courts."

Outside court, while Frank signed more paperwork, his lawyer talked to the small group of reporters scratching their pens back and forth.

"We're very confident that we will be victorious," he said, which was lawyer-speak for "We'll work out a deal where my guy pleads guilty to lesser charges and does less than five years."

"He doesn't own any stocks," the lawyer was saying. "My client doesn't even know where Wall Street is."

December 14, 1997

The border between Brooklyn and Queens was difficult to discern. Brooklyn had always been older, a place where people lived forever. Queens always seemed more transient, like a rest area on the way to the real suburbs in Long Island. Figuring out where one started and the other stopped was impossible. There were certain neighborhoods where you couldn't tell where you were, and in one such locale— Maspeth, on the Brooklyn/Queens border—the Bonanno crime family was holding its annual Christmas party at an Italian restaurant called Casablanca.

The party was taking place less than three weeks after the big arrests of Frank Lino, Boobie Cerasani, Eugene Lombardo, Claudio Iodice and all the rest, so they were likely a topic of conversation at Casablanca. Everybody was out on bail, so nobody would be spending the holidays at the Metropolitan Detention Center. Generally speaking there was a feeling that Wall Street arrests were somehow different.

No one seemed very concerned. The potential prison time hovered around five years, and pretty much everybody concerned was willing to do that kind of time and then get back on the street. Frank was in such a good mood he was hosting the party.

On paper the Casablanca was owned by a guy named Anthony. In reality it was owned by Joseph Massino, the boss of the Bonanno crime family. The Christmas party was an event that allowed all the members and associates of the Bonanno family to stop by and bring envelopes of Christmas cash for the boss. It was always well attended.

This year, when everybody was making money, the event was crowded. It started in the afternoon and went into the night.

The players paraded through: Boobie Cerasani showed up with his girlfriend and child in his usual black turtleneck/ black suit coat. Dirty Danny brought his wife. Frank's son, Joey, whom Frank had brought into the life of organized criminals, was there. Gene Lombardo showed up without his cell phones. There was a guy, Joe, who owned a school bus company, who brought his whole family. T.G. from the Bronx represented the Lucchese family; a guy named Georgie was there for the Colombo family. There was even a guy named Tutti.

In a building across the street, FBI Special Agent James Meskill sat at the window with a video camera, trying to identify as many members and associates of New York's five organized crime families as he could. He would write down the suspected name and the time shown on the video. It was all part of an ongoing procedure. It was an investigation that never ended.

For Frank Lino, it was a good holiday season. His lawyer was already working on an arrangement with the federal government that would get Frank out in forty-seven months, and by now he and his cousin, Lombardo, had made so much money, what were a few years in a comfortable federal prison? This wasn't state time. All around, the atmosphere at Casablanca was one of conviviality and general good cheer. The Wall Street bust was seen as a speed bump. Of course, nobody was too happy about Cousin Eugene. In fact, just about everybody wanted to kill him, the Genovese family in particular. By now everybody knew that the investigation was made up almost entirely of conversations on Cousin Eugene's many cell phones. Some of these conversations went on for hours and were quite detailed, with names and ranks and all the rest.

Then there was the business with Claudio Iodice and the drain cleaner. Nobody quite knew what to make of that. Claudio had been acting increasingly erratic in the days leading up to the arrest. He was picked up the same morning as everyone else, retained a lawyer and then got himself released on bail. There had been some reluctance to let him out, given the FBI tapes of him threatening to track down and stick a knife into the HealthTech CEO and his entire family, but a solution had been crafted and he was allowed to go. The only caveat was that he was required to wear a special electronic monitoring bracelet around his ankle that allowed court personnel to track his whereabouts. He was ordered to stay inside his air-conditioned home in Boca and was allowed to visit only his lawyer and his doctor. Really it wasn't so bad.

A few days after he snapped on the bracelet, the police received a 911 call. When they broke into his home, they found Claudio lying on the floor of his bathroom, passed out and very near death. At the hospital, the doctors were somewhat puzzled by what they discovered. Somehow Claudio Iodice was still alive, but he no longer had an esophagus. Some substance had been poured into Claudio—either by himself or by others—that had essentially eaten it up. It was gone. Since Claudio couldn't speak, the police who looked into the matter were the ones to determine that he had ingested a modest but effective amount of drain cleaner.

This material is essentially sulfuric acid. It is not meant to enter one's throat. It effectively burned his esophagus away.

The complications were endless and, in a certain way, fascinating. The loss of his esophagus left Claudio unable to swallow anything. This caused enormous problems because on any given day, normal human beings swallow pints of spit. This spit wound up getting into Claudio's body cavity and causing untold numbers of internal infections. In the weeks after his interaction with the drain cleaner, it was clear Claudio was going to be spending a lot of time at the hospital.

Besides wondering about all the ramifications of losing one's esophagus, the most common question that occurred to people when confronted with Claudio and the drain cleaner was simple—why had this occurred? Was it possible he feared prison so much he was willing to ingest sulfuric acid in the hopes that he would somehow survive but be so maimed as to avoid spending any time behind bars? If that were true, he couldn't have thought too much about what life would be like without an esophagus. Ultimately the doctors would have to sew his stomach directly into his windpipe, which would allow him to survive, in a way, but would make his life an endless misery. And how could he have been sure it wouldn't just kill him? Or perhaps he didn't care.

Perhaps it was a suicide attempt. It was likely that Claudio was depressed. The government had charged him with numerous counts of securities fraud and was trying to seize every dollar he owned. They even put a lien on his thirty-two-foot Powerplay speedboat. He was on several tapes making threats. He and Eugene Lombardo were practically the stars of the FBI's show. They had both implicated several members of organized crime. Even if he got a good plea deal and did a few years in prison, how could he walk the streets again without thinking that someday some guy would come up behind him and put five in his brain? Perhaps getting the job done right now would save everyone a whole lot of aggravation.

The other scenario was that someone did this to him. The FBI was very interested in this possibility and asked a lot of questions. This wasn't your usual Wall Street fraud case, after all.

Only Claudio knew for sure, and he was no longer able to speak.

Jimmy Labate, Sal Piazza and Jeffrey Pokross were sitting in the conference room at DMN talking about deals. As was always the case, the smallest guy in the room—Jeffrey Pokross—was the guy doing the most talking. He was a catalog of schemes. Every day he thought up new ways to steal. His newest brainstorm involved bribing the guys who ran some of the union locals to dump their members' pension funds into stock DMN was pushing. He wanted to start with the pension fund of Production Local 100, a union he believed would soon be available as a kind of piggy bank. It was controlled by a guy they knew, Frank Persico. Pokross had noticed a change regarding Frank Persico. When Persico's name first came up, it was no big deal. Lately—or more precisely, after the Meyers Pollock arrests—Pokross noticed that Robert Lino and Jimmy Labate would get worked up when Frank Persico's name popped up.

Jimmy stood up and said, "Just a second." He walked over and turned up CNBC on the TV in the corner.

"Okay," he said. "That's better."

After Robert Lino's cousin, Frank, and all the rest were arrested in the Meyers Pollock mess, for some reason DMN Capital had managed to stay off the radar. That was somewhat surprising, considering that Jeffrey Pokross and

Robert Lino had spent a considerable amount of time dealing with Meyers Pollock in the months preceding the arrests. Yet DMN Capital did not appear to interest the FBI.
It seemed that Robert Lino, Jeffrey Pokross, Sal Piazza,
Jimmy Labate—all of them had dodged the bullet. That
was good news, because the market was taking off.

Tech stocks were the mantra. The profits were mind-
boggling. The Internet was spawning dozens of new company
concepts each week. Everybody was dropping run-of-the-
mill jobs with real paychecks to sign up for a start-up with
not much in the way of wages but plenty in the way of stock
options. You could sell anything by just plopping a dot-com
on to the end of your idea. You wanted to use the Internet to
sell pet supplies? Kitchen cabinets? Truck parts? No problem. In fact, you could now sell anything you wanted through
the Internet. Sure it was really just another way to advertise
and attract buyers. Who cared? Just create a company and
you're off.

In so many ways, the stars had aligned for the forces of
DMN Capital. The day they busted everybody at Meyers
Pollock, the feds eliminated DMN's competition. Now
DMN could sell everything. Spaceplex was a lousy amuse-
ment park on Long Island. Beachport was a bunch of ice
shows. Country World was a ratty old casino in Colorado.
Monolite supposedly made parts for semis—supposedly.
Take 'em public, make a mint. Watch the profits soar. Sure
you could lose money, but mostly you didn't. Nobody had
seen anything quite like it. Certainly not the gangsters of
Wall Street, who knew they had a good thing going as the
market took off for the heavens.

That didn't mean it couldn't all go to hell.

This was the thought that ate away at Jimmy Labate
when he turned up the TV in the conference room. Since
the Meyers Pollock busts, he had become increasingly paranoid. Every time Pokross would begin discussing investing the detective's union pension funds or Frank Persico

over at Production Local 100, Jimmy would jump up and turn up the TV. Jimmy would tell anybody who asked that there were bugs everywhere, FBI agents on every corner and, more likely than not, an informant in their midst. He couldn't prove it. He just sensed it.

He was particularly sensitive about Frank Persico. Down at DMN Capital on Liberty Street, Robert Lino and Jeffrey Pokross understood one mission above all when it came to keeping the money flowing—keep the contraption off the regulatory radar. Now that Meyers Pollock had collapsed and DMN was free and clear, they needed to keep things low-key. Keep the wiseguys behind oak veneer walls. Keep the investors believing that they were dealing with graduates of the Wharton School, not graduates of the Brooklyn waterfront. Robert Lino and Jeffrey Pokross both knew that Frank Persico was going to make that mission a challenge.

Frank Persico was the cousin of Alfonse Persico, the more-or-less boss of the Colombo crime group. Alfonse was the son of Carmine Persico, the real boss of the family, but Carmine was behind bars for the rest of his life and he'd designated as acting boss his son, a college graduate who'd once had his minions shoot a guy in the testicles for messing around with his wife. Cousin Frank Persico was Allie Boy's official designate on Wall Street, and he'd really gotten into the role in a serious way. For instance, though Frank looked like a Teamsters foreman with his no-neck fireplug physique and nylon jogging suit wardrobe, Frank himself was an actual registered stockbroker legally approved to buy and sell stocks to the trusting public.

How Frank Persico had obtained his license was not clear. In the early 1990s, regulators had discovered a number of individuals like Frank who'd paid others to take the exam under their name. Some—but not all—were caught. Frank—whose only experience eligible for listing on a résumé was "trucking assistant"—had some made it through the Series 7 exam and was now listed as a registered broker for one esteemed brokerage house after another: Joseph Stephens, William Scott, White Rock, State Street. All sounded quite legitimate. All were as rancid as fish left lying too long in the sun. It was a mystery worth investigation that would remain unsolved why anyone would buy stock from Frank Persico, but many an investor did.

Frank Persico's real job was to represent the interests of the Colombo crime family and his cousin, Alfonse, and when Jeffrey Pokross was looking for brokers to push one of his bogus stocks, he'd heard only good things about Frank and his registered brokers' license. Jeffrey had asked Frank to come aboard to help hype Beachport stock, and at first, the marriage of the Bonanno and Colombo families had gone swimmingly.

Then the marriage careened toward divorce. Persico had a problem with his emotions, plus he was not too swift with numbers. He blew up his relationship at William Scott, so Lino, Labate, Piazza and Pokross discussed putting him at another brokerage they controlled, First Liberty. They put him in there, and he helped them push a deal called 1-800--TRAVEL. Usually these things work out well for all concerned. This time it was different. After Persico booked the stock into client accounts, the deal went up for about a day or two and then went straight down to $1.

Persico was furious, and because the deal came from a Bonanno wiseguy, he blamed DMN. He became convinced that DMN had set him up, that they were shorting the 1--800-TRAVEL stock just to screw him. All of his brokers suffered, their clients suffered, and now he was having a tough time calling customers and raising money for other house stocks.

More disputes between DMN and Persico erupted. Persico got it into his mind that a $40,000 copy machine at DMN was really his. Many citizens might have pursued the matter through litigation in small claims court or taken their dispute to a TV judge and hashed it out in front of a national audience. Frank Persico had a different approach. He came into the DMN office and demanded stock as compensation for the copy machine. Jimmy Labate gave him forty thousand personal shares of whatever they were about to pump up, but did so with the promise that Persico would give Jimmy back the money at cost after he sold the shares at profit. Persico apparently forgot about the back end of the deal, and Jimmy got not a dime. Jimmy estimated Persico owed him $80,000; ill will between the two followed.

Then Persico brought in a hustler named Albert Alain Chalem, a day trader from New Jersey who always wore baseball caps and did not seem to have a job. He claimed he'd made millions after selling a printing business in Queens and was now playing the stock market for fun and profit. He was also a friend of Alfonse Persico, the son of the boss of the Colombo family. Chalem and the Persicos hung out in Fort Lauderdale on Chalem's fifty-five-foot Hatteras, the *Miss Boombastic*. Nothing this guy owned was in his name. Frank Persico promised that Chalem would turn lead into gold, so he was allowed to work at DMN on certain deals. Soon it became obvious that Chalem was hustling everybody. He had worked with Meyers Pollock, with Philly Abramo, and now with DMN, and appeared to be playing one off the other. The rumor was he was shorting DMN house stocks in a big way. Frank Persico's latest contribution to DMN was asked to leave. That was the last time Robert Lino and Jeffrey Pokross saw Albert Alain Chalem and his baseball cap.

Now they sat in the conference room discussing the problems of Frank Persico with the TV set turned up loud. They had come to realize that Frank was short in both the temperament and intellect departments, and the deficit was causing certain frictions. He was the cousin of the boss's son, and he had come to believe his last name allowed him to tell other people what to do.

Suddenly they heard a loud *Pop!* at the front of the office. They bolted out of the conference room.

They found the front door open and the receptionist cowering under her desk. There was smoke coming out of a computer monitor. The receptionist was weeping.

She said Frank had come into the office and started ranting and raving about a copy machine. She didn't know what he was talking about. He'd pulled out a gun. She didn't see much else because she dove under the desk, but when she came back up she had figured it all out. Frank had gone and shot the computer and stormed out.

It was difficult to imagine such a scene at Bear Stearns.

CHAPTER TWENTY-SEVEN

December 1, 1999

After midnight the phone crew wearing AT&T jackets stepped out of the elevator on the eighteenth floor of an office building a few blocks from Wall Street. To the left they approached an office upon which was the title "DMN CAPITAL" in brushed, embossed steel letters. They had a key. Inside they quickly entered the office of Jeffrey Pokross and removed the plate covering a phone jack about knee-high next to his desk. They quickly installed a tiny device about the size of a pencil eraser and replaced the cover. One of the technicians used another device to test the bug installed in the wall. Then they moved to a conference room, where they repeated their task with another phone jack right next to the fax machine. The technicians looked around to make sure they hadn't left a mess, and then out the door they went.

The New York City detective and his girlfriend stood in the elevator, waiting for the number 18 to light up. He was in his fifties, silver-haired, Irish-American, the proud owner of a storied career in the New York Police Department. She was a few years younger, a divorcee with a teenaged son. She was going to marry the detective soon. He was, after all, a hero. He'd been written about in the papers, truly one of New York's finest. Fifteen years ago, he'd run an investigation of a disturbed man who'd mailed a booby-trapped book to his own mother. The mother had opened the book, and flying shrapnel, sent by her own flesh and blood, had ripped into her. The papers worried about a new mad bomber; no motive was apparent. Detective Stephen Gardell tracked down the lunatic offspring.

Detective Gardell had worked his way up through the ranks, spent too much time humping up and down urine-soaked stairwells in housing projects. He was tired of the job. That was why he and his bride-to-be were down here in the anonymous office world of Wall Street, a man and woman clearly out of their element.

The couple stepped into the lobby on the eighteenth floor of 5 Hanover Square and observed all the accoutrements of the typical small brokerage on Wall Street: the oak-paneled walls, a Federalist end table with white porcelain vase and pale blue plastic hydrangeas, an oil painting of a wild ocean at dawn. Furnishings implying old money. They noted that the fixtures were polished brass, the nameplate on the door:

"DMN CAPITAL" in a tasteful brushed steel.

The detective and his fiancée entered the office and were greeted by Lucille the receptionist, the gatekeeper who knew that anybody she didn't recognize who tried to come into the office was not making it past the door.

"Stephen Gardell," the detective said, not bothering to mention his rank in the New York City Police Department. He nodded toward his fiancée and said, "This is Sharon Kilcoin."

He did not have a warrant. He was not there to ask questions. This was no cop on the job. He was there to do business at DMN. He was expected.

Lucille the receptionist smiled and got Jeffrey Pokross on the phone in his office. She told the detective to go right into the conference room.

Detective Gardell and Sharon Kilcoin walked past the cubicles with brokers working phones, TVs with CNBC on all day long, a coffeepot eternally filled with burned coffee, a water cooler, file cabinets. There were doors leading to offices but no names on them. This was a place where business occurred with anonymity.

Jeffrey Pokross welcomed the couple into the room. Detective Gardell shook his hand and introduced his beloved. There were smiles all around. Jimmy Labate strolled in and embraced Gardell like a lost brother.

"If this fund works out right and you can open up doors for more funds, you won't have to work as long as you live," Jimmy said.

"I know," said Gardell.

"This is a hell of a parachute," Pokross said.

"I know that," Gardell said. "What they hell you think I'm going out there for? I'm not a traveler. Jimmy thinks I'm going out there for a vacation. I'm not. I don't like to travel. She does. I don't."

Pokross was a pragmatist. Some of the gangsters at DMN hated the idea of involving a cop in all of this, but Pokross had an intuitive sense that this particular cop wasn't really a cop. He was a crook with a badge, which had certain advantages. Such as the fact that Stephen Gardell was at the top of the union pension fund for New York City's detectives. One of his jobs was to invest all that money. Jeffrey Pokross and the gangsters at DMN were going to help him with this.

Gardell said he was supposed to fly out to San Francisco to meet with a new money manager who was going to handle some deal he was trying to set up. As Jeffrey Pokross saw it, the deal was going to be the future of DMN and the Bonanno crime family's piece of Wall Street.

The idea was to tap into the huge pool of money in union pension funds. Gardell was treasurer of the Detectives Endowment Association, one of the union officers responsible for deciding how to invest the DEA's $175 million pension fund. Frankie Persico was bringing in another union the Colombo family was controlling, Production Workers Local 400. They had maybe $120 million sitting in various funds and accounts. The Mafia had used unions for their own benefit at construction sites and on the waterfront, why not use them in pump and dump schemes as well? Union pension funds were the wave of the future. They were going to make them all rich—the cop, the fiancée and all the gangsters in the conference room at DMN.

It was strange to have a cop hanging around the office with all those members of the Bonanno crime family coming and going, but Gardell had adopted an odd interpretation of the thin blue line. Gardell didn't really see the need for a thin blue line. He believed that it was every man for himself. You took care of your own and you worried about the rest later. Anybody who was a victim was really just a sucker. He had a sticker attached to his phone to remind him: "RATS TALK ON PHONES." That way he could remember to say nothing important over the phone, because with phones you never knew for sure who you were talking to.

Jimmy Labate had brought Gardell to DMN. He'd met the detective through his neighbor in Staten Island, Tom Scotto, the head of the detectives union. Gardell viewed the DEA's pension fund as his ticket to the good life. He'd worked hard his entire life. Sure he'd been dubbed a hero by the papers, but what did that contribute to the bottom line? He'd risked his life for the civilian world and what did he have to show for it? The union had been his road to opportunity. He'd locked up a good job with the DEA that let him kick back as he wound up his twenty years. He was going to get the pension, then settle into semiretirement and the good life in Boca. He had it all planned out.

Jimmy Labate was going to make it happen. He'd known Jimmy for years. He was in construction on Staten Island just like his father. He was possibly connected. Possibly. Jimmy never said and Detective Gardell didn't ask. It was better not to know. When Jimmy introduced him to Jeffrey and Jeffrey started talking about all the opportunities that were available to him because of his influence in the union, Detective Gardell had promised he could steer the union pension fund's board toward hiring a brokerage controlled by DMN to manage the fund's bounteous assets.

Detective Gardell was a regular guy, for a detective.

In order for this to work, DMN needed to stay out of the picture. They needed a legitimate-looking money manager up front to set up a plan of investment for the DEA fund. It would be mostly prudent, conservative investments, but it would also involve setting aside a little to buy DMN house stocks. That was where Gardell would benefit. Jeffrey had arranged to get Gardell some private shares. Detective Gardell, after all, wasn't doing this for his health.

None of this arrangement was ever discussed out in the open. Jeffrey would say only, "We may be able to do something." Instead of saying that DMN was out and out bribing Gardell, Jeffrey would say, "We would do the right thing with him, if we got a piece of that money—putting him into some things like house stock. Some of our stuff."

The day's meeting at DMN was to make it all happen. There were issues. Getting Gardell "some of our stuff" wasn't turning out to be quite so simple. The first brokerage they tried to use was First Liberty. First Liberty planned to invest $10 million of the DEA pension fund. The investment strategy seemed reasonable: mostly conservative, a few modest risks. It promised big returns in Wall Street's best run-up ever, and promised those returns fast. There was only one problem: First Liberty was under investigation by the Securities and Exchange Commission. Gardell the detective had found out all about the investigation and that was the end of First Liberty.

Now they had a new front firm in San Francisco and were hoping to be back on track for big bucks.

"If they've got the numbers, if they can produce, then we've got a done deal," Gardell said, trying to sound like he knew a spreadsheet from a rap sheet.

"They got 'em," Pokross promised. "If we've got a done deal, then we all do wonderfully."

"Okay," Gardell said. "I won't have to work Monday, Tuesday or Wednesday."

"Will I have to work?" the fiancée chimed in. "I don't want to work."

"All right," said her betrothed.

"We'll all do wonderfully," Pokross enthused.

"We need a new car," said the bride-to-be.

"Well if this one gets pulled off, should we start looking for a convertible?" Pokross said.

"I know what I want," said the bride. "I want a Mercedes truck."

"She wants Jimmy's Mercedes," Gardell said.

"Whose name are we putting this under?" Pokross asked.

"We can put this under not the same name as mine," Gardell said, laughing.

"I got a different last name," said the bride.

"I'll use it for a parachute then," Gardell said.

"If this gets done, go get a vacation house," Pokross said.

"I got to take care of my mother," Gardell said. "She's poor."

"Your mother's got plenty," said the bride-to-be.

*   *   *

Jimmy Labate was explaining why having a cop hanging around was a good idea. He was in the conference room at DMN with CNBC on in the background, talking to Jeffrey Pokross and John Black, an associate of the Lucchese crime family. Black was a registered stockbroker who'd been working with DMN to pump up certain house stocks, and Jimmy was mentioning that his good friend and neighbor Detective Stephen Gardell of the New York City Police Department had access to these parking permits that were very useful.

"You want one?" Labate asked Black.

"I could have used one this morning going out of the Holland Tunnel," Black said.

The permits come from the Detectives Endowment Association and offer many opportunities besides free parking wherever you want on the streets of New York. If you get pulled over, the permits are a sign that you're a friend of law enforcement.

"If I give it to you, you can't abuse it," Labate said. "You put it on your dashboard. And when they see it, just salute, and if they ask where you got it, just say you work with the Endowment Association. Every year we donate $8, $9, $10,000 a year at Christmas for all the widows and orphans, yadda, yadda, yadda."

"All right," Black said. "Okay."

"If you get pulled over, you have to keep my phone number with you in case something happens. You're drunk and you get pulled over with it, they're gonna bring you in the station house, you're gonna call me and I'm gonna have you taken out of the station house."

Black laughed at that one.

"I'm serious. How do you think we got Mikey help? Mike was going to jail."

Mikey had hit a stock promoter in the head with a pool cue. It was a big mess and he was charged with assault, which with his previous record of many other assaults would mean that Mikey would go directly to jail.

"Do you understand that Mikey's on probation, that he would have did the eighteen months plus three years for a second felony offense," Jimmy said.

"He's crazy," Black said. "I told him, 'What the hell are you doing, punching a guy?'"

When Black left, Labate was alone with Pokross. Labate said he'd just spent more than four hours with Detective Gardell, and that the experienced officer of the law seemed to know something about other gangster families and their increasing involvement in Wall Street stock schemes.

"How does he know that type of business?" Pokross asked.

"Every cop's feedin' him information, every detective's feedin' him information. You're out of your mind and if you think there's not half a dozen wiseguy rats talking to him."

The way Jimmy saw it, Gardell had been nothing but positive for DMN. He'd scared up city parking permits and he'd let them know that First Security was under investigation. Once, he warned them about an upcoming bust of Bonanno family gangsters, and the very next day there was an arrest. He was always hearing about ongoing investigations and was happy to let them know what was up.

So far all Jimmy and Sal and Jeffrey had to do in return was arrange to comp the guy and his girlfriend at the Paris hotel in Vegas. They picked up some swag fur coat for the girlfriend, and arranged to have an aboveground swimming pool built for the guy. They'd promised him secret insider shares on some house stock deals once the union hired DMN's front firm. Sometimes when Jimmy looked at how much time it was taking to set up this union deal, he wasn't sure Gardell was worth all the hassle.

"I didn't say I don't like him, I just keep saying the same thing. I think that we give, give, give, give and get very little back. It's an observation," he'd told Sal Piazza. But on most days, Jimmy believed Gardell had proved to be a valuable asset to DMN.

"He asked me a funny question," Labate said. "Am I a gangster? I said, 'Do I know people? I know a lot of people.'"

"Why does he want to know if you're a gangster?" Pokross asked.

"So I won't jeopardize him," Labate said.

The more time they spent thinking about the potential money involved in these unions, the more excited they got. Besides the detectives union and Production Local 400, Labate was now bringing up yet another union, this one representing the officers who maintain order and decorum in New York City's courts. Pokross claimed to know the union's president and thought that pension fund would be fertile ground for upcoming scams. The more he thought about it, the less he was sure who was worse—the criminals like himself trying to skim cash from the pensions of hardworking civil servants, or the hardworking civil servants like Detective Stephen Gardell who were put in charge of the pension fund.

"When Mr. Gardell gets his three hundred thousand dollars at the cage in the Palace Casino in Nassau under his girlfriend's name, let him run amok," Pokross laughed. "Even though a lot of these union guys are fucking gangsters and sitting there and making tons of money running these unions, it is protocol that they gotta put these things out in advance."

Labate agreed.

Pokross said, "They won't pretenderize, meaning they're not going to go for the hard sell. They're pre-sold."

Then it was time for Jimmy to go, and Jeffrey waited a bit before punching a beeper number into his phone. When the beeper picked up, he put in a special number code and left the office. He took the elevator downstairs and walked down the block to a diner. There he sat in a booth until another man walked in without speaking and sat down across from him. The two men leaned toward each other and spoke quietly. Frequently Jeffrey looked around to see if anyone he knew was walking by. He was pretty sure none of his gangster business partners would recognize the guy he was sitting with, but he was still a bit rattled during these meetings. He fully understood the consequences if they figured out he was sipping coffee with the FBI.

Since Jeffrey Pokross had decided to secretly cooperate with the U.S. government against all his friends, the FBI had come up with a little system to keep track of their new star informant. When he arrived at work in the morning, he'd beep his agent with a code—the number one. If he left the office for a sandwich at lunch, he'd put in a different number, and do it again when he returned. He had another number for when he left for the day. Sometimes agents listening in would want to get in touch with Jeffrey to get him to bring up specific subjects or press for answers on something they believed they'd heard. They would call a cell phone Jeffrey had that was always turned off. He would check his messages repeatedly during the day, and if there was a message he would create a reason to leave the office. Then he'd call the agents from his cell phone. Every night he'd write up e-mails for the FBI summarizing the day's activities, including who was likely to visit the next day. Once a week he'd meet the agents at a diner somewhere near the office. It was risky. Somebody could have seen. But Jeffrey seemed to like it that way. It was real James Bond stuff.

"I was posing as a corrupt investment banker and as best as possible without blowing that cover. [I was to make] sure it was clear to the participants that we were engaged in illegal activity as best I could under the circumstances."

He was supposed to try and prevent violence before it

happened, but he was also supposed to stay in character, like any good liar or actor, and not appear to behave in any law-abiding way.

He was now working undercover twenty-four hours a day, seven days a week. He couldn't take time off. There was no vacation for Secret Agent Pokross. He had to keep the story line going. So far he'd done pump and dump with the Bonanno family and the Colombo family. He was constantly trying to invent new schemes that wouldn't end up with Jimmy Labate putting some broker's head in a vise. At the end of the 1990s there was the Globus deal, then Innovative Medical.

"We manipulated the stock upward and brokers put it out to their retail clients and they made undisclosed commissions that were never reported to the clients," he said.

DMN set the size of the chop. Investors in Globus lost $3 million. Pokross personally made $100,000. Pokross made $150,000 on Innovative Medical. He estimated that by 2000, he'd done fifteen corrupt deals at DMN that cost investors $20 million in losses and put $1.6 million in his pocket strictly from stock fraud. That was on top of the $1 million he made legitimately from non-manipulated stocks. He did not file income tax returns, despite his pledge to the United States government that he was on their team. He was aware of certain inconsistencies in his logic.

"Under my agreement with the government, it says that I'm not supposed to commit any illegal activity. So by not filing those tax returns, it was an illegal activity not filing those on time." It added up. By 2000, he owed $900,000 in state, local and federal taxes, plus another $500,000 in penalties.

Always he was watching his back. The gangsters constantly believed somebody was following them or listening in on the phone. Everybody around was a potential rat. Nobody could be trusted. If you hadn't committed an actual crime in front of their eyes, you were suspect. Even if you had, you might still have a secret arrangement. Pokross walked a narrow line.

"If I was talking about Frank Persico or Steve Gardell from the detectives union or any mob activity on the phone, they'd go wild," Pokross said. "Labate, Lino, to an extent Piazza, would look at me like I was crazy. Because those things in that world are not mentioned on the telephone. Because I know Lino and Labate. They are very surveillance conscious. They were always checking for bugs and tails and people following them. They would turn up the radio. They thought everything was wiretapped . . . Once, I'm sitting in the conference room with Labate and Frank Persico discussing the union activities," he recalled. "And then it starts to get a little more serious and detailed into the conversation and Labate says, 'Let's turn up the TV.'"

April 11, 2000

In the conference room, Jimmy Labate was telling Jeffrey Pokross something he'd learned from his friend and neighbor Detective Gardell that indicated DMN might have a little problem.

"He told me unequivocally the phones are tapped," Labate said.

"What would lead him to that conclusion?" Pokross asked.

"I haven't the slightest idea. He says, 'Have you ever had the phones swept?' I says, 'For what? We only do legitimate business.'"

"It's true."

The way Jimmy saw it, Detective Gardell's warning was all the proof he needed to become a full-time paranoid. A few months back the U.S. government had filed misdemeanor charges against him for not reporting income from his construction business. He owed more than $180,000 in back taxes, but so did a lot of guys like him. Why had they singled him out for such pathetic charges? Now there was this business about bugs at DMN. Of course, a bug in DMN's office meant there was an active investigation under way, which probably meant there was an informant floating around and it could be just about anybody. Then the preppy stockbroker, Francis Warrington Gillet III, had shown up at DMN with a tape of the stock promoter Cary Cimino making threats. He claimed he hadn't made any other tapes, but who knew if he made that one and if there were any more? Then two of the executives at Spaceplex had pleaded guilty a few months earlier and were probably cooperating. Until now DMN Capital hadn't surfaced on any radar screen. Now everybody had good reason to be paranoid. It was the only healthy thing to do.

"I says, 'Listen to me, Steve, my family doesn't want me to have nothing to do with organized crime,'" Labate was saying. "Matter of fact, when my name comes up, my cousin jumps in anybody's face that asked about me because I don't have nothing to do with street shit. So whoever's telling you this, get that delusion outta your fuckin' head. I don't go to no coffee clubs. I don't go to no sit-downs. I don't go to no meetings, no nothing. It gets nipped in the bud before it ever comes to me.' He says, 'Yeah, I heard that.' I says, 'So then, why do you ask?'"

"Why was he asking?" Pokross wanted to know.

"How do I know?" Jimmy replied, clearly agitated. "I can't have Steve up here no more."

CHAPTER TWENTY-EIGHT

August 3, 1999

At 4:20 p.m. Jeffrey Pokross stepped out of a yellow cab into the summer heat of Midtown Manhattan. From there he crossed the most famous piece of sidewalk in the city and entered the air-conditioned bar of Sparks Steakhouse, a restaurant known the world over for the gangster who'd died where Jeffrey had just tread.

Pokross was supposed to be meeting Cary Cimino, and Cary had picked the locale. He certainly had a crude sense of humor. Nearly fourteen years earlier, around Christmas 1985, the then boss of the Gambino crime family, Paul Castellano, had had a dinner reservation at Sparks. He didn't quite make it. On the sidewalk in front, four men wearing long white coats and black Russian hats shot down Big Paulie and his driver while shoppers with bags of Christmas gifts in hand dove for cover. There lay Big Paulie on the cold ground in his expensive winter coat, blood oozing, his reign finished and Sparks's reputation sealed. Guides on tourist buses pointed it out. Effete restaurant guides described it as a "macho bastion" with "too much testosterone," but Cary loved the place. It was real New York, not Tribeca or Soho or all those other precious neighborhoods where people like his former best friend, Francis Warrington Gillet III, hung out. This was where real men ate red meat and drank red wine and reveled in the success they had achieved on their own terms—not because Daddy gave them a trust fund.

Pokross was vaguely aware of his mission. Cary had asked for the meeting because of certain concerns he had about being arrested at any minute. As usual, all the concerns involved Francis Warrington Gillet III. Cary was convinced that Warrington was a cooperating witness. Cary barely spoke on the phone anymore and never to Warrington. He had recently become convinced somebody was following him on the street. After Cary requested the meeting, the FBI wired up Pokross and tasked him with exploring Cary's Warrington-phobia.

At the Sparks bar, Pokross ordered Absolut on the rocks with a twist of lime. This was a Tuesday in August and Manhattan wasn't its usual bustling self. The people who could afford it were already out in the Hamptons. The rest were waiting for the weekend to do the same. Still the bar was unusually crowded and Cary was late. Pokross chatted with the bartender and checked his cell phone voice mail. There he discovered a message from Cary saying he was sitting at the bar at Sparks. Pokross looked down the bar.

"Hey, Cary," he said, pushing his way through the crowd to the other end of the bar.

"How long you been sitting there?" Cary asked, startled.

"Five minutes," Pokross said. "You got to be kidding. You were sitting over there?"

They both laughed, and Cary lied about how he was turning thirty-nine in a month.

"You gotta be forty-two," Jeffrey said.

"Why?"

"Because you gotta be a year older than me 'cause your vision is worse than mine."

Pokross sipped his vodka and asked Cary what he was up to.

Cary said, "Disappearing to L.A. for six months, then I'm going to move off to London, then I'll disappear into an Eastern European country like Prague or Hungary for a year or two, let it all blow over. I'm not fleeing the law because I'm not under indictment," he said. "There's no warrant for my arrest, so if I'm in a different country, I'm not on the lam."

"What do you expect a problem from?" Jeffrey asked.

Cary replied, "Anything we've done in the past. It's going to come up and bite us in the ass."

Pokross had heard the concerns before. They had come up quite often with Cary, who could not seem to understand that fearing imminent arrest was just part of the game when you're a full-time criminal. He knew, more or less, where this was going.

The two men ordered and joked and argued about moneys owed and waited for the waiter to leave before continuing their talk. The restaurant was full and loud, and it would be very difficult to hear the substance of what Cary and Jeffrey were discussing, but any observer could tell this was not a conversation filled with laughter and good feeling. Pokross mentioned a CEO named Manas in one of their schemes who'd pleaded guilty and was testifying against others they knew.

"The U.S. attorney, fuck them," Pokross said.

"USDA," Cary joked. "Department of Agriculture."

"Fish and Wildlife," Pokross said, laughing. "In your case, it's Fish and Wildlife, the filthy animal that you are."

Pokross said he'd heard their names had come up in the other case. They discussed getting the court transcripts and splitting the cost. "This is hot off the presses," he said. "Jeffrey and Cary were the promoters. Or Cary and Jeffrey. You and I are joined like brothers."

"I like that," Cary said, scribbling something on some paper.

"You're writing down quotes now?"

"My biography," Cary said. "My life story."

Pokross asked Cary if he'd approached any of his friends to see if they'd been questioned.

"What do you mean?" Cary asked.

"Well Warrington has vanished," Jeffrey said. "Where's Warrington? Down at his folks' farm?"

"Yeah. Why don't you call him?"

"Why don't you call him?"

"I don't speak with him anymore," Cary said. "We had a huge fight."

Jeffrey knew all about Cary and Warrington. He'd heard the original tape, which he'd turned over to the FBI, and he also suspected (but did not know for sure) that Warrington was, like him, cooperating. He'd heard all kinds of things. Warrington had fled New York after his arrest, even while his case was still pending. He'd moved back to his mother's horse farm in Maryland, and despite his rich upbringing, he was actually desperate for money. Pokross pointed to his glass and ordered another Absolut, this time with tonic. Cary ordered a Diet Coke.

"Do you think it's better to let sleeping dogs lie with him or what do you wanna do?" Jeffrey asked.

"Why don't you call him?"

"And ask him what?"

"Has he been approached by the Feds? He got arrested. It was sealed."

Pokross: "What happens when something gets sealed?"

Cimino leaned forward and answered, "'Cause he's co-operating."

"Then why would you want to call him?"

"Right."

Pokross handed Cary two recent news releases from the Dow Jones newswire, about two stock promoters who'd been convicted of securities fraud in the Spaceplex deal. They discussed what Pokross called "our mutual exposure points." This was another name for anybody involved in their schemes who might now be talking to the FBI. Warrington was a "mutual exposure point."

"Let's go over Warrington for a minute."

"There's nothing to go over," Cary said. "He's about to turn state's evidence. He's untouchable. Unless you want to whack him."

"I think you broached that issue at one point before," Jeffrey said, recalling Cary's reference to a "dirt lunch" some months before. "I really don't think that's the way to do it."

"Why?" Cary persisted. "If you whack him, you, um, his testimony is no good in court. Because you can't cross-examine the witness."

Jeffrey couldn't resist: "As they say, dead men tell no tales."

"Right. So the bottom line is . . ."

"What do you suppose I do with him?" Jeffrey asked. This appeared to be a carefully worded question. He was not suggesting that he himself should do anything regarding Warrington. He was just exploring what Cary might think to do with the guy.

"Have Jimmy take care of him," Cary said, obligingly. "I don't care how it's done, just take care of him. He's not married anymore," he added, as if this might seal the case. "His wife left him."

"She did?"

"She lives in New York now."

"Who lives in New York?"

"She does," Cary said. "He can't even feed his family. He's been living in the same cottage without electricity. Go down there, have them put a gun in his mouth."

"No," Jeffrey said. "You never pull a gun unless you're willing to use it."

"No, no, no," Cary said. "You miss the point."

"What's the point?"

"Put the gun in his hand, put the gun in his mouth, pull the trigger, make it look like suicide. It's not hard to believe he committed suicide, he's so down and out."

"Oh, I mean, I think that's a little involved, don't you?"

"What's it going to cost us, ten Gs?" Cary asked. "You got to get rid of him."

"Why don't you put the whole ten grand up? I don't want any part of it."

"What are you afraid to kill someone now?"

"It's not the first thing on my wish list, no."

"But you don't want to go to jail. What would you rather have, five years in jail or whack Warrington? They are going to use the majority of his testimony against us. Do you want to destroy the case against us?"

Jeffrey asked, "Do you think he's a credible witness?"

"Yeah."

"You do?"

"He has checks," Cary said.

"Did you ever give him checks?"

"No," Cary said. He paused. "Yes. As a matter of fact, I did. He cashed a check that had a fictitious name, but it doesn't matter. He's a credible witness. The core of the case against you is Warrington. The core of the case against us requires testimony. If you eliminate the testimony, you eliminate the case."

Cary claimed that besides his own words, Warrington had their words on two hundred and thirty hours of secret recordings of phone calls implicating everyone in everything. He said, "Do you want to take care of the problem, yea or nay?"

"Personally, I have to think about it," Jeffrey said.

"Think about it. Let me know because my vote's yea.

I'm tired of, when push comes to shove, people backing down."

"Well I don't back down from shit," Jeffrey snapped. "Where we're taking us, which is like . . ."

"Naw," Cary interrupted. "He deserves it."

Pokross said he'd decide whether to mention Cary's request to Jimmy Labate. "That may spook Jimmy," he said. "So I got to think about it a few days."

"Want anything to eat, by the way?" Pokross asked.

It was clear that Cary truly believed Warrington was the source of all his problems. If there was no Warrington, there would be no problems. It was also clear that Cary was not at all like the gangsters Pokross had known for years. They would never discuss something like this in a restaurant with a million tourists and businessmen in white shirts and ties and who knows who else sitting all around them. They wouldn't use terms like "put a gun in his mouth" and "make it look like suicide." No way. It would all be arranged by implication, without anything explicit uttered. Cary, it was clear, was an amateur. A pseudo-gangster who was so trusting of his longtime pal Jeffrey Pokross that he'd say things like this and expect no one would ever know. In this regard, already he was wrong.

When they finished, Pokross left Sparks and walked around the corner. He got into a leased car parked on the street, pulled up his shirt and pulled off the wires taped to his chest. He handed the wires and the tiny recorder tucked in his waistband to Special Agent Kevin Barrows of the FBI. Jeffrey Pokross, after all, was a reliable cooperating informant, skilled at coaxing out culpability. With Cary Cimino, they were learning, you didn't need much coaxing.

CHAPTER TWENTY-NINE

October 26, 1999

By the time the sun rose across the sweeping horse country of central New Jersey's Monmouth County, there were enough cop cars in the driveway of the house to open a Crown Victoria used car dealership. There were the locals from Colts Neck and the state troopers and the unmarked variety that signaled the feds. Lights red and blue revolved in the growing autumn light, making clear to the waking neighbors that this would not just be another Tuesday in suburbia.

The house was of the classic New Jersey striver variety, an enormous beige stucco McMansion with crushed white clamshell driveway encircling a pseudo-Venetian fountain. It practically shrieked, "Look at me! I have arrived!" It sat in the middle of a horse farm subdivided when the housing market got hot. There were probably two dozen just like it, each with two acres of open space parceled out of what was once rolling green farmland, far enough apart that if you needed to borrow a cup of sugar from your neighbor you'd have to get in your car and drive over. No way you'd hear what was going on next door from that distance. Even the sound of gunshots didn't carry that far.

When the cops arrived, they viewed what would appear to be a typical upper-middle-class new-money New Jersey neighborhood a few days before Halloween. There were pumpkins on doorsteps and fake scarecrows propped against lampposts. When they approached the house, they were greeted by two workmen who had done jobs for the owner and were there to pick up his two pugs while he went to Florida on a quick trip. They had found the front door open and entered, calling out the name of the owner, Albert Alain Chalem. They found the two dogs upstairs in a closed bedroom and a good reason to call the cops lying on the floor of the dining room.

Investigators first noted that the door was unlocked. Inside they entered a grand vestibule with a fifteen-foot ceiling and a wraparound staircase leading to the upper floors. A massive crystal chandelier that would look great in a casino hung overhead. There was very little furniture and almost nothing hanging on the gleaming white walls. They walked through the living room and straight to the back of the house, where a huge, thick wood dining table dominated a room that looked out on the backyard. The table was covered with papers spread out in a way that indicated work was under way when events were suddenly interrupted. They noted that the back door was slightly ajar. On the floor of the dining room they found what they were looking for.

There were two men, blood pooling beneath both. One was the owner of the house, Chalem. He lay sprawled on the floor, the baseball cap he always wore next to him. The other was a friend of Chalem's, Maier Lehmann. He still had his cell phone in his hand.

At first it was just the locals and the state police, but within a couple of hours the FBI showed up. It was clear right away that Chalem was anything but a stranger to the Bureau. In fact, Chalem had long been involved in mul-

tiple over-the-counter stock scams and had tangential connections with multiple Mafia families and was involved
with a platoon of corrupt stockbrokers and promoters. It
was believed he'd been involved in shorting the house
stock of a mob-run boiler room and driving the price
down before they could unload and make a profit. He was
also a sometime informant for the Bureau, tipping them
off occasionally to the comings and goings of his criminal
brethren. There were many reasons why he would wind up
lying on the floor of his own expensive home. The other
guy, Lehmann, appeared to be just a guy who had really bad
timing. He was a computer whiz who worked for Chalem.
When they began to look into the matter, they started with
Chalem.

Lehmann was helping Chalem with a penny stock Internet site he'd started called stockinvestor.com. Chalem
had been sued by the Securities and Exchange Commission for his role in penny stock manipulation, and his name
had come up as a conspirator in a major arrest by the Manhattan district attorney of a boiler room known as A.S.
Goldmen. They learned that he was supposed to be driving
down to the Carolinas to meet a business associate, then
flying the rest of the way to Fort Lauderdale to meet up with
his girlfriend, Kim, at a condo he owned there. He called
her around 5 p.m. to say Lehmann would be joining him on
the trip to Florida. His last phone call had come at 8 p.m.
Monday night, to a business associate. Whatever had happened, happened sometime between that call and the early
hours of Tuesday when the two workmen showed up to get
the dogs.

There was a quite a bit of blood, but it appeared that
there had not been much of a struggle. It must have occurred
quickly, and investigators theorized that Chalem and Lehmann were shot almost at the same time. This indicated
more than one shooter. There was no sign that anything was
missing, and the papers on the table appeared to have been

left alone. It seemed that Chalem, at least, knew whoever had killed him, and that after they were done, they merely walked out of the house and drove away.

Chalem's girlfriend, Kim, learned what had happened when she awoke around 7 a.m. She had seventeen messages on her cell phone, all from their neighbor in Colts Neck. She called back, and the woman said there were about one hundred cop cars outside Kim's house and two dead people inside. She got a ticket back to Newark Airport right away, and when she stepped off the plane two FBI agents were waiting at the gate.

The appearance of the FBI was not exactly shocking to the girlfriend. She was vaguely aware of Al's involvement with criminals and those who wanted to be criminals. She'd been with him when they hung out with Allie Boy Persico, the acting boss of the Colombo family, in the Hamptons, and had once attended the wedding of one of Persico's relatives. She was vaguely aware that a guy named Phil Abramo who Al said was "connected" was involved in some of Al's business deals. Al was not your average businessman. The house in Colts Neck was in her name; the Florida condo was in the name of one of Al's employees. Al had made it clear he had certain credit issues, but it was also clear he wasn't crazy about having too many known assets.

The FBI was very interested in everything she had to say about when Al had planned to be in Florida and why that hadn't worked out. They asked about his friends, his family, his business associates. She didn't really get into Allie Boy Persico and Phil Abramo. They asked about his work habits. He would disappear into his office inside the house in the morning and emerge after the closing bell on Wall Street, having spent all the hours day trading. She would write down each trade to help him track his money. As far as she knew they were all real companies. She was happy to have the money, and didn't ask a lot of questions.

The story hit the papers in a big way. This was not your usual Wall Street tale of merger and acquisition. This was more *America's Most Wanted* than the *Wall Street Journal*. Here were two stock pickers murdered by the mob. There were no gambling wire rooms, no corrupt union leaders, no tainted captains of the carting industry. This was the mob on Wall Street. Although the cops and the FBI really had no idea who specifically to blame for Chalem and Lehmann, and certainly could not say that it was a mob hit, it sure looked like one, and that was the way it got written. The manner of killing—no robbery, no big mess—made it obvious this was just business. This was clear evidence that the gangsters of New York had, like millions of law-abiding Americans, decided to get their slice of the Wall Street boom. They just did it a little differently than everyone else.

A day or two after the Colts Neck murders hit the papers, Frank Persico called up DMN. Pokross took the call. All Frank would say was "I want to talk." Pokross met with Frank, and Frank asked a lot of questions about what Chalem did for DMN and what kind of records there were to connect Chalem to Frank. It was Frank, after all, who had introduced Chalem to DMN three years earlier.

The FBI knew all about this call and had no reason to think Frank Persico was involved in the murder of Al Chalem any more than about a dozen other gangsters across New York. Chalem had been into so many schemes with so many different organized crime families it was hard to tell who wouldn't want to kill the guy. Besides Persico they quickly saw connections with Phil Abramo, the self-proclaimed father of pump and dump. But Abramo himself was sitting in a prison cell in Tampa, Florida, where he faced charges that had nothing to do with DMN. Instead the FBI began pulling together information on the exact whereabouts of some of

Abramo's mob cohorts during the evening of October 25, 1999. They'd found blood at the scene that did not belong to either Chalem or Lehmann, and while they awaited the test results they took blood and hair samples from several members of the DeCavalcante crime family, to which Abramo belonged. Nothing came of any of it.

Francis Warrington Gillet III didn't really care who killed the two guys in New Jersey. He didn't know them. He'd never even met them. Whoever put a bullet into them probably had his reasons, and Warrington was not in a position to know those reasons. He was simply upset that such a thing could occur to guys who were, in a way, just like him.

Two years after the FBI had come to his apartment and taken him away, Warrington's world was continuing its downward spiral into the abyss. Nothing was going as it should. He'd split from his wife. His mother wouldn't talk to him. His father didn't return his calls. His half-brother made fun of him every chance he could. He'd been forced to quit Wall Street and couldn't go near the securities industry. These days he was working around the stables at his mother's home in Maryland, living there in a converted barn. He had just turned forty-one. He was the father of a three-year-old. He was supposed to be a responsible member of society, contributing to the tax base and participating as an able-bodied consumer of goods and services. Instead he was struggling to get control of his life, and now there was this awful thing in New Jersey.

What caught his eye was the mention of a possible theory in the deaths of the two guys in Colts Neck. One of them, Chalem, was believed to have been an informant. The word jumped off the page like a hand to the throat.

For months, Warrington had been spending long hours in anonymous government offices, sitting and talking with

Special Agent D. True Brown of the FBI. He had been telling Brown everything he could remember about all of his
former friends in the underworld and nearby environs. It
hadn't been easy. He'd gone back and forth, trying to decide for himself whether he was a victim or a conspirator.

Sometimes he blamed others. For a time, he launched a
lawsuit against a Florida law firm that had been involved in
helping him set up the Discovery Studios model search
debacle. He'd alleged fraud and assorted skullduggery,
claiming that the law firm he'd hired had a conflict of interest that ultimately blew up the deal. In a newspaper
story in the *Palm Beach Post*, Warrington didn't mention
his arrest by the FBI but instead whined that he was just
another working man stiffed by greedy lawyers.

"Even though I have had well-off family in Palm Beach,
I've had to struggle and work my way up like everyone
else," he told the reporter. "I'm a regular guy just trying to
make it."

Sometimes he felt sorry for himself.

"I was an actor turned stockbroker and I didn't know
what the hell I was doing."

The more he thought about it, though, the more he felt
he had no choice but to cooperate with the government.
None of these guys were his friends, not even Cary Cimino,
his former best friend. What sealed the deal for Warrington
was the realization one morning that Cary would turn on
him in a heartbeat if he were faced with the possibility of
going to prison. And if Cary turned, Warrington was sunk.

In the room with Special Agent True Brown, Warrington
told all about Cary Cimino—especially about Cary. He
also told about Jimmy Labate and his guns and Sal Piazza
and Jeffrey Pokross (whom he referred to as "the militant
angry little gangster") and about all the stockbrokers and
stock promoters involved in all the schemes. He told about
the rinky-dink amusement park that was behind Spaceplex

Amusement Centers International and the ridiculous roofing shingle recycling outfit in Tampa called Reclaim Inc. Then there was the ludicrous ice skating venture, Beachport Entertainment Corp. They already knew about his goofy modeling agency idea that had been Discovery Studios Inc. He'd even had to admit to his embarrassing nom de guerre, Johnny Casablanca, scribbled on all the bribe checks he'd cashed.

The idea was to stay out of jail at all costs. If they could use what he told them to make other cases and put other people in jail, Warrington might not have to join his former friends behind bars. He was inspired. He'd even tried to bolster his position by taping phone calls with Cary Cimino, the only one of his fellow co-conspirators who would talk to him after his arrest. He would call up Cary and complain about money and lawyers, and Cary would tell him to sell the Ferrari and as many horses on his family farm as he could ride out of the stable. All the tapes he made went straight to D. True Brown of the FBI, potential currency in Warrington's bid for redemption.

For months this had gone on. Warrington would take the train up to New York City, submit to one of these all-day sessions with the FBI and various assistant United States attorneys, unburdening himself of all that he had done. That was important. They made it clear he had to tell them everything. He even mentioned the tickets he'd gotten for running a red light and talking on his cell phone while driving. Nothing was hidden. In the white light of truth, Warrington was—perhaps for the first time—as vulnerable as a child.

He had still not signed an actual plea agreement. He had yet to testify in open court. He and his lawyers were trying to work out the details. The prosecutors told him little and made few promises, except to say they'd ask the judge not to make Warrington do time. The prosecutors needed him to take some form of punishment, and they'd more or less agreed that would be monetary. He would have to join his fellow conspirators in coming up with some form of restitution for all the old ladies in Wisconsin they'd ripped off. The figure being kicked around was $1 million, plus a $75,000 fine payable to the United States government for all their hard work. The prosecutors were certainly not Warrington's friends.

Clause by clause they were working it out. They'd hoped to sign a final plea agreement within a few months, if all went as planned.

Now there was this business in New Jersey. Warrington was vaguely aware that what he was doing was dangerous. Although he'd made a point to never ask too many questions of Jimmy Labate and Sal Piazza and Jeffrey Pokross, their inclinations were certainly obvious to him.

"Finally when they got around to paying you, you'd look at the people who were paying your commission and you knew. They're all proud that they're from Brooklyn. They get their nails done, they walk the walk and talk the talk. They're all John Gotti wannabes. That's what they aspire to. Do you know why Monitor was called Monitor? If you get beaten, you get put on a life support system. You're on a monitor. That's why it was called Monitor."

Somehow after he was arrested and the FBI offered to keep him out of jail if only he would help out a little, he'd felt the risk was worth it. As far as he knew, nobody was absolutely sure that he was cooperating. Now there were two guys dead in Colts Neck, New Jersey. If they were willing to do that, why wouldn't they come after him? When he'd been arrested, he'd thought that was pretty bad. When he was told he might have to cough up a million dollars in restitution, that was pretty bad. When he lost his ability to earn a living on Wall Street, that was as lousy as it could get. Or so he thought. Now Warrington found himself with two options, both lousy. He could pull out of his deal with the government and face the possibility of going to federal prison. Or he could continue in his role as a secret FBI informant knowing that soon enough, that role would be anything but secret. Soon enough Sal would know, Jimmy would know, Jeffrey would know, and Cary would know.

Once again, Warrington found himself unable to choose between bad and worse.

CHAPTER THIRTY

June 14, 2000

The morning of the big takedown FBI agents and New York City cops spread out across the five boroughs of New York City, ventured deep into New Jersey and fanned out across Florida. They picked up Jimmy Labate at his home in Staten Island, which was very convenient because they were able to stop right down the street and also pick up his neighbor, NYPD Detective Stephen Gardell. Sal Piazza they found in New Jersey, and Robert Lino they picked up in his native borough of Brooklyn. Frank Persico, the guy who shot up the computer, they found in Howard Beach, Queens. They were to be the stars of what Mary Jo White, the United States attorney for the Southern District of New York, would later that day call the largest securities fraud takedown in history.

The breadth and scope of law enforcement's efforts became clear at 8 a.m. when a federal magistrate unsealed not one but sixteen indictments and seven criminal complaints making allegations of securities fraud, extortion, death threats and all around bad behavior against 120 people. All five of New York's organized crime families—the Gambinos; the Luccheses; the Genovese, Bonanno and Colombo groups—all were named in the indictments. It took all day to bring all of them through the courts. They couldn't fit them all on a school bus.

In the top indictment, the one with the most gangsters, Robert Lino was listed as "Little Robert," not Robert from Avenue U. Sal Piazza was just plain Sal, and Jimmy Labate just plain Jimmy. Two names that were not on the indictment were Jeffrey Pokross and Francis Warrington Gillet III. Right away everybody knew what that meant. Immediately they all began thinking about how much time it would take for Jeffrey and Warrington to tell the FBI everything. Right away they realized that could take days.

Everything was there in one place—all the pump and dump schemes, the threats against uncooperative or simply clueless brokers who tried to put in sell orders, the bribes for the corrupt brokers and stock promoters, all the money wire-transferred to accounts on Grand Cayman. The prosecutors were talking about $15.9 million in losses caused to hundreds of victims all across America, most of whom were senior citizens so lonely they'd listen to the nice salesmen tell them about the stock that was going to make them rich tomorrow. They were only talking about a handful of the bogus schemes. There were probably thousands of victims, too many to count, between all the greed and avarice assembled in sixteen indictments and seven criminal complaints. They put out a chart with all the stocks the gangsters and their white collar cohorts had used to steal. Spaceplex alone netted $3.5 million in scam profits.

DMN Capital was called "the fraud magnet" at the center of all the scams. There was a chart for the TV people with little bundles of cash, and there was DMN right in the middle with arrows pointing off to Robert Lino of the Bonanno family and Frank Persico of the Colombo family. Robert's name was everywhere, and he was given the rank of Mafia captain while Sal Piazza was listed as a mere associate. Jimmy Labate was listed as an associate of both the Bonanno and Gambino families, and Frank Persico only made it to the associate level, too. Some of these alleged gangsters were even listed as registered stockbrokers, including Frank, who also got his own nickname, Frankie. Detective Gardell was not listed as a member or associate of any family and he didn't get a nickname, but his name came up quite often nonetheless.

One name that was on the indictment but was not mentioned at all during the press conference was Cary Cimino. That morning the FBI had gone to his apartment in the East Village and found no Cary. His sister had no idea where he was. None of his friends could help either. He'd just disappeared. Technically, he was a fugitive, until later in the day when his lawyer called up and said he'd arrange to have Cary come right away.

What the FBI did not know at the time was that Cary Cimino had somehow figured out the game was over and checked into a luxury suite at the Grand Hotel in Manhattan's Soho neighborhood. He put the $500-a-night room on his credit card. It was a strange choice. It wasn't walking handcuffed out of your apartment in the predawn darkness, but it also wasn't Mexico. It was, instead, a place to buy time. Since Cary had run up so much debt and used up so much goodwill, there wasn't a whole lot else that he could buy.

THE VICTIMS

They came from across America. They were extremely wealthy or moderately wealthy or not wealthy at all. Many were elderly citizens who'd saved up their money and were happy to get free advice on what to do with it. They lived in Stamwood, Washington, and Middle Village, Queens. There were investment partnerships based in London and Switzerland, and there were retired postal workers and schoolteachers. They all had one thing in common: they'd thought they were investing their money in the stock market that was carefully regulated and policed for fraudulent activity. They gave up their money believing that they would make even more, and perhaps quickly. They did so willingly. They wanted to get rich quick. They got screwed instead.

Anil Deshumukh, retired electrical engineer. He bought Spaceplex and other stocks through a broker relatives recommended.

"I never saw him. I'm in Philadelphia, and he's in New York. Over the phone he sounded all right. For every wiseguy, there's a sucker. I'm not experienced in stock. He tells me, 'You're going to make thousands of dollars on these shares. It's going to go up dramatically.' Some stocks did . . . He forced me. He kind of pressured me to buy stocks. Those people who were involved kind of cashed out. The stock went up, and they sold off, and my stock was worthless. And he said, 'Why don't you take it as a tax loss?' He was telling me that the stock is going to go up so high and you will make thousands of dollars. And then he said I don't know why it is going down. Then I found out later this was what you call a pump and dump scheme.

"The thing is, looking back, always you can see the con. But even at present, there are cons you cannot recognize. Years from now, I'll probably see it's a scheme, but I don't know it at the moment. The stocks started collapsing. He kept on saying it's going to go up, it's going to recover. But it went down so quickly it was hopeless. I suspect he did [unauthorized trades]. I'm not familiar with stocks. I was going not to trade any stocks and sell them and get my money back. Once when I called back, somebody else picked up the phone. They told me this is what happened [to my broker], that somebody killed him. The guy I talked to he told me what stocks I owned, and I had no idea I had these stocks. I said I never owned them. I was sick at the time. This new guy, I told him to sell, to close the account. And that was the end of it. I lost $10,000 to $15,000.

"Shame on me for being a fool. It's not a question of me making easy money. It was taking advantage of your trust. I wasn't looking to become a millionaire or such, but I wasn't expecting outright fraud like that."

Dr. Leonid Rubinov, New Jersey dentist: "The call was when the market was going up and you got a lot of calls. For some reason he talked me into something, into investing with him. One transaction was successful and then, not only did they overcharge me on commissions and everything else—they put in illegal transactions so I end up losing thousands of dollars. They told me it was just a mistake but then it wasn't corrected for so long."

Bill Bernard, retired lawyer from a small town in Minnesota: "I'd been in and out of the stock market for years. I was never a big investor. I was a real estate lawyer in the 1960s. I didn't have brokerage accounts. Then in the 1990s I thought I was going to retire so I started selling everything. Of course the 1990s were kind of an upside for stocks and I didn't know what to do with my money, so I put it in stocks. And oh boy! I took a bath . . . One broker, he would belittle you if you didn't take his recommendation. These guys are so pompous, they say they're executive vice president of the firm. Others brag about how much money they're handling for well-known people and they get your confidence . . . [Another broker] promised the moon and this is where I guess personal greed comes in. But he always had a story that I guess wasn't true. None of it was investment grade . . . I imagine that I lost $1 million and I never had $1 million. I was just a small town lawyer. I bought older buildings downtown, fixed them up and rented them out. Corporate America and the stock market are filled with thieves and the Mafia and everything else. I wish I had never got out of real estate. It didn't appreciate but at least you can see it . . . These guys would never have contacted me except that the Bank of Minnesota sells lists of customers. I'm out here in small town America. How else are they gonna find me? I'm on somebody's list. We've got a lot of people selling lists and that's why I won't fill out anything anymore . . . I don't take cold calls anymore, and if I get one, I give them holy hell." Bernard filed a complaint with the NASD in 2000. A year later a settlement was entered: $85,948 in compensatory damages, $17,905 in interest and $69,235 in attorney's fees. "Nothing's been paid on that award and nothing ever will."

Manny Pragana, retired from his job working maintenance at the post office. He put the family's savings—$45,500—into stocks. "I'm a World War II veteran, Battle of the Bulge, kid. This guy, he said that the people in East Chester invest with him, everything would be in good shape. We have nothing to worry about. He said he had people in Westchester investing with him. And I listened to him. I got sick from this. What are you gonna do? You live and learn. You know how it is. They tell you it's a sure thing . . . What can I do now? They said if we had to go into court, we would have had to pay the lawyer's fees. I said nothing doing. Before these lawyers took over, if we got anything, they got a third. We went to arbitration way down there in New York. I went there so many times, and we lost out. What are you gonna do?"

Five days after the big takedown Cary Cimino surrendered at the U.S. Attorney's Office in Lower Manhattan with his lawyer. He was held overnight at the Metropolitan Detention Center a block away, a dark and foreboding place where Cary immediately started complaining about the mild case of glaucoma he'd suffered from in recent years. When he showed up in court to request bail the next day, he was shocked to hear a young prosecutor named Patrick Smith request that Cary be detained without bail. By now he knew quite a lot about what he was facing, but all the charges he was facing were white collar. There were no murders, no broken arms. Just money stolen. He was aware that Jeffrey Pokross had been cooperating for years and that he'd recorded hours and hours of tape inside DMN and who knows where else. He knew that the amount the feds considered to be stolen profits was in the millions and that he could be held responsible for some of that. He knew that this was not going to be a repeat of 1996, when he'd seen all the charges against him dismissed within a month. But he figured he could get bail.

Prosecutor Smith stepped forward and asked the magistrate if he could play a tape recording made by an informant. He didn't name the informant, but Cary knew right away it would have to be Jeffrey. Prosecutor Smith explained in earnest that the tape would show how Cary Cimino was a danger to the community. He plunked in the tape, and soon Cary heard his own voice fill the room.

"Put a gun in his hand, put it in his mouth," Cary heard himself say. "Pull the trigger and make it look like suicide."

It was all a big misunderstanding, his lawyer argued. Had anything come of this idle threat made in conversation at Sparks Steakhouse with crowds of people all around? No. Of course not. Cary Cimino wasn't capable of hurting a fly, never mind a stockbroker who was at one time his best friend. The only individual Cary presented a danger to was himself. Mostly Cary needed the judge to know how his eye problems were getting worse inside the prison where, his lawyer argued, conditions were simply unacceptable.

Back and forth they went, with Prosecutor Smith insisting that Cary really did mean to have Francis Warrington Gillet III murdered by a gangster, and Cary's lawyer insisting it was just macho hyperbole by an insecure guy. The judge pushed for a compromise, and the prosecutor came up with extreme bail conditions for someone accused of nonviolent criminal activity: a $2 million bail bond backed by three people who would consider Cary to be a responsible person. Plus he'd have to remain confined all the time to his home in the Village, wearing an electronic monitoring device and staying away from securities deals, real or proposed. Cary's lawyers agreed to the requirements and promised to make the arrangements right away. Cary wondered where he was going to find three people to help him get out of jail.

CHAPTER THIRTY-ONE

November 13, 2002

Francis Warrington Gillet III, great-grandson of the World War I flying ace, son of the Palm Beach playboy, father of Francis Warrington Gillet IV, former owner of a red Ferrari, stood before a judge to receive his due. It was late on a Wednesday afternoon, a miserable day of rain after a miserable week of rain. Warrington had just turned forty-four the month before and now he was about to learn from a stranger—United States District Court Judge John G. Koeltl—whether he'd have to spend any time inside a federal prison. He was beyond nervous. He was nearly insane with fear.

After all this time, it was still difficult for him to see that where you are is mostly a function of who you are. Standing in the federal courtroom in lower Manhattan with the rain pattering at the window, Warrington couldn't possibly explain why he was there. All he could hope to do was tell the judge it was his fault and hope for the best.

When he'd stood before this same judge and pleaded guilty to securities fraud charges two years earlier, Judge

Koeltl had asked him straight out, "Mr. Gillet, are you pleading guilty because you are in fact guilty?" He had answered in the affirmative because you had to. The judge wouldn't accept the plea otherwise. Even as he said those words, Warrington was still at that point where he wasn't sure if he had really done anything wrong other than try to make a living in a difficult and greedy world. He'd merely said what he was supposed to say.

Today was different. Today he had to be sincere. He had to let the judge know that what he now felt was not mere regret but true remorse. It would not be easy. As he stood there with the prosecutor and his lawyers and not a single family member present to hear his words, he knew that his ability to convince the judge to keep him out of prison would be the result of two people in his life.

The first was Cary Cimino. The first time he learned of Cary's repeated discussions about giving him a dirt lunch, he was stunned into silence. He knew Cary liked to spout off, but he couldn't believe he would go that far. When he actually heard the tape of Cary's chat with Pokross at Sparks Steakhouse, he was even more upset. There was his former best friend going on and on about putting the gun in his hand and putting the gun in his mouth and so on. His sense of betrayal was profound.

By now Warrington had made several public appearances as a snitch. He'd finally resigned himself to going public with his status as an FBI informant after the U.S. attorneys he was dealing with made it clear that if he didn't, he would, in fact, go to prison. They would make sure of it. Warrington came to understand that U.S. attorneys really dislike guys who promise to help and then change their minds.

In one of his public appearances, the U.S. attorney had him come to court to testify against Cary Cimino. They were playing the Sparks tape for the judge to make sure that Cary would go away for many years. Warrington had come to court and sat in an anteroom knowing that Cary was sitting next door, learning his fate. The prosecutors were more or less sick and tired of Cary Cimino. Cary himself had briefly offered to be a cooperating witness and testify against anyone he'd ever met. They listened and wrote down everything he said, and he'd promised to plead guilty and even did. But it hadn't worked out. Ultimately they didn't need him, and now he and his lawyer were doing everything they could to spread blame and mitigate punishment.

At one point, Cary even tried to use the terrorist attacks on the World Trade Center as a means of staying out of jail. He'd been several neighborhoods above the twin towers when the planes struck on September 11, 2001, but claimed he'd been traumatized by the whole event. So traumatized, he whined, that going to jail would likely push him over the edge. The judge listened to this, than heard the prosecutors say they wanted Cary in prison for fourteen years. For a white collar crime, this was a significant amount of time. The prosecutors offered to play the Sparks tape again, but the judge really didn't need to hear it. He gave Cary a small lecture and sentenced him to ten years in prison while Warrington sat in the room next door.

Now Warrington sat before another judge as his lawyer, Philip Pitzer, talked about the education—in fact, the transformation—of Warrington.

"And I can say to the court that the Warrington Gillet who is before this court today is not the same Warrington Gillet that I started representing five years ago," Pitzer said.

It was true. The Warrington Gillet busted by the FBI had truly believed for quite a while that anybody but Warrington Gillet was to blame for his troubles. Cary Cimino was to blame for misleading him. Jeffrey Pokross was to blame for involving the gangsters without asking Warrington's permission first. Jimmy Labate was to blame simply for being Jimmy Labate. Pitzer the lawyer admitted that, even when Warrington had entered his plea and the judge had asked him that question about whether he was really guilty, Warrington wasn't so sure.

"He was rationalizing his conduct and was unable to accept the fact that he had committed violations of criminal law. He was in such denial that even by the time he was standing before this court entering his plea, I know that word 'guilty' was hard for him to speak. I know that articulating for the court exactly what he had done of a criminal nature was difficult for him to do, even though it was true."

Pitzer went on about Warrington being embarrassed, humiliated and—most important—"willing to accept full responsibility for the conduct that he entered into and accepting the fact that he and he alone is to blame for the consequences of that conduct."

He described Warrington as "a young man who was born, frankly, of privilege. A young man who was blessed with so many extraordinary, God-given gifts, is now forever branded a felon. That will never change. This experience, without a doubt, has been the most traumatic thing that has ever happened to Warrington Gillet."

It was certainly true that Warrington had come a long way to arrive at this place. He had absolutely started with more than most. He had the prep school pedigree. He went off to Villanova and could have, if he had chosen to do so, picked up a college degree. Instead he chose to quit college and try acting. He chose to quit acting to pick stocks. He chose to work with the likes of Jeffrey Pokross and Sal Piazza and Jimmy Labate and Cary Cimino and, without even knowing it, Robert from Avenue U. Now look at them. Jeffrey Pokross had become an FBI informant and was in the witness protection program. So was Sal Piazza. Jimmy Labate had pleaded guilty to securities fraud and extortion charges and was off to federal prison. Even Robert Lino— Robert from Avenue U—had pleaded out and taken his punishment—eighty-three months in prison. Cary Cimino got it worse than anybody—ten years.

In a way, Warrington was just like them. They all cut corners and got caught, then had their own explanations for how they ended up in such a mess. Here he was, a wealthy man living in a country that believed it was the guiding light for the entire world. He was born into money and began his journey believing that he could have pretty much anything he wanted because, well, he just could. He had not realized until much later that it was all his to lose.

The lawyer reminded the judge of the hefty packet of letters sent by the many influential and respectable friends and family of Warrington Gillet. There was a letter from his mother and a letter from his uncle, a United States senator, and even his ex-wife.

Jason Sabot, the assistant United States attorney, a young man bearing the standard phlegmatic demeanor required by the United States Justice Department of all its employees, stood and squared his paperwork. He was there to make the case to keep Warrington out of prison. He made it clear that Warrington's assistance had been crucial to the federal prosecution of the mob on Wall Street case because his testimony had provided a key to a crucial first door that allowed them convince others to cooperate and open all the doors necessary to bring an effective indictment that inspired nearly everyone charged to plead guilty. By the date that Warrington faced his sentence, more than sixty defendants had pleaded guilty to various charges. A handful had gone to trial and been acquitted, but in all those cases it was Jeffrey Pokross who'd been the star witness—not Warrington Gillet. Warrington had offered what Sabot called "substantial assistance"—the key phrase to obtaining leniency from federal judges.

Plus, Prosecutor Sabot noted, Warrington had promised to contribute to the $1 million in restitution owed by multiple defendants who'd been convicted and now needed to reimburse some of the people they'd ripped off. It helped, perhaps, that Warrington's customers had not been mom and pop investors from Weehawken, but were instead international banks and other institutional investors that had, in some cases, participated in the scheme. And he had agreed to pay a $75,000 fine, even though he was to be, for a time, barred from the securities industry and would have to come up with another means of paying that one off.

And then it was time for Warrington to speak. The judge said, "I'll listen to you for anything that you wish to tell me in connection with sentence, any statements that you'd like to make on your own behalf, anything at all you'd like to tell me."

No more hired guns, no more delay. Warrington stood up, arranging and rearranging papers on the table before him.

"Obviously I have a lot of thoughts on this," he said. "My life has been through so much."

He opened with remorse.

"I would like to apologize to those persons that suffered as a result of my bad choices and my greedy choices, and I would like to apologize to the victims of my schemes. I apologize to my family, my wife, my son. I apologize to the court. I apologize to the assistant U.S. attorneys who have worked with me for the last five years."

He was just warming up.

"I'm in total embarrassment, disgrace, total humiliation. I could never have been beaten down lower as a human being. What a catastrophic lesson to learn. I'm shocked, and I had it coming."

He veered back to shifting blame. He picked the usual target—his upbringing.

"I don't know. It was probably something since childhood that had evolved. My parents were divorced when I was three, so I kind of grew up myself, sort of under the trappings that both of those persons provided for me with who they remarried, so I was always on this mission to acquire. They led a well-to-do lifestyle, but it wasn't mine. But I just did what I could do to keep up, to win their approval. And the journey took me through life and I ended up being a stockbroker and it was the first time I started to make money."

Here he was back with Cary Cimino on New Year's Eve on St. Bart's. It was a thousand years ago, a lifetime. His crossroads. His date with the devil.

"People looked at me like I was a good person. It led me into an engagement and then I was, I suppose, confronted with temptation and the temptation was 'Here's some money in front of you, do you want it?' And it kills me that I said yes, and it nearly killed me. And if Jeffrey Pokross was not a cooperator for the government, I would have been killed."

Now he brought up his child, Francis Warrington Gillet IV. It might seem a bit unseemly to bring up one's offspring in an effort to escape punishment, but it would also be fair to say that Warrington appeared to be truly moved by the fact that he had a child to raise. The idea that he was supposed to be a role model for another human being had certainly changed him. Not completely, but enough.

"These greedy choices I made at the time I didn't have a child, but this child would have grown up without a father. I mean, what a catastrophic lesson to be given to somebody." And then he began to drift. "And I've had every day since I first came into this building to reflect on that and to try to put the pieces of my life back together." He made a point to remind the judge of the "mercy of the court," and ended by requesting "another chance to prove myself, you know? That I can be a good person and a good father."

"Thank you," he said, and he did not sit down. He just stood there, pushing the papers around in front of him, waiting.

In the federal system at this time, defendants faced a

range of years in jail based on a complex mathematical formula known as "the guidelines" that took into account the offense they were convicted of, their prior criminal history and several other outstanding factors such as how much money you stole. If you stole a lot—as Warrington did—you could get extra time in prison. The best way to reduce that range of years was to cooperate with the prosecutors, who would then be inspired to ask the judge to reduce the sentence. But all they could do was ask. The judge had the final say, and in this case, the guidelines required that Warrington receive a sentence of fifty-one to sixty-three months. That could mean five years and three months inside a federal prison somewhere out there in America. That could mean an orange jumpsuit and mixing it up in the yard with the other nonviolent miscreants—the corrupt cops, the fallen CEOs, the drug mules, the tax cheats.

The judge asked the prosecutor if there was anything else he needed to say, and they went back and forth about the peculiarities of restitution and whether any of the trivial facts placed on the record in the probation department's pre-sentence report were accurate and fair, and it was all excruciating for Warrington. He needed resolution. He needed a final word. He needed to know right away just how bad it was going to be.

Judge Koeltl, in methodic monotone, began his important monologue in this little bit of theater. Right away, Warrington heard the magic words he was hoping for— "substantial assistance."

"It is plain that the defendant has provided substantial assistance in the investigation and prosecution of others," Judge Koeltl said. "The cooperation helped in the return of two indictments against numerous defendants. The defendant in this case was prepared to testify and did provide extensive cooperation. His assistance was truthful, reliable and prompt."

Judge Koeltl even took note of the threat to Warrington's

safety implied by Cary Cimino's ultimately empty threats at Sparks Steakhouse.

"It is clear that the defendant's cooperation brought with it a risk of significant personal danger, which raises the credit that should be given the defendant in this particular case."

And then, more than five years after the FBI woke up Warrington from a deep sleep in his Central Park West apartment, Judge Koeltl cut Warrington the break of his life.

"It is the judgment of this court that the defendant, Francis Warrington Gillet III, is hereby placed on probation for a term of three years," the judge said. "The defendant shall also comply with the conditions of home confinement for six months."

This meant Warrington would have stay in his apartment on the Upper East Side of New York for six months except to look for or work at a job. His phone couldn't have call-forwarding, caller ID or call-waiting. It had to be plugged into a wall. A cordless phone and a cell phone were out of the question. After that he could come and go as he pleased, as long as he remembered to follow the requirements of the U.S. Department of Probation for another two and a half years. Not a single day would he have to spend in a federal prison for the crimes he had committed during his time as Johnny Casablanca at DMN. Warrington had officially dodged the bullet.

Outside court he began making calls to let friends and family know how he'd fared. It was nothing but good news, as far as he could tell. Sure, he'd have to stay away from Wall Street for a while, which would make coughing up money for restitution and fines tough. Sure, he'd have to meet regularly with a probation officer and let him know all about how he was trying to earn money and contribute to society. Sure, he was a felon, but he would never be an inmate. Sure, he'd be barred from purchasing and owning a firearm for the rest of his life, but he could live with that. Sure, he'd have to put down this little matter on every job application he ever filled out until the day he died, but so what? His only prison would be his apartment, with cable and air-conditioning and fully stocked liquor cabinet.

Damn, Warrington thought. This is a great country.

There was only one problem. Warrington Gillet IV. Little Warry. He would have to explain it all to Little Warry. Explaining this to his fellow adults was relatively simple. Life is complicated. Sometimes you make bad decisions. Sometimes you get a little too selfish and forget your way. Adults understand these things. Kids really don't. They see things on a much simpler level. Warrington would have to let Little Warry know that his father had made huge mistakes and then gotten lucky. He would have to find just the right words, and that—more than anything—would be the most difficult task of all. In the end, after all was said and done, it really came down to one thing.

"The biggest job with your kids is the biggest job with my kid," he said, "and that is, you have to teach them the difference between right and wrong."

CHAPTER THIRTY-TWO

2004

At 6 p.m. on a spring day in March, Robert from Avenue U found himself once again standing in a courtroom, wrangling over words with lawyers. It was after hours in the federal court in downtown Brooklyn and the issue was the organization to which Robert belonged. In the opinion of the United States attorney, Greg Andres, the organization was the Bonanno crime family and Robert Lino was a captain with supervisory responsibilities. The prosecutor was insisting that Robert from Avenue U say the actual words, "Bonanno crime family." Robert from Avenue U was not pleased at this development. He'd agreed to plead guilty to several crimes and say he was a member of a group, but he was not about to say anything about any Bonanno crime family.

None of this had anything to do with Wall Street and pump and dump and corrupt brokers and stock promoters and DMN. This was all about everything going on behind the curtain, and the reason they were all assembled was because of Robert's uncle and mentor, Frank Lino. Frank had gone and turned himself into a cooperator for the FBI and started talking about all his friends, including his nephew, the kid from Midwood he'd helped raise as a favor to his cousin, Bobby Lino Sr.

Frank had given up Robert from Avenue U in a heartbeat. He'd told the FBI all about the murder of Louis Tuzzio, the one in which Robert was the shooter. He'd also remembered the business about Robert Perrino, the guy from the *New York Post* Robert helped with. There were many other stories to recall, harkening all the way back to dark winter nights digging into the frozen ground of Staten Island to find a final resting place for Gabe Infanti, then trying again a few years later to find Gabe and not succeeding. Frank had a remarkable memory for detail, and as a result, Robert now faced the possibility of spending the rest of his life in prison.

Robert had agreed to admit to certain activities at this particular court session. And at first, things had gone along as planned. His lawyer, Barry Levin, and the prosecutor, Greg Andres, did not seem to get along at all. The judge, Nicholas Garaufis, kept stepping in to smooth things over. The task at hand was fairly simple: Robert had to plead guilty to four counts related to a lengthy racketeering indictment brought against much of the Bonanno crime family, which Robert did not wish to acknowledge the existence of.

"The defendant needs to acknowledge that the enterprise charged in the indictment is the enterprise with which he associated," said the prosecutor.

"But he need not allocute to the name of the enterprise?" the judge asked.

"Correct, Judge," replied the prosecutor.

They came up with a plan to give Robert twenty-seven years in prison. He was thirty-seven, so that meant if he behaved in prison and got a little time off as a reward, he still wouldn't be walking out on to the streets of America until he was sixty. A sobering thought for a man not yet forty.

Lino—who barely got out of elementary school—began to read a prepared statement describing his crimes.

"Your Honor, I am not such a good reader and I don't have prescription glasses, so bear with me."

"Take your time," said the judge.

"I, Robert Lino, withdraw my previous plea of not guilty under case number 03 CR 0307 S20 and enter a plea of guilty to Count One of the superseding indictment . . . charging me with violation of Title 18 of United States Code Section 1962 D. That I joined an association of individuals and I conspired to commit the following criminal acts."

"Go ahead," said the judge.

"I was involved in illegal gambling and sports betting. Acts 15." Lino stopped. He couldn't read what was written. His lawyer, Levin, jumped in.

"Between January 1, 1989, and January 1, 2003. Your Honor, it is my chicken scratch, so I have to apologize to the court."

Robert summed it up: "I was taking bets on sports and that is it."

The judge asked, "Were you taking bets?"

"On sports," Lino replied.

"Did this activity involve five or more people?"

"Five or more bets? Yes."

And so on. Soon it got around to the murder of Louis Tuzzio, the same Louis Tuzzio that Robert Lino personally shot in the face. The judge said, "As to Racketeering Act 16, the conspiracy to murder and the murder of Louis Tuzzio."

Robert Lino said, "I participated in the conspiracy to murder and the actual murder of Louis Tuzzio between December 1989 and January 3 of 1990."

The prosecutor interjected: "The government would prove at trial that Mr. Lino was, in fact, the shooter on the Tuzzio murder."

"All right," said the court.

Next up was Robert Perrino, a man who died by another's hand. Robert Lino merely helped clean up afterward, which in a murder conspiracy was more or less as bad as being the guy who pulled the trigger.

The judge: "What did you do in furtherance of the conspiracy, what activity?"

Lino said, "I cleaned up the . . ."

The judge: "You cleaned up?"

Lino: "Yes, I cleaned up the . . ."

The judge, turning to the prosecutor, asked, "Is that sufficient for you?

Prosecutor: "Yes, sir."

Then came the usual confusion that erupts when defendants are asked to admit that they are part of an "enterprise" that existed solely to commit crime. Often members of these types of enterprises prefer to wrap themselves in the gauze of euphemism instead of actually admitting the existence of, say, the Bonanno crime family. It is a quaint tradition.

The judge said, "In order for you to plead to the Rico count, the conspiracy count, it is necessary to acknowledge that such an institution or organization existed without any specificity—no specificity is needed as to who the members of the organization were. You are not being asked to state that this one was or that one was, just that the activities were pursuant to the activities of an enterprise, that these were not some unrelated acts of criminal violence."

"Okay," said Robert Lino.

"So you understand what has to be done here? It is a structural—it is a question of admitting, which you must do in order for me to accept the plea, that you were part of a racketeering enterprise."

"Okay. Can I state something for the record?

"Sure."

"Nobody ever told me I was part of the Bonanno family or a Massino family, for the record."

This was a mistake. His lawyer tried to keep things

moving, but it was not to be. Prosecutor Andres started in by claiming Lino had just committed perjury.

"Judge, I just—I don't want to make this worse for Mr. Lino. He certainly can't perjure himself. He is under oath. He certainly was told that he was part of the Bonanno family. I am not asking him to say that."

"No," insisted Lino.

Prosecutor: "He is not being asked to admit that to the court."

The judge: "I am not asking him to admit that."

Prosecutor: "I understand. But he is making statements that are false under oath. All he has to admit is that—or to acknowledge that he was part of the enterprise that is charged in the indictment." He actually said at one point, "He doesn't have to say it is the Massino family or the Bonanno family. But he has to acknowledge his membership. He has to acknowledge the existence of the membership— excuse me, the existence of the enterprise."

Finally they agreed on language, and Lino admitted that he was part of an unnamed organization made up of unknown people who got together and shot people like Louis Tuzzio and Robert Perrino. Robert Lino was then allowed to go back to his prison cell to await his sentence.

Eight months later, they were all together again in downtown Brooklyn. Four FBI agents and Assistant United States Attorney Greg Andres arranged themselves in an efficient government manner on one side of court. Robert Lino's wife, Carla Vitucci, her mother, and three other Lino family members occupied the other half of the courtroom. Both sides did their best not to look at one another. Outside a frigid rain fell from a sky as gray as a hearse. Both groups sat in more or less silence for forty-five minutes, until Judge Nicholas Garaufis finally took his place behind the bench.

A side door opened and Robert Lino was led in by two

United States marshals. He wore a khaki prison suit and blue canvas laceless shoes. He waved with a small anxious smile and pulled on glasses. His lawyer, Barry Levin, and Prosecutor Andres stood in front of the judge at his bench and listened to a lecture on the difficult job of being a federal judge.

The problem was Judge Garaufis hated the deal worked out between the prosecution and the defense attorney. He wanted to be the judge. The agreement he hated was that Lino should get twenty-seven years in prison.

"I could get a clerk to come up here and sentence Mr. Lino," the judge bellowed. He'd presided over a trial in which witness after witness described the inner workings of the Bonanno crime family, and in particular the nasty murders of Perrino and Tuzzio, and he was not satisfied with twenty-seven years.

"When I see there's plenty of evidence of the brutal nature of these crimes, it gives me pause to swallow this kind of agreement," he said.

Prosecutor Andres apologized again and again, but insisted that twenty-seven years in prison was not a walk in the park. And he praised Lino for actually taking responsibility for his actions, stating, "It's such a rarity for somebody to accept responsibility and agree to a sentence like this."

Robert Lino had a new daughter named Cassidy Rose. He'd sold off the house he'd inherited from his father and given the money to his wife. She had moved back in with her aging parents to raise their daughter, who—if the deal the judge hated actually happened—would likely be thirty-two when she got to see her father outside prison walls.

His wife, Carla, had written letters to this judge and the last judge, who'd sentenced Robert to eighty-three months for his role in the Wall Street case. Now this new judge would be adding to her misery. In her letters, she first pointed out that she had gone to school and graduated Brooklyn College with a degree in psychology. She then described her husband like this:

"I must admit, upon meeting Robert, his dry sense of humor and subtle sarcasm could have been quite unappealing. But it did not take me very long to see the side of Robert that is admired by many. He is a gentleman in the true sense of the word. He has a heart of gold and always a kind word or a kind gesture to those in need. He is the first to stop the car and help a pedestrian in need of assistance. He would not think twice about handing a homeless man the jacket off his back and has time and time again bought food from restaurants to give to a destitute person on the street. Robert would always be the one to talk to when you had a dilemma; he always has an honest opinion and is always straightforward with his thoughts. He would also try to lend a helping hand whenever possible.

"Lately Robert's demeanor has been very calm and pensive. Over these past ten months I have regularly discussed with Robert what has been happening with his case and offering him advice on how to deal with his troubles. But Robert is very ashamed of his actions and constantly belittles himself for what he has done. He feels he is not worthy of my love and the love of his daughter. I could empathize with what he is feeling but I, as his wife, know that Robert is a good man who made a bad decision. I in no way feel he should be excused from his responsibility, but do hope you can find it in your heart to have some compassion for Robert. His daughter is blameless but unfortunately the children of the incarcerated suffer the most.

"I will do my best to raise my daughter on my own to be well-adjusted socially, emotionally, intellectually and spiritually, etc."

Then it was Robert Lino's turn. He stepped up and kept repeating, "I don't know what to say. I don't know what to say." His lawyer took him aside, and he tried again. As he began to speak, his wife, Carla, put her hand over her mouth, closed her eyes and leaned forward.

"Your Honor, I would just like to put this behind me. I'm very sorry for anyone I offended. I'm sorry."

The judge then cleared his throat and called the whole matter "a Greek tragedy."

"No happiness comes from these events. I hope that you can put this behind you and you can have some solace in the future. This is an extremely large chunk of your life."

And twenty-seven years it was. The judge stood to leave, and everyone followed suit. When the judge was gone, Robert Lino turned and shook his lawyer's hand, then turned toward his wife and relatives and shrugged as if to say "What did you expect?" His wife smiled and waved as he walked through the door and was gone. She had not brought their daughter to see this.

Outside in the brightly lit white limestone hallway, the Lino family considered the fate of the young man who would not walk again as a free man until he was sixty years of age. He would go in with brown hair and come out with gray or none at all. In the hall, the family was asked why Robert Lino didn't try to get away from all that business with the Mafia and the killings, etc.

Carla's mother interjected, "He was born into that life. How do you go against your family? How do you go against your father? Your mother? All your cousins? Robert is not a coward. He did what he had to do and took it like a man."

All that Robert had admitted, the murders of Tuzzio and Perrino, the burying of bodies in the middle of the night with his father, the lying, the cheating, the perpetual state of deceit—none of that mattered. What mattered—what really mattered—was the fact that Robert's cousin Frank, a blood relative, a member of his own family, had gone and told the FBI all about Robert's life as a criminal. This fact made the Lino family crazy.

"The betrayal of your family is the worst thing you can do in your life. There is nothing worse," said one of the Lino cousins, who'd decided it was best not to reveal his name. "These informants, they walk away with no time."

Robert Lino was certainly not going to walk away with no time. This was the fact that his family would have to live with—that he would spend twenty-seven years in prison. The family Lino contemplated how much time cousin Frank would spend inside a prison cell.

"He won't get twenty-seven years, I can tell you that," said Robert Lino's wife, Carla, with not a little bitterness in her voice.